RIGHTS AND PARLIAMENTARY SYSTEMS IN CANADA AND BEYOND

Edited by Emmett Macfarlane

Rights and Parliamentary Systems in Canada and Beyond brings together political scientists and legal scholars to explore rights and their limitations, along with the governmental and legislative processes affecting them, within Canada's parliamentary system. It also examines how these elements shape broader institutional relationships under the Canadian Charter of Rights and Freedoms and in comparative perspective.

This interdisciplinary volume offers valuable, in-depth analyses of timely issues, cases, and controversies involving rights and institutional dynamics. The book employs an array of methods, including legal analysis, qualitative case studies, content analysis, legal theory, research interviews, and policy analysis.

With a forward-looking perspective, *Rights and Parliamentary Systems in Canada and Beyond* investigates how rights-based processes influence specific policies and offers new insights into the framing of rights, including administrative law and Aboriginal treaty rights during the COVID-19 pandemic. It also explores how aspects of parliamentary democracy affect governments, legislators, and the public. The book ultimately reveals how the institutional relationships at stake operate to protect – or fail to protect – rights in relation to government policy objectives.

EMMETT MACFARLANE is a professor in the Department of Political Science at the University of Waterloo.

Rights and Parliamentary Systems in Canada and Beyond

EDITED BY EMMETT MACFARLANE

UNIVERSITY OF TORONTO PRESS
Toronto Buffalo London

Toronto Buffalo London
utppublishing.com

ISBN 978-1-4875-5953-3 (cloth)
ISBN 978-1-4875-5954-0 (paper)
ISBN 978-1-4875-5956-4 (EPUB)
ISBN 978-1-4875-5955-7 (UPDF)

Library and Archives Canada Cataloguing in Publication

Title: Rights and parliamentary systems in Canada and beyond / edited by Emmett Macfarlane.
Names: Macfarlane, Emmett, editor
Description: Includes bibliographical references and index.
Identifiers: Canadiana (print) 20250196549 | Canadiana (ebook) 2025019662X | ISBN 9781487559533 (cloth) | ISBN 9781487559540 (paper) | ISBN 9781487559557 (PDF) | ISBN 9781487559564 (EPUB)
Subjects: LCSH: Canada. Canadian Charter of Rights and Freedoms. | LCSH: Canada. Parliament. | LCSH: Civil rights—Canada.
Classification: LCC KE4381.5 .R56 2025 | LCC KF4483.C519 R56 2025 | DDC 342.71/085—dc23

Cover design: Heng Wee Tan
Cover image: Oganic SL/Shutterstock.com

University of Toronto Press acknowledges the financial assistance to its publishing program of the Canada Council for the Arts and the Ontario Arts Council, an agency of the Government of Ontario.

Canada Council for the Arts
Conseil des Arts du Canada

ONTARIO ARTS COUNCIL
CONSEIL DES ARTS DE L'ONTARIO
an Ontario government agency
un organisme du gouvernement de l'Ontario

Funded by the Government of Canada
Financé par le gouvernement du Canada
Canada

Contents

Acknowledgments

This volume is about how rights, and in particular bills of rights like the Canadian Charter of Rights and Freedoms, have informed policymaking, institutional processes and relationships, societal discourse, and the work of courts, legislatures, and governments across a wide range of issues. Although this is a substantive volume covering a range of topics under the theme of "rights and institutional relationships," the chapters in this collection were presented at a workshop in honour of the career of Janet Hiebert. Janet is a leading scholar of the politics of rights and the impact of rights on executive and legislative processes in Canada and in other Commonwealth countries. Her work is thus prominent in many of the chapters presented here, providing a cornerstone for the analyses, findings, and prescriptions that emerge in this book.

I want to thank Janet for her invaluable scholarly legacy, for her mentorship, and for her friendship. My thanks as well to all of the contributors for the insightful work they have presented in these pages.

This is my fifth book with the University of Toronto Press. I am grateful for the work of the entire editorial team, and especially for Dan Quinlan, who is instrumental to a smooth and positive publishing experience. My thanks as well to the anonymous peer reviewers for their helpful comments and suggestions, and to Beth McAuley for her copyediting work.

My thanks to the Department of Political Science at Waterloo for supporting the workshop leading to the collection of papers for this book, and in particular to Jasmin Habib and Shelby Davies.

As always, this book would not have been possible without the support of my family, especially my wife, Anna, and our daughter, Thea. I am also grateful for the continued support of my parents, Don and Eileen, and my sister, Aingeal.

Foreword

It seems like only yesterday that a bright young woman from Nanaimo who had turned from sports writing to political science burst into my office at the University of Toronto to introduce herself and tell me, the Director of Graduate Studies, what she was going to do for her PhD. Never before or since that first encounter did I encounter a young scholar with such a strong and intelligent sense of what she would study and write about. That was Janet Hiebert.

Janet fully understood that comparative studies are the political scientist's laboratory. Accordingly, off she went to Australia, a country in so many respects like Canada, except for the way it dealt with the fundamental rights of a liberal democracy – Australia did not have a national or a constitutional bill or a charter of rights. How then did it deal with fundamental rights? What roles did courts and legislatures play in defining and protecting fundamental rights such as freedom of speech, equality before the law, and due process of law? And what difference did all this make between the enjoyment of rights in countries with constitutional codes of rights and liberal democracies like Australia, New Zealand, and the United Kingdom.

After completing her PhD dissertation, Janet went on to be a world leader in the study of the politics of rights. She also became a leading Canadian political scientist. She rose quickly through the ranks at Queen's University in Kingston, Ontario, to become the chair of the Political Science Department and, not long after that, the president of the Canadian Political Science Association.

On the personal side, Janet married Wayne, a highly accomplished news photographer. They love the opera, and on several occasions we have been able to share that passion with them when attending performances of the Canadian Opera Company at the Four Seasons Centre for the Performing Arts in Toronto. I don't know anyone else whose knowledge of the Blue Jays and Supreme Court of Canada decisions matches their knowledge of Mozart. And to top all this off, when Janet opens the door, her cheery face lights up the room.

Peter H. Russell,
Professor Emeritus, Department of Political Science,
University of Toronto

RIGHTS AND PARLIAMENTARY SYSTEMS IN CANADA AND BEYOND

Introduction: Governing with Rights

EMMETT MACFARLANE

More than four decades after the entrenchment of the Charter of Rights and Freedoms, empirical study of the way governments justify limits on rights, the way rights influence the legislative process, and the broader institutional relationships surrounding judicial review is, in important ways, only now blossoming. For a long time, and for obvious reasons, the study of the Charter was largely judicial-centric,[1] focusing on jurisprudential developments and, especially within political science, on judicial power and the role enjoyed by courts to affect public policy in ways that go well beyond the settling of federalism disputes.[2]

Debates over judicial activism,[3] often reflecting similar and parallel discussions in academia and the popular media, were both empirical and normative, but they typically shed more light on particular outcomes under the Charter than the effects it was having on institutions and their processes. In the Canadian context, a scholarly debate over the notion of a dialogue between courts and legislatures somewhat supplanted the activism debate, querying whether courts really do enjoy the final say over the policies implicated by judicial review.[4] Canada is unique among Westminster parliamentary systems for having a constitutionally entrenched bill of rights and courts empowered to employ strong form remedies like striking down legislation. The two main features of the Charter that theoretically operate to preserve a degree of parliamentary sovereignty and allow for a "dialogue" between courts and legislatures are section 1's reasonable limits clause and section 33's notwithstanding clause. The former might allow creative legislative responses to negative judicial decisions that preserve the government's initial policy objectives, so long as different and minimally impairing measures are employed. The latter allows Parliament and the provincial legislatures to temporarily immunize legislation against the effects of judicial review as it relates to certain sections of the Charter. However, because section 33 has, until recently, been rarely used – and never at the federal level – and because there is evidence that courts frequently do have the final say over the policies implicated by the Charter,[5] many scholars regard Canada as exhibiting strong form review in practice.

As with earlier debates, disagreement over dialogue – presented as meaningful legislative responses to judicial decisions that, at least in part, preserve governmental policy objectives – was both empirical and normative, but in many ways proved less nuanced, illuminating, or conceptually useful[6] than the amount of attention it received might otherwise imply. One of the limitations pertained to fundamental disagreements between dialogue proponents and critics about whether legislatures could legitimately disagree with how courts interpret the Charter's requirements. An alternative theory to dialogue, coordinate constitutionalism, posits that the other branches of government can assert independent judgment about the Constitution's requirements and act on those, such that neither the courts nor legislatures enjoy finality in that sense.[7] This is different than how dialogue proponents envision dialogue, in that they assume judicial supremacy in interpretation.

Despite the seemingly irreconcilable nature of the debate over how dialogue operated in practice, it drew attention for its broader suggestion that the Charter offered a potential middle ground approach or distinctive "model" of judicial review, falling somewhere between traditional parliamentary sovereignty and American-style judicial supremacy. Janet Hiebert refers to this as the parliamentary model, as first Canada, then New Zealand, the United Kingdom, and subnational jurisdictions in Australia adopted bills of rights that either included features that preserved some space for parliamentary sovereignty or that stopped short of granting courts the power to invalidate laws that impugned enumerated rights.[8] Also referred to as the Commonwealth model or "weak form" judicial review,[9] the core implication of the parliamentary model is that legislatures engage in rights scrutiny along with courts. Legislative features of the parliamentary model include ministerial reporting obligations or statements concerning bills thought to impose limits on rights; rights-based vetting of legislation in development by government lawyers and cabinet; rights-based scrutiny by parliamentarians, especially in committees; and a capacity for legislative responses to negative judicial rulings.

Hiebert was one of the first scholars to engage in comprehensive study of the role Parliament plays under the Charter. Her book *Charter Conflicts*[10] provided an analysis generally hopeful of parliamentarians' capacity to incorporate procedural and cultural changes in the legislative process to instil Charter-sensitive scrutiny and amendments to legislation. The book was realistic, however, about the nature of legislative work in practice, and she criticized a mixed record when it came to Parliament's ability to play a rights-protecting role in a manner that was independent and complementary of the role of courts. Occasionally, parliamentary responses to judicial rulings provided some hope of this normative ideal. For example, in the area of sexual assault, Parliament asserted a defence of survivors' rights on issues like defendant's access to accuser's therapeutic records and in relation to the extreme intoxication defence (although two decades later the Supreme Court struck down the provisions on the latter).[11] In general, however, Hiebert criticized a risk-averse approach by government as well as a concern that parliamentarians were often too reliant on judicial norms when assessing legislation. By contrast, her more recent work, including our book *Legislating under the Charter* (co-authored with Anna Drake), finds that executive-dominance of Parliament generally offers limited room for either independent judgment about legislative initiatives' consistency with the Charter or Parliament's capacity for holding government to account on rights-based grounds.[12] In that book, we propose a number of reforms to improve transparency and accountability around executive and legislative rights-based scrutiny of legislation, including separating the attorney general and minister of justice portfolios, waiving solicitor-client privilege when it comes to the bureaucratic advice governments receive about the constitutionality of legislation, enhancing the use of Charter statements by the Department of Justice, and creating a joint committee on rights modelled somewhat on the United Kingdom's Joint Committee of Human Rights.[13]

Analysis of the bureaucratic Charter-vetting process by James Kelly in his 2005 book, *Governing with the Charter,* similarly avoids judicial-centricity and suggests that executive power risks marginalizing Parliament. His analysis is relatively laudatory about the extent to which Department of Justice vetting has "improved the quality of legislation in Canada."[14] Hiebert and Kelly's later study of the experience of New Zealand and the United Kingdom is critical of the parliamentary model's success, as they conclude that it has failed to function "in a manner that substantially increases parliaments' willingness and capacity to hold governments to account for decisions that implicate rights adversely."[15]

Although the executive has received relatively scant independent attention in terms of its approach to the Charter, Matthew Hennigar has explored government decisions to concede Charter violations, appeal lower court losses, and employ litigation strategies.[16] Two recent books by Kate Puddister and Carissima Mathen provide in depth analyses of governments' use of the reference power, and Charter cases comprise a significant portion of reference opinions since 1982.[17] And Hennigar, Macfarlane, and Christopher Manfredi have each examined specific governments' relationships with the Charter and the courts.[18]

A distinct but related area of scrutiny involves analysis of the way rights and their limits are conceived. A considerable amount of attention has been devoted to the development and evolution of the famous "Oakes test," the two-pronged approach the Supreme Court adopted to engage in proportionality assessments under the Charter's reasonable limits clause.[19] Yet as Hiebert argues, there is evidence that the executive and legislative branches have considerable influence on how the courts conceive of limits on rights.[20] Moreover, many of the analyses of how governments and legislatures go about justifying limits on rights are embedded in the frames described above, with attention to how legislative responses to judicial invalidation of statutes are formulated under dialogue theory,[21] or the ways in which parliamentary debate incorporates rights considerations.[22]

Empirical study of the way the public or the media understands rights and their limits remains surprisingly limited in the Canadian context,[23] although recent uses of the notwithstanding clause by Saskatchewan, Quebec, and Ontario sparked scholarly scrutiny of media coverage and public opinion in that context.[24] Use of the notwithstanding clause may not constitute a mere "limit" on a right, in that it can work to allow the operation of laws that would otherwise be found unconstitutional, but it was conceived at least in part as a safety valve to address egregious judicial decisions or contexts where legislatures wish to assert their own view about the balance between competing rights, something that is usually part of section 1 analysis. In that view, the notwithstanding clause could be theoretically seen as placing limits on rights or even protecting rights in certain contexts where judicial decisions are seen as violating them (the sexual assault cases noted above are arguably examples of this, and some scholars argue section 33 should have been employed as part of those legislative responses).[25]

The collection of chapters in this volume seeks to build on this foundation of scholarship to examine rights and institutional relationships. The chapters offer analyses of the way in which we conceive of rights, how they are limited, and of government and legislative processes that are part of the parliamentary model and that inform broader institutional relationships under the Charter. Several chapters push the boundaries on these issues by framing legislative rights review in contexts beyond Charter law, such as in relation to Aboriginal and treaty rights, by assessing the limitation of rights in the context of administrative law, or by exploring both institutional relationships and the implications for rights in relation to the exercise of prerogative powers. The collection also analyses key institutional features of the parliamentary model, including chapters that examine Charter statements by the federal Department of Justice, and alternative ways of understanding the potential impact of the notwithstanding clause. Other chapters examine a host of related rights issues and policy areas, including an empirical study of rights discourse by the news media, users of social media, and parliamentarians during the COVID-19 pandemic; third-party advertising restrictions and the use of the notwithstanding clause in Ontario; federal regulation of pre-election advertising; police powers; and criminal sentencing policy. While diverse in the topics and issues they explore, each of the contributions fall squarely within this book's overriding theme of rights and institutional relationships.

Written by a diverse group of political scientists and legal scholars ranging from senior leaders in their field to junior scholars and graduate students, these contributions provide rich, new empirical study and analysis of timely issues, cases, and controversies implicating rights and institutional relationships under the Charter. Several chapters adopt explicitly comparative or international perspectives by considering rights instruments like the United Nation's Universal Declaration of Human Rights, legislative rights review in the Scottish Parliament, or case examples exploring Australia and the United Kingdom. They also offer an array of methods or approaches, including jurisprudential analysis, qualitative case studies, content analysis, legal theory, research interviews, and policy analysis. The contributions are also broadly accessible, and the book is meant to be read by a wide audience, including researchers, university students, decision-makers, and the general public. The chapters are generally forward-looking, offering insights into the impact rights-based processes have on specific policies; into new ways of understanding how certain features of the parliamentary model inform governments, legislators, and the public; and into how the institutional relationships at stake operate to protect (or fail to protect) rights as balanced against government policy objectives or other values and interests, from electoral fairness to criminal justice policy to decisions to engage in war.

Outline of the Book

Grégoire Webber explores how rights and their relationship to the law are conceived in chapter 1. Drawing on the UN Universal Declaration of Human Rights, which recognized that the rights and freedoms set out in it shall be secured "by progressive measures," Webber explores how this conception of rights and law "failed to animate the jurisprudence of the Supreme Court of Canada and much of the scholarship interpreting the work of our Court." The law is regularly framed in opposition to rights, as the object of rights' potential infringement or limitation, rather than the thing that helps to secure rights and ensure they can flourish. It is a conception of rights and the law that is often lost in debates about the Charter and the dominant perception of the role of courts as defenders of rights against governments and their legislative agendas.

In chapter 2, Minh Do examines whether the parliamentary model of rights review could serve as an effective check on the executive's legislative priorities that implicate section 35's Aboriginal and treaty rights. A key problem Do elaborates on concerns the nature of section 35 rights, which are not properly understood as individual rights but as relating to governments' jurisdictional authority. Limits on section 35 rights can only occur "through political, nation-to-nation negotiations between Crown representatives and an Indigenous nation through instruments like treaties," something that means Parliament lacks the authority to impose limits. In Do's view, Parliament's role may come into play where it can ensure the executive upholds the honour of the Crown, especially in contexts where executive actions implicate section 35 rights. Do explores institutional reforms that might enshrine such considerations in the legislative process.

G. Elizabeth Bergman assesses the limitation of rights in the context of administrative law in chapter 3. Pushing beyond the traditional focus on the Court-Parliament relationship, Bergman explores the role that administrative actors play within Charter jurisprudence. She notes that the concepts of judicial activism and dialogue theory offer an incomplete picture of judicial review absent consideration of these actors. Bergman argues that the emphasis on judicial deference in the administrative context has "changed the standards by which rights evaluations are made" and serve to weaken rights protection while threatening to diminish the courts' role as "guardian of the Constitution."

In chapter 4, George Williams and Winsome Hall examine the prerogative power to declare war and commit the Armed Forces to conflict overseas. Noting that the human rights implications of such decisions are considerable and complex, the authors examine the evolution of the prerogative power and the relationship between the executive and respective parliaments in Australia, Canada, and the United Kingdom. The different experiences in these countries suggest evolving, or potential evolution in, core conventions around this particular prerogative power, but the authors note that if parliaments are to play a greater role then they must assert it through their lawmaking function.

Brendan Dell and Mark Harding investigate the introduction and use of Charter statements by the federal Department of Justice in chapter 5. Charter statements were introduced by the Liberal government in 2016 as a means of demonstrating that rights were considered during the legislative drafting process and to improve public awareness and understanding of the Charter itself. Employing an original dataset of 105 Charter statements issued since that time, the authors find some evidence to support the idea that the government has met its basic objectives. However, the statements rarely explain in any detailed way how certain provisions of bills might implicate particular rights. Dell and Harding are also somewhat critical of the extent to which the Charter statements rely on past judicial constructions of rights rather than independent assessments of the rights at stake in relation to legislative objectives.

Chapter 6, authored by Andrew McDougall, examines the notwithstanding clause. Unlike many analyses that focus on the institutional or democratic implications of the clause, McDougall reminds us that one of the key features of section 33 as a central political compromise leading to the entrenchment of the Charter was the space it gave to provincial governments to protect certain policy areas from the potentially centralizing effects of judicial review. In this light, McDougall argues, the notwithstanding clause has a role beyond the preservation of parliamentary sovereignty or ensuring dialogic judicial review: the preservation of national unity. The chapter explores the historical underpinnings of section 33's national unity function, recent uses of the clause in Quebec, and a "federalist" understanding of the power.

In chapter 7, Nancy Hills and I provide an empirical study of "rights talk" in the context of the COVID-19 pandemic. Rights talk is understood as the tendency to portray moral, social, and policy issues as fundamentally about rights.[26] While rights claiming comes with obvious benefits, not least of which is the protection of rights, the inflationary tendency to transform public policy debates into winner-takes-all rights disputes can be detrimental to the health of political discourse, raising the stakes of political disagreement, inhibiting opportunities for compromise, and increasing tensions in pluralistic societies. We present three distinct analyses of rights talk: a content analysis of news media reporting of public health mandates; content analysis of social media users' framing of rights on Twitter (now known as X) through an analysis of tweets about pandemic restrictions; and an examination of debate in the Legislative Assembly of Ontario. Our findings confirm that, even in the context of a global health emergency, absolutist rights talk exists and, in certain contexts, flourishes in the Canadian context.

In chapter 8, Andrea Lawlor and Erin Crandall investigate the regulation of third-party election advertising and the Ontario government's decision to use the notwithstanding clause in response to the judicial invalidation of provisions in the *Election Finances Act*, which was found to violate the Charter's free expression guarantee. Lawlor and Crandall conduct an exploration of third-party spending and the Ontario government's approach as a case study to consider the evolution of election spending regulations in Canada. They use this case study to reflect on the Royal Commission on Electoral Reform and Party Financing of 1991 and its recommendations, which continue to inform the policy landscape. Their analysis reveals the ongoing challenges and debates around third-party election advertising as well as the partisan motivations that may trigger reform, and how they have changed over time.

On a similar theme, in chapter 9 Tamara Small examines the regulation of third-party election advertising at the federal level, with a focus on pre-election limits under the *Electoral Modernization Act*. After tracing the legislative changes ahead of the 2019 federal election, Small conducts a systematic analysis of third-party behaviour during the pre-election period, noting that most third parties effectively opted out of the pre-election period by not incurring any expenses, but for a key category of third parties: labour unions. These findings are potentially significant for the central objectives of the "egalitarian model" of electoral regulation: fairness between political parties and third parties, and among third parties.

Troy Riddell examines the relationship between Parliament and the courts in defining and regulating police powers in chapter 10. Although his analysis confirms the dominant role of courts, Riddell also identifies nuances in the relationship, including examples of Parliament acting on its own initiative and not always following judicial decisions about police power. After arguing in favour of a coordinate relationship where Parliament takes a lead role through the development of a code of police power, Riddell then briefly outlines some prospects and challenges for comprehensive reform.

In chapter 11, Brendan Dell and Kate Puddister analyse legislative rights review in the context of sentencing policy and the upwards of fifty mandatory minimum sentences created under the federal Conservative government of Stephen Harper. Via an examination of parliamentary debates and committee hearings for all bills passed by the Harper government that contained mandatory minimum sentences, the chapter explores the role Charter rights played in the legislative process, the government's justifications for potentially rights-infringing provisions, and the role of the opposition in raising rights-based concerns. Dell and Puddister find that the government rarely provided substantive responses or justifications and that the Charter failed to play a significant role in this area, reinforcing for them the relative weakness of Parliament in legislative rights review. They conclude by briefly exploring the implications of this finding.

In the twelfth and final chapter, Chris McCorkindale and Janet Hiebert examine the framework for pre-introduction checks and cross-checks in the executive and legislative processes in relation to bills in the Scottish Parliament, including by the Presiding Officer. These are designed to ensure both that the legislation operates within the legislative competence of the Scottish Parliament in the context of devolution and that it is compatible with the European Convention on Human Rights. Based on interviews with government lawyers, parliamentary lawyers, and legislators, McCorkindale and Hiebert's analysis lead them to argue that the statutory function of the Presiding Officer "provides an independent check on the executive that is missing in other jurisdictions with executive-only requirements and provides a source of independent scrutiny by lawyers that – unlike governmental legal advice – can be made known to legislators in the exercise of their legislative and scrutiny functions." Although it is not yet clear if the pre-introduction reporting requirements have achieved the goal of better informing the Scottish Parliament to take legislative review seriously, and despite some serious transparency issues, the authors conclude that the Presiding Officer's role serves as a promising innovation within the parliamentary model.

Together, the chapters in this volume provide rich new empirical evidence and insightful analyses of myriad issues surrounding the protection of, and limitations on, rights, as well as of institutional relationships within parliamentary systems. Although largely focused on Canada, this collection illustrates various dimensions, institutional processes, and rights and policy issues certain to inform scholars and practitioners in other jurisdictions. The collection's more explicitly comparative elements also shed light on the ways other countries might provide fruitful insights for the Canadian experience. By both building on, and moving beyond, the established body of scholarship on rights and institutional relationships, this collection also sets out a host of new research agenda pathways that should prove valuable for years to come.

NOTES

1 One early exception was Peter H. Russell's inquiry into the political purposes of the Charter, implicating national unity and the way society conceives of the protection of rights, both of which continue to require further empirical validation today. Peter H. Russell, "The Political Purposes of the Canadian Charter of Rights and Freedoms," *Canadian Bar Review* 61 (1983): 30–54. See, for example, Mark S. Harding, "The Political Purposes of the Charter: Four Decades Later," in *Constitutional Crossroads: Reflections on Charter Rights, Reconciliation, and Change*, ed. Kate Puddister and Emmett Macfarlane (Vancouver: UBC Press, 2022), 23–40.

2 Michael Mandel, *The Charter of Rights and the Legalization of Politics in Canada* (Toronto: Thompson Education Publishing, 1994); Allan C. Hutchinson, *Waiting for Coraf: A Critique of Law and Rights* (Toronto: University of Toronto Press, 1995); Ian Greene et al., *Final Appeal: Decision-Making in Canadian Courts of Appeal* (Toronto: Lorimer, 1998); Peter McCormick, *Supreme at Last: The Evolution of the Supreme Court of Canada* (Toronto: Lorimer, 2000); F.L. Morton and Rainer Knopff, *The Charter Revolution and the Court Party* (Toronto: University of Toronto Press, 2000); Christopher P. Manfredi, *Judicial Power and the Charter: Canada and the Paradox of Liberal Constitutionalism*, 2nd ed. (Oxford: Oxford University Press, 2000); Patrick James, Donald E. Abelson, and Michael Lusztig, eds., *The Myth of the Sacred: The Charter, the Courts, and the Politics of the Constitution in Canada* (Montreal: McGill-Queen's University Press, 2002); Paul Howe and Peter H. Russell, eds., *Judicial Power and Canadian Democracy* (Montreal: McGill-Queen's University Press, 2001); Emmett Macfarlane, *Governing from the Bench: The Supreme Court of Canada and the Judicial Role* (Vancouver: UBC Press, 2013).

3 Emmett Macfarlane, "Revisiting Judicial Activism," in *Constitutional Crossroads: Charter Rights, Reconciliation, and Change*, ed. Kate Puddister and Emmett Macfarlane (Vancouver: UBC Press, 2022), 41–57; Sujit Choudhry and Claire E. Hunter, "Measuring Judicial Activism on the Supreme Court of Canada: A Comment on *Newfoundland (Treasury Board) v. NAPE*," *McGill Law Journal* 48 (2003): 525–62; Christopher P. Manfredi and James B. Kelly, "Misrepresenting the Supreme Court's Record? A Comment on Sujit Choudhry and Claire E. Hunter, 'Measuring Judicial Activism on the Supreme Court of Canada,'" *McGill Law Journal* 49 (2004): 741–64.

4 Peter W. Hogg and Allison A. Bushell, "The Charter Dialogue between Courts and Legislatures (or Perhaps the Charter of Rights Isn't Such a Bad Thing After All)," *Osgoode Hall Law Journal* 35, no. 1 (1997): 75–124; Christopher P. Manfredi and James B. Kelly, "Six Degrees of Dialogue: A Response to Hogg and Bushell," *Osgoode Hall Law Journal* 37, no. 3

(1999): 513–27; Matthew A. Hennigar, "Expanding the 'Dialogue' Debate: Canadian Federal Government Responses to Lower Court Charter Decisions," *Canadian Journal of Political Science* 37, no. 1 (2004): 3–21; Peter W. Hogg, Allison A. Bushell Thornton, and Wade K. Wright, "Charter Dialogue Revisited – or 'Much Ado About Metaphors,'" *Osgoode Hall Law Journal* 45, no. 1 (2007): 1–65; Emmett Macfarlane, "Dialogue or Compliance? Measuring Legislatures' Policy Responses to Court Rulings on Rights," *International Political Science Review* 34, no. 1 (2012): 39–56; Kent Roach, *The Supreme Court on Trial: Judicial Activism or Democratic Dialogue*, rev. ed. (Toronto: Irwin Law, 2016); Geoffrey Sigalet, Grégoire Webber, and Rosalind Dixon, eds. *Constitutional Dialogue: Rights, Democracy, Institutions* (Cambridge: Cambridge University Press, 2019).

5 Macfarlane, "Dialogue of Compliance?"

6 Emmett Macfarlane, "Conceptual Precision and Parliamentary Systems of Rights: Disambiguating 'Dialogue,'" *Review of Constitutional Studies* 17, no. 2 (2012): 73–100.

7 Dennis Baker, *Not Quite Supreme: The Courts and Coordinate Constitutional Interpretation* (Montreal: McGill-Queen's University Press, 2010).

8 Janet L. Hiebert, "Parliamentary Bills of Rights: An Alternative Model?," *Modern Law Review* 69, no. 1 (2006): 7–28.

9 Stephen Gardbaum, *The New Commonwealth Model of Constitutionalism: Theory and Practice* (Cambridge: Cambridge University Press, 2013); Mark Tushnet, *Weak Courts, Strong Rights: Judicial Review and Social Welfare Rights in Comparative Constitutional Law* (Princeton: Princeton University Press, 2008).

10 Janet L. Hiebert, *Charter Conflicts: What Is Parliament's Role?* (Montreal: McGill-Queen's University Press, 2002).

11 Ibid., 224.

12 Emmett Macfarlane, Janet Hiebert, and Anna Drake, *Legislating under the Charter: Parliament, Executive Power, and Rights* (Toronto: University of Toronto Press, 2023). See also, Janet L. Hiebert, "The Charter, Policy, and Political Judgment," in *Policy Change, Courts, and the Canadian Constitution*, ed. Emmett Macfarlane (Toronto: University of Toronto Press, 2018), 81–102.

13 Macfarlane, Hiebert, and Drake, *Legislating under the Charter*, chap. 7.

14 James B. Kelly, *Governing with the Charter: Legislative and Judicial Activism and Framers' Intent* (Vancouver: UBC Press, 2005), 262.

15 Janet L. Hiebert and James B. Kelly, *Parliamentary Bills of Rights: The Experiences of New Zealand and the United Kingdom* (Cambridge: Cambridge University Press, 2015), 407.

16 Matthew A Hennigar, "Exploring Complex Judicial-Executive Interaction: Federal Government Concessions in Charter of Rights Cases," *Canadian*

Journal of Political Science 43, no. 4 (2010): 821–42; Matthew A. Hennigar, "Why Does the Federal Government Appeal to the Supreme Court of Canada in Charter of Rights cases? A Strategic Explanation," *Law & Society Review* 41, no. 1 (2007): 225–50; Matthew A. Hennigar, "*Reference re Same-Sex Marriage*: Making Sense of the Government's Litigation Strategy," in *Contested Constitutionalism*, ed. James Kelly and Christopher Manfredi (Vancouver: UBC Press, 2009).

17 Kate Puddister, *Seeking the Court's Advice: The Politics of the Canadian Reference Power* (Vancouver: UBC Press, 2019); Carissima Mathen, *Courts without Cases: The Law and Politics of Advisory Opinions* (Oxford: Hart Publishing, 2019).

18 Christopher Manfredi, "Conservatives, the Supreme Court of Canada, and the Constitution: Judicial Government Relations, 2006–2015," *Osgoode Hall Law Journal* 52, no. 3 (2015): 951–84; Emmett Macfarlane, "Conservative with the Constitution? Moderation, Strategy, and Institutional Distrust," in *The Blueprint: Conservative Parties and Their Impact on Canadian Politics*, ed. J.P. Lewis and Joanna Everitt (Toronto: University of Toronto Press, 2017), 221–41; Matthew A. Hennigar, "Unreasonable Disagreement? Judicial-Executive Exchanges about Charter Reasonableness in the Harper Era," *Osgoode Hall Law Journal* 54, no. 4 (2017): 1245–73; Emmett Macfarlane, "'You Can't Always Get What You Want': Regime Politics, the Supreme Court of Canada, and the Harper Government," *Canadian Journal of Political Science* 51, no. 1 (2018): 1–21.

19 Leon E. Trakman, William Cole-Hamilton, and Sean Gatien, "*R. v. Oakes* 1986–1997: Back to the Drawing Board," *Osgoode Hall Law Journal* 36, no. 1 (1998): 83–149; Marshall Rothstein, "Section 1: Justifying Breaches of Charter Rights and Freedoms," *Manitoba Law Journal* 27 (2000): 171–83.

20 Janet L. Hiebert, *Limiting Rights: The Dilemmas of Judicial Review* (Montreal: McGill-Queen's University Press, 1996).

21 Roach, *Supreme Court on Trial*; Macfarlane, "Dialogue or Compliance?"

22 Macfarlane, Hiebert, and Drake, *Legislating under the Charter*.

23 But see Janet Hiebert, "Rights and Public Debate: The Limitations of a 'Rights Must be Paramount' Perspective," *International Journal of Canadian Studies* no. 7–8 (1993): 117–35; Emmett Macfarlane, "Terms of Entitlement: Is There a Distinctly Canadian 'Rights Talk'?," *Canadian Journal of Political Science* 41, no. 2 (2008): 303–28; Erin Crandall, Andrea Lawlor, and Kate Puddister, "Charter Talk: How Canadian Media Cover Rights and Politics," in *Constitutional Crossroads: Reflections on Charter Rights, Reconciliation, and Change*, ed. Kate Puddister and Emmett Macfarlane (Vancouver: UBC Press, 2022), 102–20.

24 Eleni Nicolaides and Dave Snow, "A Paper Tiger No More? The Media Portrayal of the Notwithstanding Clause in Saskatchewan and Ontario,"

Canadian Journal of Political Science 54, no. 1 (2021): 60–74; Michael McGregor, Cameron Anderson, and Scott Pruysers, "Partisanship, Motivated Reasoning and the Notwithstanding Clause: The Case of Provincially Imposed Redistricting in the City of Toronto," *Commonwealth & Comparative Politics* 59, no. 1 (2021): 94–117; Dave Snow and Eleni Nicolaides, "Notwithstanding the Media: Section 33 of the Charter after *Toronto v. Ontario*," in *Constitutional Crossroads: Reflections on Charter Rights, Reconciliation, and Change*, ed. Kate Puddister and Emmett Macfarlane (Vancouver: UBC Press, 2022), 121–39.

25 Janet Hiebert, "Is It Too Late to Rehabilitate Canada's Notwithstanding Clause?" *Supreme Court Law Review* 23, 2nd ser. (2004): 169–89; Janet L. Hiebert, "Compromise and the Notwithstanding Clause: Why the Dominant Narrative Distorts Our Understanding," in *Contested Constitutionalism: Reflections on the Charter of Rights and Freedoms*, ed. James B. Kelly and Christopher P. Manfredi (Vancouver: UBC Press, 2009), 107–25; Dwight Newman, "Canada's Notwithstanding Clause, Dialogue, and Constitutional Identities," in *Constitutional Dialogue: Rights, Democracy, Institutions*, ed. Geoffrey Sigalet, Grégoire Webber, and Rosalind Dixon (Cambridge: Cambridge University Press, 2019), 209–34; Macfarlane, Hiebert, and Drake, *Legislating under the Charter*, 173–6.

26 Mary Ann Glendon, *Rights Talk: The Impoverishment of Political Discourse* (New York: The Free Press, 1991); Macfarlane, "Terms of Entitlement."

1 Rights and the Law's Progressive Measures

GRÉGOIRE WEBBER

Suppose you think, as I do, that the right to abortion requires more than the absence of a criminal prohibition; that the right to education requires the provision of free schooling; that the right to be free from discrimination on the basis of sex, race, sexual orientation, gender identity, and more requires protection in matters of employment, accommodation, services, and more; that the pursuit of equality between persons requires "taking full account of social, political, economic and historical" circumstances;[1] and that a social welfare system is a requirement of justice, of what we owe each other, and so of what we each have a right to. If you think this, then you likely think, as I do, that our rights are to be realized and secured by law.[2] From this thought arises a series of others: that our rights are to be secured by government and legislature, that law and the rule of law are necessary for the full realization of our rights, and that the absence of law and the rule of law spells the violation of our rights. These are thoughts that, though they are at some level plain, are often obscured and in important measure contradicted by the way in which we have come to conceive of our rights and our laws and of their relationships to each other.

The relationships between rights and laws here explored are not contingent on your endorsement of the above examples. I offer a range of other examples below, examples that turn on matters that invite less moral and political disagreement, such as mandating disclosure of contents of food products, designating certain medication as available "over-the-counter" or by prescription, and even sewer systems and waste removal. The conception of rights and of laws here explored is open to a range of moral and political commitments and so the reference to "progressive" in the chapter's title is not to a set of such commitments. The title's reference is instead to the UN General Assembly's proclamation of the Universal Declaration of Human Rights "as a common standard of achievement for all peoples and all nations," with the aim that the "universal and effective recognition and observance" of the rights and freedoms set out in it shall be secured "by progressive measures."[3] As will be explored, the Declaration conceives of a relationship between rights and laws according to which "human rights should be protected by the rule of law."[4] It is a conception of rights and of laws that is not at the heart of the jurisprudence of the Supreme Court of Canada and of much of the scholarship interpreting the work of courts developing human rights law. There is here no suggestion that our Court has failed to arrive at conclusions that favour the rights of each and all. But the frame of analysis under the Canadian Charter of Rights and Freedoms favours a conception of law that opposes law to rights, that sanctions the infringement of our rights by the law, and that regularly finds that laws are justified in their infringement of our rights. It is an understanding that is at some distance from the understanding of rights and of law favoured by the Declaration.

The chapter begins by reviewing how the Declaration secured a universal commitment to human rights and then reviews how a similar strategy animates many domestic bills of rights, like our Canadian Charter. The chapter then reviews how the law's progressive measures complete the incomplete commitment to rights captured in the Declaration and the Canadian Charter before comparing that understanding of the relationship between rights and laws with the understanding that animates the Supreme Court's jurisprudence. The chapter concludes by suggesting that inherent to the very idea of law is this somewhat complex thought: that our rights are law's point and purpose and measure.

On the Universality of Rights

The Universal Declaration of Human Rights almost failed at various stages in its hesitant journey to the United Nations General Assembly on 10 December 1948. Yet, on that fateful day, the Assembly adopted the Declaration without a single dissenting vote. The making of the Declaration illuminates not only the precariousness of world politics following a world war, but also – and critically for the ideas here explored – the relationship between rights and what the Declaration refers to as "progressive measures," measures that, being progressive, secure the "universal and effective recognition and observation" of our human rights. The ultimate success of the Declaration's improbable achievement can be attributed to any number of considerations, but one holds special status for understanding the Declaration's claim to universality. It is a consideration that speaks to the relationship between a commitment and its implementation and a corresponding relationship between the general and the specific, all of which speaks to the relationship between rights and their realization by the law's progressive measures.

The wording of the Declaration was initiated by a draft prepared by the first director of the UN Secretariat's Human Rights Division, John Humphrey, who instructed his staff "to study all the world's existing constitutions and rights instruments."[5] The result of this protracted study of rights instruments – past and present, local and regional – was a "list of forty-eight items that represented, in Humphrey's view, the common core of the documents and proposals his staff had collected."[6] In the director's exaggerated words, his draft included "every conceivable right which the Drafting Committee might want to discuss."[7] Included were "political and civil rights found in the British, French, and American revolutionary declarations" and "economic and social rights found in late nineteenth- and early twentieth-century constitutions such as those of Sweden, Norway, the Soviet Union, and several Latin American countries."[8] In this way, the making of the Declaration proceeded from the local and the regional as it aspired to the universal: local and regional attempts to set out rights and freedoms for local and regional communities informed the grander appeal to universality for all communities. The Declaration's content was developed, at least initially, not by appealing to natural reason or ethical and moral thought but instead by reference to the study of instruments made in times and places less ambitious than the one then confronting the United Nations. Perhaps because of this methodology, when questioned what philosophy had guided the work of the Human Rights Division in setting out a first draft of universal rights, Humphrey responded that the draft was based on "no philosophy whatsoever."[9]

When the Human Rights Committee set to work on Humphrey's draft, René Cassin, the French delegate to the committee and an important member of the drafting subcommittee, sought "to make sense of how the various rights fit together" and to promote clarity "in their presentation."[10] Cassin was mindful "to find a formula that did not require the Commission to take sides on the nature of [the human person] and society, or to become immured in metaphysical controversies."[11] The challenge was to affirm rights common to all human persons, to affirm that each right is to be read in relation to every other, and to do so in a manner that would be acceptable to the world's many political communities.

This theme of a common standard to be realized by local and regional specification can be traced from Humphrey's agnosticism regarding the philosophical foundations of his draft to Cassin's conscious effort to review the draft so that it could be agreed to by countries with differing understandings of how best to realize rights in their different communities. As will be explored below, the resulting commitment to the universality of human rights is in no way inconsistent with the recognition that universal rights can be specified in a variety of different ways. As Cassin would emphasize in the course of the committee's deliberations, "a 'universal' document would ... have to leave room for an ample degree of pluralism in the understanding and implementation of many of its rights."[12] A more poetic formulation of this thought was offered by Jacques Maritain, who said that "different kinds of music" can be played on the Declaration's many strings.[13]

For this reason, much of the Declaration leaves unspecified what human rights require of us and of others. Few contested questions animating rights are answered in the Declaration, which is not to say that the final draft lacks a governing philosophy. A most significant philosophical understanding is articulated in Article 29, in which the Declaration affirms that every person "has duties to the community" and that it is only in community that "the free and full development of [one's] personality is possible." Notwithstanding this all-important conception of the human person and of our relationships to each other in community, there is a general lack of specificity in the Declaration's text as to the content and scope of our rights. That lack of specificity enabled twenty-three of the thirty articles to be unanimously approved in the General Assembly and nays never totalling more than seven were registered for only three of the Declaration's articles. On the final, most important vote on the Declaration as a whole, the success of seeking a commitment to human rights that could be implemented in a plurality of ways was manifested in the absence of a single dissenting voice: forty-eight votes in favour, eight abstentions, none opposed.[14]

The Declaration highlights how a commitment to human rights stated at a sufficient level of generality can allow for different approaches to the implementation of our rights as different political communities undertake the difficult task and responsibility of specifying the general. That task and responsibility are to be realized by the adoption of what the Declaration calls "progressive measures," measures that have as their point the realization of human rights for each and every one of a community's members. Though there are a plurality of measures that may be adopted in political communities to this end, one stands out for its unparalleled contribution to human rights: the law.

Domestic Bills of Rights

The relationship between the Declaration and domestic law can be contemplated as one of universality in commitment and plurality in implementation. The Declaration's universality set out a general commitment to human rights common to all persons and their communities that allowed, in turn, each community and its members to specify the content of that general commitment. Among the various progressive measures pertinent to evaluating how a community has sought to specify the open-ended commitments of the Declaration, a domestic bill of rights would appear to be an obvious starting point and especially so for those bills of rights, like the Canadian Charter of Rights and Freedoms, that were adopted after 1948. And yet, with few exceptions, domestic bills of rights like our own do little to specify further the variously worded rights affirmed in the Universal Declaration of Human Rights.

Open to the authors of domestic bills of rights is a possibility closed to those concerned with affirming the universality of rights for all political communities: the possibility of specifying rights that, though universal in their generality, are not universal in every respect once specified and implemented. Yet, despite this opportunity, indeed despite the responsibility incumbent on all political communities to realize and give life to the rights of the Declaration for all members of their communities, no domestic bill of rights does so to any considerable degree. In this way, little differs between the universal and the local in terms of the scope and content of the rights instruments, and this despite the fact that the motivation for leaving general matters unspecified is of a different order.

Unhindered by a commitment to set a common standard for all political communities and confronted by a responsibility to settle upon a specific standard for their political community, the architects of domestic bills of rights the world over have nonetheless formulated rights in a manner that leaves their scope and content open and unresolved. They have favoured the less studied but no less compelling account of an incompletely theorized agreement: an agreement on an "abstraction" despite "disagreement on particulars"; indeed, this genre of incompletely theorized agreement is illustrated by reference to bills of rights, which often leave "room for many possible specifications of underlying rights."[15]

With few exceptions, bills of rights have been framed by their architects and adopted by political authorities in a manner that leaves the specification of rights *to a later day*.[16] Why have they done so? It is likely that these architects and authorities were live to many of the same sensibilities that animated the commitment to generality in the making of the Declaration. The various members of a political community charged with adopting a bill of rights aim to affirm rights in a manner that will secure broad assent despite the persistence of disagreement over how best to specify rights for the community. After all, the many debates animating rights are not anticipated to dissipate the moment a bill of rights is drafted and adopted: while the responsible authorities agree to the rights to life, liberty, and security and more, they do so despite continuing disagreement on how those rights bear on contested questions. It would seem that the aspiration is to avoid, as the authors of the Declaration so aptly avoided, the registration of opposition to the very commitment to rights themselves when a domestic bill of rights is adopted.

Thus, echoing Article 3 of the Declaration, our Canadian Charter affirms that "Everyone has the right to life, liberty and security of person" in a way that avoids providing definite answers to questions over the death penalty, abortion, assisted dying, and more. Echoing the Declaration's Article 19, our Charter affirms that "Everyone has the right to freedom of opinion and expression" in a way that offers no determinate answers to debates surrounding hate speech, pornography, libel, and more. And so it is with the various formulations of various other rights, more or less echoing similar formulations in the Universal Declaration in a manner that avoids resolving disputes over a familiar range of contested claims of rights. While it would be too strong to suggest that bills of rights play no part in resolving these and other disputes over rights, it nevertheless remains the case that the formulations of rights in bills of rights bear on without contributing much more to the resolution of these contested questions. The disputes are left to be resolved by way of progressive measures, measures that aim to settle what, on the whole, neither the Declaration nor domestic bills of rights have sought to settle: the implementation of a commitment, a specification of the general, a delimitation of the scope and content of our rights.

It is a general feature of international and domestic bills of rights that they proceed largely in abstractions, seeking agreement on grand formulations in a way that avoids many of the great debates and disagreements animating rights in political communities. The commitment by the architects and authorities responsible for domestic bills of rights to leave the relationship between rights and disputed claims of rights open and unresolved appears to mirror, in outcome and perhaps also in motivation, the commitment made by authors of the Declaration to secure broad consensus around the idea expressed in the Declaration's first article: that we are all "born free and equal in dignity and rights." The resolution of disputed claims of rights is thus not avoided because these contests are unimportant or unforeseen or because they are predicted to abate with time, though some will. It rather seems that the common hesitation among those responsible for domestic bills of rights to go very much farther than the Declaration in specifying our rights relates, perhaps paradoxically, to the importance of such specifications for the community. Given such importance, there is reason to favour a scheme according to which the specification of our rights remains in ready reach so that we can correct the errors of times past, all without denying or underpaying the ever-present risk of errors here and now.

Law's Progressive Measures

The decision to avoid undertaking the difficult, contested, and contingent specification of rights within a bill of rights does not relieve a political community of its responsibility to do so. After all, even if neither the Declaration nor our Charter resolves questions about assisted suicide, hate speech, pornography, libel, and more, there remains a responsibility to settle the scope and content of the rights to life and to free expression and to more in these and other respects. Absent such specifications, our rights remain inchoate and we remain without the protection of the rule of law in affirming our rights, in claiming what is due to us by right. So where is such specification undertaken? Which are the progressive measures that will implement our general commitment to human rights so that these rights can be claimed in a manner that settles, at least provisionally, some disputed questions?

Given the general absence of such efforts within bills of rights, the effort must be pursued elsewhere. As was the case before and as continues to be the case after a bill of rights is adopted, members of a political community look to their legal system to determine much of the specified scope and content of their rights. As is well understood even when it is not acknowledged, much of the work specifying and implementing the universal rights set out in a bill of rights is to be found in everyday law – law that is unremarkable in status and title when compared with such grand instruments as a Universal Declaration of Human Rights or a constitutional Charter of Rights and Freedoms.[17] Yet, despite lacking in special status or heightened dignity, the law's progressive measures give universal rights life in a political community. Through various enactments in criminal law, labour law, family law, tort law, and other fields of overlapping legal regulation, the law's progressive measures specify the open-ended, general commitment to human rights by articulating who owes what to whom. The law's measures set out modes of criminal, civil, and other responsibilities; they define the scope and the content of protected and forbidden and regulated instances of human activity; they settle the time, place, and manner of engaging in such activity.

The law's progressive measures are part of a political community's efforts to complete that which remains open and unresolved in a bill of rights. In so doing, the law gives the various rights and freedoms legal life – it constitutes those rights by delimiting their scope and content and by harmonizing them one with the other, so that everyone has rights and can do right by every other person.

To illustrate this understanding of the law's progressive measures to realize human rights, consider the Declaration's affirmation, in Article 3, that "Everyone has the right to life," an affirmation recalled in section 7 of the Canadian Charter. The positive law's special responsibility to protect everyone's right to life is pursued in a variety of ways, sometimes directly by prohibiting actions inimical to life and sometimes less directly by regulating activities that pose significant risks to human life. The criminal law of murder, the tort of wrongful death, occupational safety regulations, and traffic rules all realize and specify the right to life, as do the policing, investigatory, and prosecutorial responsibilities to prevent the loss of life and to seek justice when this right is violated.

Consider, in turn, the Declaration's Article 25, which provides that "Everyone has the right to a standard of living adequate for the health and well-being of himself and of his family," captured in part by the right to security of the person in the Charter's section 7. The responsible legislature sets out to protect the health and well-being of persons against general threats and specific dangers, all the while acknowledging that its authority is not like that of a parent, who can require a child to observe healthy eating habits, to exercise, and to sleep reasonable hours. The legislature acts to realize the right to health and well-being by many direct and indirect measures, including requiring testing and approval for new drugs; regulating the medical profession; categorizing medication as available "over-the-counter" or only by prescription; licensing commercial food preparation and imposing hygienic standards; mandating disclosure of contents of food products, nutritional information, and negative health effects; authorizing and funding various educational programs on healthy lifestyles and vaccination; and, as in Canada, by directly providing medical care and insurance through public funds. Less directly but not less importantly, the right to health is secured and promoted by laws on pollution and clean air and water, and even in establishing public works like sewer systems and waste removal.

Consider now the Declaration's Article 21, which provides that "Everyone has the right to take part in the government of his country, directly or through freely chosen representatives," which is specified in part by the Canadian Charter's guarantee that "Every citizen … has the right to vote." That right will be impossible to exercise unless there are provisions on the frequency of elections, the qualifications of candidates, the eligibility requirements of voters, the demarcation of electoral constituencies, the system by which voters elect representatives, the regulation of spending during the election, and more.[18]

While the Declaration and domestic bills of rights may avoid specifying the scope and content of these and other rights, a free and democratic political community cannot and so lawmakers are called upon to complete the task left open in rights instruments. In so doing, lawmakers not only set out to resolve in law the questions animating the rights to life and health and to vote, they also appeal to law's distinctive devices to set out bright lines respecting eligible medical procedures, drug approval processes, the hours of voting, the registration of voters on electoral rolls, and other specifications of our general, abstract commitment to rights.

To recognize that there are innumerable ways of going right in the specification of our rights is not to suggest that reason is abandoned in favour of erratic or adventitious choices. Just as no painter or builder or composer will succeed unless each choice that is free and open in the painting of a canvass or the building of a home or the composing of a symphony is made with a view to the overall project at hand and to coherence with all of the choices that have come before the one now present, so too with the lawmaker. Every alternative that is live for adoption is supported by its contribution to realizing the general right and so by its relationship to protecting and promoting the life and health of the person and of that person's participation in government, among other ends. Once the law's progressive measures have specified the scope and content of a human right, it becomes, in law, a fully "legislated right,"[19] which is not to deny or to underplay that it warrants its place in our law because, in advance of any such legislative specification, there was a general right in need of such specification.

More examples could be given for the "immensely complex" and "intricate regimes" that characterize the law's social security measures, health care and education measures, and more.[20] But the organizing idea is a constant: the law's progressive measures are necessary for realizing our rights. Without the law's progressive measures, many human rights would fail to be realized and secured. That is true not only of what some refer to as positive rights (rights that are only realized with progressive measures, such as the right to vote or to primary and secondary education) but also of what is sometimes referred to as negative rights (rights that award immunity against legislative interference). Among such negative rights is the right of persons to freedom of expression. As intimated above, this right is in need of specification in order to demarcate the boundaries of that freedom and thus to award to persons confidence in expressing themselves freely within the scope of the right.[21] It will be accepted by all that no person may, in the name of freedom of expression, "advocate some public policy … by interrupting a church service, or a classroom, or a sickroom, or a session of Congress or of the Supreme Court, or by ringing a doorbell and demanding to be heard."[22] Yet the general declaration that "Everyone has freedom of expression" does not establish such boundaries without more. The law's regulation of libel, defamation, intellectual property, contempt of court, incitement to religious hatred, publication of confidential documents, disclosure of state secrets, and so forth expresses judgments on what is needed to realize this and other rights in community. Although libel and defamation may indeed constitute expressive activity, it is too simple a reading of our rights to conclude that we have the "freedom" (read: are subject to no constraints) to express ourselves on such matters to anyone at any time, all without regard to the rights of others. As expressed by Article 29 of the Declaration, our "duties to the community" – including with respect to the reputation of others, for example – informs the scope and content of our right to free expression, so that everyone has rights and can respect the rights of others.

To say that the law's progressive measures realize rights in community is in no way to deny that barbarous acts have been perpetrated by and in the name of the law. It is no way to deny that the law has been a tool for the strong to prey on the weak and for majorities to oppress minorities. It is in no way to deny that, even with good will and a commitment to do right by all, the law's makers are liable do wrong and to violate the rights of persons they are duty-bound to protect. But it is to affirm that when the law's measures are progressive – when they justly specify general rights in community – they complete the rights project initiated but left unfinished by the Declaration and the Canadian Charter. In so doing, the law does what the Declaration calls on all political communities to do: to recognize every member of one's community "everywhere as a person before the law," to make all "equal before the law," and to award to everyone the "equal protection of the law."[23] As expressed by the Declaration's makers, "it is essential, if [the human person] is not to be compelled to have recourse, as a last resort, to rebellion against tyranny and oppression, that human rights should be protected by the rule of law."[24]

"Most Rights Where There Is the Least Law"

It has been a surprising development in legal thought that, soon after the Canadian Charter was adopted, judges and scholars developed a conception of our rights and of our law according to which the law's progressive measures are at some distance from the specification of human rights. As faithfully reported by Janet Hiebert in *Limiting Rights*, a distinction has been drawn between, on the one hand, "defining rights" by "giv[ing] scope to the Charter's vague provisions" and, on the other hand, "limiting rights" with a view to "accommodat[ing] and reconcil[ing] conflicting rights and policy values."[25] According to this distinction, the first task – that of defining rights – falls to the judiciary, as it sets out to define the scope of the many general, abstract rights of the Canadian Charter. The second task – that of limiting rights – encompasses the legislature's law-making, but it is not a task that contributes to the right's definition, its specification, its implementation. The law's measures may limit but not help to define our rights.

What, then, is it to "limit" a right on this understanding? Much is disclosed by the favoured terminology of the Supreme Court of Canada in evaluating the relationship of law's measures to the limitation of the Charter's rights and freedoms. Even when such measures are held to be justified, legislation is said to "infringe,"[26] "*prima facie* infringe,"[27] "violate,"[28] "derogate from,"[29] "breach,"[30] "contravene,"[31] "trench,"[32] "abridge,"[33] "impair,"[34] "deny,"[35] "override,"[36] "trammel,"[37] or "incur" upon our rights.[38] If these many words have overlapping meaning, it is that the law's progressive measures are inconsistent with rights, denying them a scope and content that they would otherwise have but for the law's measures. From the point of view of the rights themselves, the law's measures are regressive, not progressive: the measures oppose rather than realize rights in community.

The seed of this legal thought was planted in the 1986 case of *R. v. Oakes*, in which the Supreme Court awarded to the Charter's limitation clause its most authoritative interpretation. Contrary to the Declaration's sound affirmation that every person has duties to others in community because it is only in community that "the free and full development of [one's] personality is possible,"[39] the Court reasoned that it is necessary to limit rights "in circumstances where their exercise would be inimical to the realization of collective goals of fundamental importance."[40] The implication of such a conception of rights is that the human person has rights that can be injurious, harmful, damaging, destructive, and ruinous for others, rights that can be opposed to what we owe others and that can be opposed to the very community in which one's free and full development of human personality is enabled. In this opposition, the Court appeals to a conception of rights that opposes "the interests of society with those of individuals and groups."[41]

It is a conception of rights and of law and of their general opposition that has been endorsed by many. Aharon Barak, former president of the Supreme Court of Israel, writes for example that a "limitation of a constitutional right by law also means its infringement," there being "no difference between" the limitation and the infringement of a right.[42] Stephen Gardbaum tracks much human rights case law by drawing a distinction between the "internal" and "external" limitations of a right, explaining that internal limits are about the "scope and definition" of rights as determined by legal interpretation of text, whereas external limits are "constitutionally permissible restrictions on rights" or their "infringements" as set out in legislation.[43] The chapter of *The Oxford Handbook of the Canadian Constitution* devoted to surveying the Charter's limitation clause frames its analysis of rights' limitations as the "justification of rights violations."[44] The settled view, for many,[45] is that law's measures may be justified – indeed, may be required in the name of a free and democratic society – but that, even when justified, such measures do not secure and promote our rights: the law infringes or violates our rights and the only question is whether the law's measures do so permissibly.

On such an understanding of the relationship between law and rights, we have the most rights when there is the least law, but our rights are not always worthy of the law's respect. The price of admission into a society in which the law secures the conditions necessary for everyone's free and full development of personality is the infringement and violation of our rights. This understanding risks distorting the relationship of rights to law set out in the Declaration. Missing from the conception of rights and their relationship to law under the Canadian Charter is the understanding of a "limitation" of a right disclosed by its Latin root *limes*, communicating "boundary" and "frontier." So framed, the law's progressive measures set out to settle the just and justified boundary and frontiers of our rights – their scope and content so that the rights of every person may be fully secured and realized.

Soit droit fait

The motto of the Faculty of Law at Queen's University is *soit droit fait*, being the classic statement of the monarch when granting royal assent to bills passed by the Houses of the Westminster Parliament. This French expression admits of no single English translation and is often rendered either as "Let right be done" or as "Let law be done." The instability of any single English translation can be traced to the root of the French *droit*, which captures in a single word what in English is captured by the words "right," "rights," and "law." In signifying more than one meaning, the French *droit* is a homonym: it has more than one meaning, though the word communicating each meaning is pronounced and spelled the same way. However, unlike chance homonyms like "savings bank" and "river bank," the homonyms of *droit* are closely related. Though they are not synonyms like "gift" and "present," *droit(s)* as in "right(s)" and *droit* as in "law" have conceptually related meanings.

Human rights are law's point and purpose and measure. But this measure is a multifaceted one, for law is both to conform to and to realize rights in community. The most straightforward relationship between the measure of rights and the law's content is one of conformity: human rights are superior and prior to the law's progressive measures. No matter the content of the law in our community, no one has the right to violate another's human rights and no law should survive if it is inconsistent with our rights. But in addition to this relationship is another, the one explored throughout this chapter according to which the relationships of superiority and priority between rights and the law are more complex insofar as human rights require the law's progressive measures for their realization.

Those relationships are understood by understanding the multiplicity of ways in which the law relates to human rights. The criminal and tort laws on assault and the wide range of health regulations reviewed above realize and specify in part the human right to security of the person. The provision of a publicly funded school system and the availability of government bursaries and loans realize and specify in part the human right to education. Freedom of information laws, privacy legislation, and competition laws in relation to ownership and control of the media realize and specify in part the human right to freedom of expression. The law of contract; the provision for limited liability corporations and partnerships; the regulation of publicly traded companies; the regulation of collective bargaining; limitations on working hours; the law of unfair dismissal; and provision for overtime pay all realize and specify in part the human rights to work and to fair and just working conditions.

Without the clarity and direction provided by the law's progressive measures in these and other ways, our human rights would be inchoate in our political communities and neither right nor law would be as both should be. The expression "human rights law" should not be taken primarily to denote a specialized subset of legal materials; properly understood, it expresses the special role of law and its progressive measures in securing and realizing human rights for all.

NOTES

1 *Withler v. Canada (Attorney General)*, 2011 SCC 12, para. 39.

2 I explore some of these thoughts in Grégoire Webber, "The Charter Party and the Work of Parliament," *Policy Options*, 27 January 2016, https://policyoptions.irpp.org/2016/01/27/the-charter-party-and-the-work-of-parliament/. In the fall of 2016, I sought to participate in the vision of government and legal responsibility for realizing our rights articulated in that essay, and in my scholarship more generally, by joining the ministerial office of Jody Wilson-Raybould as Legal Affairs Advisor to the Minister of Justice and Attorney General of Canada. That experience reinforced my conviction that, though there is much wrong that can be done by government and by law, there are rights and freedoms that cannot be realized in the absence of government and of law.

3 United Nations, "Universal Declaration of Human Rights (1948)," Preamble, accessed 25 September 2024, https://www.un.org/en/about-us/universal-declaration-of-human-rights.

4 Ibid.

5 Mary Ann Glendon, *A World Made New: Eleanor Roosevelt and the Universal Declaration of Human Rights* (New York: Random House, 2001), 56.

6 Ibid., 57.

7 Ibid., 57.

8 Ibid., 57–8.

9 Ibid., 58.

10 Ibid., 63.

11 Ibid., 68.

12 Ibid., 69.

13 Jacques Maritain, introduction to *Human Rights: Comments and Interpretations: A Symposium edited by UNESCO* (London: A. Wingate, 1950), viii. In Maritain's introduction to this analogy, he writes that, when "we are no longer dealing with the mere enumeration of Human Rights," then

"the difficulties and arguments begin" (vii–viii). On how a universal right "does not, by itself, entail the existence of any specific rights of specific persons," see the excellent discussion in Joel Feinberg, *Social Philosophy* (Englewood Cliffs, NJ: Prentice-Hall, 1973), 71.

14 Glendon, *World Made New*, 169–70.

15 Cass R. Sunstein, *Legal Reasoning and Political Conflict* (New York: Oxford University Press, 1996), 47.

16 Grégoire Webber, *The Negotiable Constitution: On the Limitation of Rights* (Cambridge: Cambridge University Press, 1999), 1–12, 160–73.

17 See Grégoire Webber, "Human Goods and Human Rights Law," in *The Cambridge Handbook of Natural Law and Human Rights*, ed. Tom Angier, Iain Benson, and Mark Retter (Cambridge: Cambridge University Press, 2022), 324–37.

18 These examples are explored in Grégoire Webber and Paul Yowell, "Introduction: Securing Human Rights through Legislation," in Grégoire Webber et al., *Legislated Rights: Securing Human Rights through Legislation* (Cambridge: Cambridge University Press, 2018), 17.

19 See Grégoire Webber et al., *Legislated Rights: Securing Human Rights through Legislation* (Cambridge: Cambridge University Press, 2018).

20 Jeff King, *Judging Social Rights* (Cambridge: Cambridge University Press, 2012), 42–3.

21 See Grégoire Webber, "Proportionality and Limitations on Freedom of Speech," *The Oxford Handbook of Freedom of Speech*, ed. Frederic Schauer and Adrienne Stone (Oxford: Oxford University Press, 2021), 173–92.

22 Alexander Meiklejohn, "The First Amendment Is an Absolute," *Supreme Court Review* (1961): 261.

23 United Nations, Universal Declaration of Human Rights, Articles 6 and 7.

24 Ibid., Preamble.

25 Janet L. Hiebert, *Limiting Rights: The Dilemma of Judicial Review* (Montreal: McGill-Queen's University Press, 1996), 150.

26 *RJR-MacDonald v. Canada*, [1995] 3 S.C.R. 199, para. 129.

27 *Canadian Foundation for Children, Youth and the Law v. Canada*, [2004] 1 S.C.R. 76, para. 73.

28 *Vriend v. Alberta*, [1998] 1 S.C.R. 493, para. 108; P.W. Hogg, "Interpreting the Charter of Rights: Generosity and Justification," *Osgoode Hall Law Journal* 28, no. 3 (1990): 826.

29 *M v. H*, [1999] 2 S.C.R. 3, para. 333.

30 *Gosselin v. Quebec*, [2002] 4 S.C.R. 429, para. 140.

31 *Edmonton Journal v. Alberta*, [1989] 2 S.C.R. 1326 at 1342.

32 *R. v. Edwards Books and Art*, [1986] 2 S.C.R 713, at 795 and 768.

33 Ibid., 768; *Vriend v. Alberta*, 1998, 108.

34 *Vriend v. Alberta*, 1998, 108.

35 *Ford v. Quebec*, [1988] 2 S.C.R. 712, 773; *Sauvé v. Canada*, [2002] 3 S.C.R 519, para. 1.
36 *Irwin Toy v. Quebec*, [1989] 1 S.C.R. 927 at 1007; *RJR-MacDonald v. Canada*, 1995, 129.
37 *Sauvé v. Canada*, 2002, para. 1.
38 *R. v. Keegstra*, [1990] 3 S.C.R. 697 at 735.
39 United Nations, Universal Declaration of Human Rights, Article 29.
40 *R. v. Oakes*, [1986] 1 S.C.R. 103, para. 65.
41 Ibid., para. 70. See Grégoire Webber, "What *Oakes* Could Have Said (or How to Read a Limitations Clause)," *Supreme Court Law Review* 112, 2nd ser. (2023): 61.
42 Aharon Barak, *Proportionality: Constitutional Rights and their Limitations* (Cambridge: Cambridge University Press, 2012), 101.
43 Stephen Gardbaum, "Limiting Constitutional Rights," *UCLA Law Review* 54 (2007): 795, 801.
44 Charles-Maxime Panaccio, "The Justification of Rights Violations: Section 1 of the Charter," in *The Oxford Handbook of the Canadian Constitution*, ed. Peter Oliver, Patrick Macklem, and Nathalie Des Rosiers (Oxford: Oxford University Press, 2017), 657.
45 See, for example, Robert Alexy, *A Theory of Constitutional Rights* (Oxford: Oxford University Press, 2002); David M. Beatty, *The Ultimate Rule of Law* (Oxford: Oxford University Press, 2004); Kai Möller, *The Global Model of Constitutional Rights* (Oxford: Oxford University Press, 2012); Francisco J. Urbina, *A Critique of Proportionality and Balancing* (Cambridge: Cambridge University Press, 2017). Many of these themes are surveyed in Grégoire Webber, "On the Loss of Rights," in *Proportionality and the Rule of Law*, ed. Grant Huscroft, Bradley W. Miller, and Grégoire Webber (Cambridge: Cambridge University Press, 2014), 123–54.

2 An Honourable Parliament? Section 35 and Legislative Rights Review

MINH DO

Policymaking under the Canadian Charter of Rights and Freedoms is argued to result in the dominance of the Department of Justice (DOJ), and the executive more generally, to shape legislation with the aim of avoiding potential legal challenges arising from judicial review.[1] To reduce the executive's dominance over policymaking and the democratic deficit resulting from this dominance, Parliament should review legislation to scrutinize and hold accountable the government's balancing of various rights and interests.[2] Parliament, which includes the House of Commons as the primary representative institution of government, thus has a coordinate role to engage in debates around rights protections and balancing.[3] By including elected representatives in policy debates with implications on individual rights, the executive's power might be more constrained from making unilateral decisions on contentious issues, although the extent to which this occurs in practice is debatable.[4] To date, the literature on legislative rights review has focused on individual rights enshrined in a Constitution or parliamentary bill of rights. This scholarship has not considered whether parliamentary review of Aboriginal rights is required to correct the democratic deficit in executive-dominated policymaking. This oversight is significant considering that Aboriginal rights were also formally enshrined and recognized under section 35 in the *Constitution Act, 1982* alongside individual human rights found in the Charter.

This chapter asks the following question: Would legislative rights review be an effective check on the executive's legislative priorities to ensure the protection of section 35 rights? Although legislative review is intended to correct a democratic deficit in rights balancing, I argue that legislative review faces *legitimacy* deficits that render it ill-equipped to sufficiently protect section 35 rights. Parliament's illegitimate status to review section 35 rights is due to both the nature of section 35 rights themselves and, by extension, the lack of authority vested in Canadian elected representatives to limit section 35 rights. Section 35 rights are not individual rights but relate to governments' jurisdictional authority. As such, section 35 rights can only be limited through political, nation-to-nation negotiations between Crown representatives and an Indigenous nation through instruments like treaties. Representatives in Parliament thus do not have the authority to limit the jurisdictional authority of Indigenous nations that existed before the assertion of Crown sovereignty. Instead, Parliament may play a role in consistently and intentionally upholding the honour of the Crown, even if it lacks the legitimacy to interpret section 35 rights.[5] Parliament can uphold the honour of the Crown by urging the executive to enter negotiations with Indigenous nations, particularly in contexts when executive actions appear to affect section 35 rights. Parliament can accomplish this task more consistently and intentionally if significant reforms were pursued that institutionalized Indigenous representation. If these reforms are pursued, Indigenous representation within Parliament must reflect Indigenous peoples' nationhood status and be given sufficient powers and autonomy to advocate the continuing existence of Indigenous peoples as distinct political entities.

The chapter will proceed as follows. First, the chapter will outline the key ideas that make legislative review of rights an attractive option for correcting democratic deficits from executive dominated decision-making. The aim is to show that the primary motivation for legislative rights review is to directly bring elected representatives into debates that have important rights-based dimensions because these representatives have important perspectives that should be brought to bear on these policy questions. Second, the chapter will explain why the protection of Aboriginal rights under section 35 does not suffer from a democratic deficit problem, making legislative rights review unsuitable. These sections will detail why section 35 should be understood as delineating jurisdictional authority rather than as analogous to Charter or individual rights. As such, it would be *ultra vires* for the Parliament of an external governing authority to limit or unilaterally interpret section 35 rights. Third, the chapter will outline some potential institutional reforms that would enshrine the consideration for the honour of the Crown during the legislative process. Rather than replace nation-to-nation negotiations as the primary way to negotiate the parameters of section 35 rights, upholding the honour of the Crown in the legislative process could help facilitate these important negotiations and prevent unilateral executive action on matters that affect section 35 rights.

Legislative Rights Review and the Democratic Deficit

The addition of the Charter in Canada's Constitution has garnered extensive scholarly attention because of the concern that unelected judges using the power of judicial review can unduly interfere with governmental policymaking. Judicial review may increase the threat of judicial incursion into policymaking, which is considered the primary site of governance, but government possesses many tactics to continue advancing its agenda despite an additional check on executive power. Indeed, scholarship interested in finding ways the judiciary constrains executive decision-making draws attention to the complex ways in which judicial review shapes existing Westminster parliamentary dynamics.

This literature that focuses on the interplay between legislative behaviour and judicial review finds that judicial review exacerbates the existing centralization of power in government.[6] When proposing bills, line departments must conform to drafting instructions that are approved by Cabinet, and then turn to the DOJ for the drafting of legislation in accordance with those instructions. When departments submit a memoranda to Cabinet, they must identify any potential legal risks associated with their proposal. Cabinet's control over drafting instructions and the DOJ's role in facilitating Cabinet's directives is also aimed to assess the legal risks the government is willing to take on.[7] The DOJ's control over drafting legislation to ensure its constitutional compliance effectively transforms it into a "central agency" because of its powers to intervene in other departments' affairs.[8] Matthew Hennigar details the specific instruments by which the DOJ has taken on a central agency role. Each federal department has a Legal Services Unit that is tasked with providing legal advice and collaborating with drafting legislation.[9] Legislation from other departments then gets vetted through the DOJ's more specialized Charter experts.[10] The DOJ further maintains its centralized oversight of policymaking by establishing legal guidelines or parameters that policymakers must follow.[11] Consequently, the DOJ coordinates with other departments hierarchically because it exercises top-down authority to identify instances of possible unconstitutional legislation across line departments.

Judicial review may enhance the power of the "centre" of government, but it does not follow that the executive will only conform to judicial rulings or prioritize compliance with the Constitution when drafting legislation. Janet Hiebert finds that governments have varying tolerance for legal risk, such that advice from the DOJ about legally risky legislation may not be accepted by other ministers.[12] Some key reasons why a government may be willing to pass legally risky legislation include the weak accountability mechanisms in Parliament to scrutinize government bills based on Charter compliance, the government's primary goal of passing its legislative agenda, and the reality that only a fraction of legislation will be challenged in court.[13] Even if legal challenges are pursued, the party in power may have already changed, the judiciary can be blamed for changing Parliament's intent, and the executive has extensive resources to effectively defend its legislation in court.[14] For example, attorneys general can strategically decide whether to appeal judicial decisions and the legal arguments to be made in court, typically without legislative input.[15]

Due to both the power of unelected courts to strike down legislation and the power of the executive to strategically respond to judicial oversight by further centralizing policymaking powers, some scholars advocate for an expanded role for Parliament to provide its perspective on how legislation can uphold Charter rights and values. Under a coordinated approach to constitutional interpretation, the power to interpret the Constitution is shared between the judicial, executive, and legislative branches of government and is exercised over time as constitutional issues unfold through inter-institutional exchanges.[16] Each institution should have the means to interpret and uphold the Constitution according to its unique vantage point and capacity since there is often reasonable disagreement over the appropriate means to uphold Charter rights and values.[17] It follows, then, that Parliament, as the primary representative institution in government, should have a role in proffering perspectives that might otherwise be neglected by other institutions like the executive or the judiciary. Although the executive is also comprised of elected officials, the fact that majority governments can be formed with less than 50 per cent of the popular vote bolsters the imperative to include the views of the legislature in shaping legislation. Parliament will correct democratic deficits associated with policymaking that are controlled by the executive. In this way, a legislative rights review offers a counterbalance to other institutions and facilitates deliberation and collaboration between institutions on important rights and values.[18]

Coordinate constitutionalists assert that the judiciary, executive, and legislature should have equal interpretative powers, but there is a recognition that current institutional dynamics between these institutions do not reflect such an equality. Between these three institutions in Canada, the legislative branch has the fewest opportunities to meaningfully shape legislation to advance its interpretations of Charter rights. When introducing a bill to the House for debate, the minister of justice under section 4.1.1 of the *Department of Justice Act* must inform Parliament if a legislative bill is inconsistent with the Charter. A minister has never tabled a statement of Charter inconsistency before, and there is a presumption against a minister ever making such a statement.[19] This lack of reporting combined with the fact that the government may advance legislation that could be legally vulnerable to a Charter challenge[20] means that members of the legislature are not given a clear signal to scrutinize legislation for potential Charter violations. Moreover, information about a bill's legal risk could also be presented too late in the legislative process for Members of Parliament (MPs) to effectively demand changes.[21] Canadian legislatures are also known to have limited measures to hold a government to account and shape legislation.[22] Rigorous scrutinizing of government legislation during Question Period or in parliamentary committees may not lead to meaningful legislative changes. Due to strong party discipline, members of the government's party will be whipped to ensure that the government's legislative agenda gets passed through the legislature with relative ease.

For these reasons, coordinate constitutionalists assert that the role of the legislature in shaping policy with potentially significant rights implications should be strengthened. The Canadian executive and legislature are not so fused as to mean that there is no meaningful distinction between the two institutional roles; even though the executive currently wields immense policymaking powers, it cannot be said to possess the entire legislative power as there is the theoretical opportunity for legislatures to reject or amend executive policies.[23] The ability of legislatures to assert more policymaking influence need only be expanded to enhance their role as legitimate interpreters of the Constitution due to their representative, law-creating function. With an empowered legislature, competing interpretations of the law can be managed through each institution's respective roles. Indeed, the constitutional values and principles that emerge from political compromise and accommodation may endure longer than those that are imposed by one institution over others.

The Colonial Turn in Section 35 Rights Interpretation

The legislative rights review scholarship is preoccupied with questions around how policymaking in Westminster parliamentary systems is affected and shaped by judicial review. A significant portion of that literature is concerned with the appropriate roles of institutions that exercise constitutional authority to ensure one body does not impose its interpretation of rights and values onto other institutions. The assumption is that the executive, legislative, and judicial branches of government have the equal authority to interpret the Constitution and may reach different conclusions about how to appropriately balance Charter rights. Does legislative authority extend to balancing and possibly limiting section 35 rights in the *Constitution Act, 1982*?

Section 35 states that "the existing aboriginal and treaty rights of the aboriginal peoples of Canada are hereby recognized and affirmed." The content and scope of the rights that are recognized and affirmed are not outlined in the *Constitution Act, 1982*. After section 35 was entrenched, a series of constitutional conferences were held that included Indigenous leadership and first ministers across Canada to clarify the scope of Aboriginal rights. The recalcitrance of the first ministers to recognize Indigenous self-government rights starkly demonstrated that comprehensive negotiations to delineate the scope and nature of section 35 rights would not be successful. Indeed, Aboriginal self-government as outlined in the Charlottetown Accord also failed to pass in 1992, which was a subsequent attempt to amend the Constitution. Instead of recognizing an inherent right to self-government across all Indigenous groups, the state has established modern treaty processes whereby a specific Indigenous nation may enter a modern treaty with the Crown. These agreements outline how Canadian and Indigenous authority interface and the jurisdictional boundaries of each order of government. The process to finalize a modern treaty takes several years and the process is fraught with challenges, including inadequate resources for Indigenous nations to negotiate as equals with the state; the state's refusal to address issues of competing claims between various Indigenous nations before initiating negotiations; and the relinquishing of Aboriginal title over land in treaties; that is, the *sui generis* ownership rights exercised by Aboriginal peoples by virtue of their prior occupation before the assertion of Crown sovereignty. Due to the glacial pace of finalizing modern treaties and the disagreements between Indigenous and settler governments over their terms, the judiciary has become a main venue to define the scope and nature of section 35 rights on a case-by-case basis.

When section 35 rights disputes first entered the Supreme Court of Canada in the 1990 *Sparrow* case, the Court characterized Aboriginal rights as a vehicle for the just settlement for Indigenous peoples, particularly as Aboriginal rights had been previously ignored by the Crown.[24] As such, section 35 should be given a liberal, purposeful interpretation[25] that alters how other parts of the Constitution should be interpreted. For instance, the Court stated that the federal government's powers to legislate in relation to "Indians, and Lands reserved for the Indians" as outlined in section 91(24) must be "read together with s. 35(1)" so that "federal power must be reconciled with federal duty."[26] Consequently, section 91(24) is recast as another means to advance reconciliation with Indigenous peoples whose rights were reaffirmed under section 35. Section 91(24) allocates responsibility "to provide for the welfare and protection of native peoples" to the federal government.[27] Given that section 35 provides the constitutional base on which political negotiations can take place to recognize proven and claimed Aboriginal rights, federal actions taken under section 91(24) must respect the constitutionality of Aboriginal rights, even as the full scope of those rights are undefined. A way for the government to ensure their actions recognize and respect Aboriginal rights is to undertake political negotiations with Indigenous nations to determine the scope of those rights.[28]

However, the Court also did not dare challenge the primacy of Crown sovereignty in this early decision by unreservedly accepting the Crown's underlying title after the *Royal Proclamation, 1763*.[29] Indeed, the Court unilaterally devised a framework that allows the Crown to justify its infringement of Aboriginal rights if there is a valid legislative objective,[30] despite the assertion that section 35 rights are not subject to section 1 of the Charter.[31] If a valid legislative objective is found, then the legislation must be considered in light of the Crown's fiduciary obligation towards Aboriginal peoples.[32] Other aspects of the justificatory framework include whether there has been as little infringement to the section 35 right as possible, if fair compensation is available in situations of expropriation, and whether the relevant Aboriginal group was consulted.[33] The acceptance of the Crown's underlying sovereignty over all territory regardless of Indigenous peoples' prior occupancy and the import of a justificatory framework to infringe Aboriginal rights set the stage for future decisions that would diminish the promise of Aboriginal rights to produce a just settlement for Indigenous peoples. Indeed, the primacy of the state to shape section 35 has arguably prioritized settler-colonial interests by limiting and managing the state's legal obligations to Indigenous nations.[34] Subsequent judicial decisions reveal how section 35 has since been interpreted narrowly as rights to certain practices and customs,[35] ignoring the sovereign authority of Indigenous peoples to govern their territory with their own legal customs.[36]

Importantly, the Court later amended the justificatory scheme that allows the Crown to infringe section 35 rights. Rather than emphasize the unique relationship between the Crown and Indigenous peoples, as was done in *Sparrow*, the *Gladstone* decision in 1996 inserted the interests of non-Indigenous peoples and broader society when considering valid legislative objectives.[37] Reweighing the justificatory framework to include non-Indigenous interests and denying Indigenous nations' jurisdictional authority results in the Court treating section 35 rights as analogous to *Charter* rights that can be infringed using a similar logic as a section 1 test: the interests of non-Indigenous Canadians can limit the exercise of Aboriginal and treaty rights by denying Indigenous peoples are a distinct, politically autonomous population.[38] Under this interpretation of section 35, Parliament may have the authority to limit and interpret Aboriginal rights when reviewing legislation. This approach to rights review would continue the colonial trajectory of Aboriginal rights interpretations, whereby non-Indigenous interests can override the rights of politically autonomous communities and nations.

Parliament and the Canadian State's Legitimacy Deficit

Although the Court has structured the jurisprudence of Aboriginal rights as non-jurisdictional, there is some evidence that this position may be shifting. In the 2018 *Mikisew Cree Nation* decision, Justice Abella writes that section 35 "allocates power between governing entities, such as the visions of powers between the provincial and federal governments, or the separation of powers between the branches of government."[39] This is the clearest statement from a judge that section 35 rights are jurisdictional in nature[40] and therefore cannot be unilaterally limited by another government. The view that Aboriginal rights must be understood as jurisdictional has been consistently advanced by Indigenous legal scholars.[41] Viewing rights in this way would help undo the perpetuation of colonial logic throughout Aboriginal law. For instance, Crown sovereignty in other Aboriginal law cases, like the 1997 *Delgamuukw* decision, is simply conjured like a spell that magically makes Indigenous peoples' rights to land subservient to the Crown's underlying title.[42] If section 35 rights were understood as jurisdictional rights, the contours of the Crown's asserted authority and Indigenous authority would be negotiated through nation-to-nation political processes as the section itself does not articulate the precise nature and scope of Indigenous jurisdictional authority. An external government, federal or provincial, taking any action to unilaterally limit or affect section 35 rights would be *ultra vires*.

Unfortunately, due to the *Sparrow* decision, state regulation and policies can justifiably infringe on or limit Aboriginal rights. And yet, even within the colonial structure of section 35, the Court is divided over whether legislatures have legal responsibilities to ensure that the Crown's honour towards Indigenous peoples is upheld. The concept of the honour of the Crown means that all the state's interactions with

Indigenous peoples must be grounded in good faith and integrity.[43] The honour of the Crown compels the Crown to reach a just settlement with Indigenous peoples through honourable negotiations.[44] Other duties may arise from the Crown's honour, including the duty to consult. The duty to consult is a legal obligation to consult Indigenous peoples if a Crown action may affect section 35 rights or rights claims. In the 2018 *Mikisew Cree Nation* decision, the majority asserted that the duty to consult does not apply to the legislative process, but only applies to executive actions. According to the majority decision, accepting the duty in legislative contexts would violate the separation of powers and parliamentary sovereignty.[45] It is argued that judicial oversight in lawmaking would cause constitutional deadlock over the lawmaking process, a process which is generally understood to be beyond the scope of judicial review.[46] The Court was divided over whether legislatures had *any* legal obligations to act honourably towards Indigenous peoples, even if the duty was found to be unapplicable. For Chief Justice Wagner and Justices Karakatsanis and Gascon, other legal obligations that flow from the honour of the Crown may apply to the legislative branch[47] but were beyond the appeal's scope to articulate. In contrast, in separate decisions, Justices Brown, Moldaver, Côté, and Rowe firmly asserted that to suggest any prospect of judicial review into the lawmaking process would ultimately invite uncertainty in the law and breach parliamentary privilege.[48]

Nevertheless, some justices asserted that the duty applies to the legislative context. For Justices Abella and Martin, legislatures cannot be excluded from the expectation of honourable dealing towards Indigenous peoples,[49] as that would leave a void in the section 35 framework. Abella writes, "If legislative decisions were only subject to the *Sparrow* framework, Indigenous groups with established rights would be required to meet the more onerous infringement threshold in order to access consultation rights, and those with unproven claims would be excluded entirely."[50] These judges envision the duty to apply in legislative contexts in limited ways to ensure a balance between the judicial and legislative branches. Under such a framework, Indigenous groups could only challenge existing legislation on procedural grounds, with the courts deciding whether the legislative process "accords with the special relationship between the Crown and Indigenous peoples."[51] The duty to consult case law has arguably evolved to overly emphasize procedural fairness, thus granting the Crown a wide latitude to meet its constitutional obligations without substantively changing its course of action.[52] As such, the minority opinion's assertion that legislatures should be bound by the duty in its current form may not result in giving Indigenous groups a meaningful role in lawmaking.[53]

Given the current interpretation of section 35 rights, legislatures either do not have the authority to limit section 35 rights because it would be *ultra vires* if section 35 rights are understood as jurisdictional in nature, or, legislatures are bound by the honour of the Crown to consider section 35 rights in a currently unspecified way, as per the majority decision in *Mikisew Cree*. There is no indication as to what kind of obligation legislatures must uphold to ensure their actions are consistent with the honour of the Crown. What is more certain is that section 35 rights should be understood as jurisdictional, as argued by Indigenous legal scholarship and some of the justices in the *Mikisew Cree* decision. If section 35 rights are jurisdictional, then nation-to-nation political negotiations are needed to determine how Indigenous and non-Indigenous authorities should interface. As such, it would be inappropriate for legislatures to have a coordinate role to interpret section 35 rights. It would similarly be inappropriate for a legislature to limit another government's jurisdictional authority and governing decisions. Instead, the legislative branch can hold the executive to account to ensure that the honour of the Crown is upheld when executive actions may have an impact on section 35 rights.

Parliamentary Reforms: Pathway to Honourable Rights Review?

Parliament should not have a coordinate role to negotiate the parameters of section 35 rights as it would be *ultra vires* for democratically elected representatives of another political community to limit or interpret the jurisdictional authority of Indigenous nations. However, it is possible that Parliament may be reformed to become a more appropriate forum to facilitate the negotiation of section 35 rights if Indigenous nations, as politically autonomous entities, are represented. This section considers how Parliament might have a legitimate role to play in ensuring federal lawmaking upholds the honour of the Crown. A specific mandate to uphold the honour of the Crown throughout the legislative process could ensure that the executive's actions within its own jurisdiction reflect honourable intentions towards Indigenous peoples.

Representatives in Parliament and legislatures typically do not represent the interests of particular groups, like Indigenous nations. Elected officials in a Westminster system support their political party's agenda, constraining them from supporting their own constituency (regional or otherwise) without party approval.[54] Moreover, Indigenous individuals may be reluctant to participate in electoral politics because of the perception that legislatures are colonial institutions designed to exclude, alienate, and co-opt Indigenous peoples and their political goals.[55] Indeed, advocating self-determination and rejecting settler-colonial state control is not seen by many Indigenous scholars as compatible with participation in settler-colonial politics, as Indigenous demands and claims will simply be neutralized.[56]

The colonial quality of Parliament helps explain Indigenous peoples' aversion to participating in electoral politics, but it may be possible to decolonize Parliament so it can deliberately and consistently uphold the honour of the Crown during lawmaking. Any attempt to reform Parliament to include Indigenous participants must be grounded by a commitment to decolonization. This includes treating Indigenous groups as distinct political entities with legitimate governing authority and to allocate sufficient power to Indigenous representatives to protect against state encroachment.[57] Crucially, Indigenous nations must be able to exercise self-determination by determining for themselves the forums and processes used to interact with the colonial state.[58] It may very well be the case that, rather than participate in existing legislative processes that are largely understood as hostile to Indigenous worldviews,[59] Indigenous nations may seek to create new institutions and practices that better reflect their values.

Indeed, the Royal Commission on Aboriginal Peoples (1996) envisioned a pathway to both promote Indigenous nation-building and self-determination alongside boosting Indigenous representation within Canadian institutions. The report prescribed the creation of a House of First Peoples, which would enable Indigenous peoples to participate in the legislative process parallel to the House of Commons and Senate.[60] Such an institution would grant Indigenous peoples power to shape national legislation that affects section 35 rights without disturbing regional representation in the Senate.[61] Crucially, Indigenous peoples themselves must design such an institution with sufficient legislative power. Although Norway, Sweden, and Finland have Indigenous representation in their parliaments, those bodies are merely advisory and lack clout.[62] Meaningful legislative power in an Indigenous legislative body would help ensure that the other branches of government are held to account with regards to upholding the honour of the Crown throughout lawmaking. Therefore, the task would not be to review legislation to consider how to balance the specific section 35 rights of a particular Indigenous nation, but to direct legislative review to consider whether the Crown is acting honourably and with good faith in its lawmaking capacity.[63] Such a review may entail the House of First Peoples to establish its own committees with the ability to call witnesses or initiate a question period where representatives can directly ask questions to the government. A vote from this House against a bill could then compel the executive to initiate nation-to-nation negotiations with relevant Indigenous groups when section 35 rights may be at stake.[64] Rather than understand this power as a "veto," it may be more fruitful to view it as a way for Indigenous representatives to oblige the state to revisit or foster a relationship with relevant Indigenous groups grounded in respect and equality. This approach is more consistent with Indigenous legal traditions, which employs an ethic of responsibility that is derived from various interconnected relationships.[65] No specific policy outcome is mandated by the House of First Peoples; instead, the Crown can be compelled to demonstrate its good faith and honourable conduct towards Indigenous peoples, which is consistent with Canadian constitutional law as well. Institutional reforms of this calibre are a significantly more robust pathway to ensure legislative processes uphold the honour of the Crown than the limited prescriptions to integrate the duty to consult in the drafting of legislation as outlined by Justices Abella and Martin in the 2018 *Mikisew Cree* decision.

The inclusion of a House of First Peoples would also preserve Parliament's relevancy as governments engage with Indigenous peoples on a nation-to-nation basis. It is widely known that Parliament exhibits weak mechanisms of intrastate federalism because territorial interests are ineffectually represented within the central government.[66] In the context of federal-provincial relations, intergovernmental negotiations are relied upon to manage competing interests between governments.[67] Although bilateral relations between governments ensure each sovereign entity is represented, Parliament's ability to help avoid an impasse throughout negotiations is underexplored.[68] In the context of Indigenous-Crown relations, negotiating section 35 rights and self-government is likely to be threatened by deadlocks. Creating another venue in which Indigenous concerns are routinely discussed can help foster trust over time, which is crucial to successful nation-to-nation negotiations.

Although a House of First Peoples would be an additional House in Parliament to help ensure legislation is upholding the honour of the Crown, it does not follow that such an institution would legitimate the government to limit or unilaterally interpret section 35 rights without the participation of the relevant Indigenous nation(s). Recall that various Indigenous groups across the country have different treaty and legal relationships with the Crown. A House of First Peoples would not adequately represent the wide variation of Indigenous peoples to replace nation-to-nation negotiations with the affected Indigenous group(s). Moreover, some nations have internal conflicts about the exercise of their rights, particularly between band council governments and members of traditional governments. It is not possible for one or two representatives in a House of First Peoples to sufficiently give voice to those various perspectives within communities. Some Indigenous groups also have competing claims to certain rights and territory, so it is possible that representatives in a House of First Peoples could have conflicting interests against certain nations whose rights may be at stake. These reasons would make such a body ill-suited to substitute nation-to-nation negotiations.

If section 35 rights are understood as jurisdictional, then governments through negotiated agreements should decide how their authorities will interface. Building Indigenous autonomy distinct from the colonial state is a primary objective of decolonization that cannot be fixed by simply adding Indigenous peoples into state structures and processes of decision-making. Treaty federalism is a process of both sharing and respecting each government's sovereign authority. Adding explicit Indigenous representation in legislative processes is one way to acknowledge the constitutional interdependency between Indigenous and settler communities.[69] Indeed, the historic treaties signed between the Crown and Indigenous peoples represent a shared commitment between nations to protect peace and good order, which could be actualized through Indigenous representation in national institutions like Parliament.[70] Treaty relationships are the constitutional foundation upon which Canadian federalism rests; respectful relations between treaty partners must be vigilantly upheld to ensure Canadian sovereignty is legitimately exercised. However, this imperative to check executive power throughout lawmaking must not supplant the authority of self-determining Indigenous nations. Indigenous nations are often not respected as sovereign political entities even though their rights flow from their prior occupancy of the land, and therefore originate outside of the Canadian state.[71] Fostering equal nation-to-nation exchanges to delineate jurisdictional authority under section 35 rights is a significant measure to undo colonial logic within Aboriginal law. Legislative rights review to uphold the honour of the Crown can help facilitate this goal, but it is ultimately not the primary pathway to decolonizing and legitimating Canadian constitutional law.

Conclusion

Legislative review of Charter rights is intended to ensure that the representative branch of government exercises its equal authority to interpret the Constitution. Therefore, legislative review corrects a democratic deficit in current constitutional interpretation due to the existing dominance of the executive and the judiciary. The scholarship preoccupied with considering Charter rights review has not considered whether the same institutional arguments can be made for reviewing other types of rights in the Constitution.[72] This chapter argues that legislative review would not be appropriate in the context of section 35 rights because Parliament does not have the authority to limit or delineate the jurisdictional boundaries of other political societies. MPs reviewing legislation regarding how to balance section 35 rights with other rights and interests would be *ultra vires*. This argument is supported by an interpretation of section 35 rights as jurisdictional in nature rather than based on Indigenous peoples' distinctive cultures. The judiciary may be pivoting to accept this interpretation of section 35 rights, as the 2018 *Mikisew Cree* decision suggests. Yet the Supreme Court of Canada also provides little guidance about how Parliament may have responsibilities to uphold the honour of the Crown during lawmaking.

Rather than reviewing legislation for its balancing or interpretation of section 35 rights, Parliament can review legislation and executive action to ensure the honour of the Crown is upheld when section 35 rights may be at stake. This task can be undertaken if reforms are directed at creating new institutions, like a House of First Peoples, where Indigenous peoples are represented as distinct political entities with powers to hold the executive to account when Indigenous nations' rights may be affected. This additional House in Parliament would serve as a powerful check to compel the executive to reach a just settlement with Indigenous nations through nation-to-nation negotiations. Nation-to-nation negotiations between equal political entities remain the primary practice to bring about a decolonial interpretation and exercise of section 35 rights.

NOTES

1 James Kelly, "Bureaucratic Activism and the Charter of Rights and Freedoms: The Department of Justice and Its Entry into the Centre of Government," *Canadian Public Administration* 42, no. 4 (1999): 476–511; James Kelly, *Governing with the Charter: Legislative and Judicial Activism and Framers' Intent* (Vancouver: UBC Press, 2005); Kent Roach, "Not Just the Government's Lawyer: The Attorney General as Defender of the Rule of Law," *Queen's Law Journal* 31, no. 2 (2006): 598–643.

2 Janet Hiebert, *Charter Conflicts: What Is Parliament's Role?* (Montreal: McGill-Queen's University Press, 2002).

3 Dennis Baker, *Not So Supreme: The Courts and Coordinate Constitutional Interpretation* (Montreal: McGill-Queen's University Press, 2010).
4 Janet L. Hiebert, "The Charter, Policy, and Political Judgment," in *Policy Change, Courts, and the Canadian Constitution*, ed. Emmett Macfarlane (Toronto: University of Toronto Press, 2018), 81–102.
5 Arguably, the judiciary also faces the same legitimacy deficit around interpreting the content of section 35 rights. The Supreme Court of Canada in *Sparrow* could have acted with more sensitivity to the judiciary's own lack of legitimacy, by, for instance, ruling that the federal regulation over Aboriginal rights was *ultra vires*, thus facilitating nation-to-nation negotiations; see Joshua Nichols and Robert Hamilton, "In Search of Honourable Crowns and Legitimate Constitutions: *Mikisew Cree First Nation v. Canada* and the Colonial Constitution," *University of Toronto Law Journal* 70, no. 3 (2020): 350n57. Instead, the *Sparrow* decision preserves the Court's position as the interpreter of section 35 rights.
6 Donald Savoie, *Governing from the Centre: The Concentration of Power in Canadian Politics* (Toronto: University of Toronto Press, 1999).
7 Kelly, "Bureaucratic Activism"; Kelly, *Governing with the Charter*; Roach, "The Attorney General as Defender."
8 Paul G. Thomas, "Central Agencies: Making a Mesh of Things," in *Canadian Politics*, Alain-G. Gagnon and James Bickerton, 2nd ed. (Peterborough, ON: Broadview Press, 1994).
9 Matthew Hennigar, "Conceptualizing Attorney General Conduct in Charter Litigation: From Independence to Central Agency," *Canadian Public Administration* 51, no. 2 (2008): 199.
10 Kelly, *Governing with the Charter*, 228.
11 Ibid., 223; Hennigar "Conceptualizing Attorney General Conduct," 199–200.
12 Janet Hiebert, "The Charter's Influence on Legislation: Political Strategizing about Risk," *Canadian Journal of Political Science* 51, no. 4 (2018): 735.
13 Ibid., 737–8.
14 Ibid., 738.
15 Andrew Petter, "Legalise This: The *Chartering* of Canadian Politics," in *Contested Constitutionalism: Reflections on the Canadian Charter of Rights and Freedoms*, ed. Christopher Manfredi and James Kell (Vancouver: UBC Press, 2009), 37. See also Grant Huscroft, "Reconciling Duty and Discretion: The Attorney General in the *Charter* Era," *Queen's Law Journal* 34, no. 2 (2009): 809.
16 Baker, *Not So Supreme*; Mark Tushnet, *Taking the Constitution Away from the Courts* (Princeton, NJ: Princeton University Press, 1999); Christopher Manfredi, *Judicial Power and the Charter: Canada and the Paradox of Liberal Constitutionalism* (Oxford: Oxford University Press, 2001); Grant Huscroft,

"Constitutionalism from the Top Down," *Osgoode Hall Law Journal* 45, no. 1 (2007): 101.

17 Rosalind Dixon, "The Supreme Court of Canada, Charter Dialogue, and Deference," *Osgoode Hall Law Journal* 47, no. 2 (2009): 235–86; Jeremy Waldron, "Some Models of Dialogue between Judges and Legislators," *The Supreme Court Law Review* 23, no. 2 (2004): 7.

18 Alison Young, "Dialogue and Its Myths: 'What Peoples Say I Am, That's What I'm Not,'" in *Constitutional Dialogue: Rights, Democracy, Institutions*, ed. Geoffrey Sigalet, Grégoire Webber, and Rosalind Dixon (Cambridge: Cambridge University Press, 2017), 35–67.

19 Hiebert, "The Charter's Influence on Legislation."

20 Janet Hiebert and James Kelly, *Parliamentary Bills of Rights: The Experiences of New Zealand and the United Kingdom* (Cambridge: Cambridge University Press, 2015).

21 Charles Feldman, "Beyond Charter Statements: Constitutional Communications in the Parliamentary Context," in "Canada's Constitutional & Governance Challenges after 150 Years," ed. Radha (Radhakrishnan) Persaud and Gregory Tardi, special issue, *Journal of Parliamentary and Political Law* (2018): 37–66.

22 C.E.S. Franks, *The Parliament of Canada* (Toronto: University of Toronto Press, 1987); David Docherty, *Legislatures* (Vancouver: UBC Press, 2005); Jonathan Malloy, "High Discipline, Low Cohesion? The Uncertain Patterns of Canadian Parliamentary Parties," *Journal of Legislative Studies* 9, no. 4 (2003): 116–29.

23 Baker, *Not So Supreme*, 13.

24 *R. v. Sparrow*, [1990] 1 SCR 1075, 1106.

25 Ibid.

26 Ibid., 1109.

27 *Mitchell v. Penguis Indian Band* [1990] 2 SCR 85 at para. 78.

28 Brian Bird, "Federal Power and Federal Duty: Reconciling Sections 91(24) and 35(1) of the Canadian Constitution," *Appeal: Review of Current Law and Law Reform* 16, no. 1 (2011): 3–14.

29 *R. v. Sparrow*, [1990] 1 SCR 1075, 1103.

30 Ibid., 1113.

31 Ibid., 1108.

32 Ibid., 1114.

33 Ibid., 1119.

34 Jeremy Patzer and Kiera Ladner, "Indigenous Rights and the *Constitution Act, 1982*: Forty Years On and Still Fishing for Rights," in *Constitutional Crossroads: Reflections on Charter Rights, Reconciliation, and Change*, ed. Kate Puddister and Emmett Macfarlane (Vancouver: UBC Press, 2022), 361.

35 *R.* v. *Van der Peet*, [1996] 2 SCR 507, para. 46.

36 Michael McCrossan, "Shifting Judicial Conceptions of 'Reconciliation': Geographic Commitments Underpinning Aboriginal Rights Decisions," *Windsor Yearbook Access to Justice* 31, no. 2 (2013): 155–79.
37 *R. v Gladstone*, [1996] 2 SCR 723, para. 73.
38 D'Arcy Vermette, "Dizzying Dialogue: Canadian Courts and the Continuing Justification of the Dispossession of Aboriginal Peoples," *Windsor Yearbook Access to Justice* 29, no. 1 (2011): 55–72.
39 *Mikisew Cree First Nation v. Canada (Governor General in Council)*, [2018] 2 SCR 765, para. 88, 2018 SCC 40 [*Mikisew Cree*].
40 Nichols and Hamilton, "In Search of Honourable Crowns and Legitimate Constitutions," 348.
41 Kiera Ladner, "Up the Creek: Fishing for a New Constitutional Order," *Canadian Journal of Political Science* 38, no. 4 (2005): 923–53; Gordon Christie, "A Colonial Reading of Recent Jurisprudence: *Sparrow, Delgamuukw* and *Haida Nation*," *Windsor Yearbook Access to Justice* 23, no. 1 (2005): 17–53.
42 John Borrows, "Sovereignty's Alchemy: An Analysis of *Delgamuukw v. British Columbia*," *Osgoode Hall Law Journal* 37, no. 3 (1997): 537–96; John Borrows, *Recovering Canada: The Resurgence of Indigenous Law* (Toronto: University of Toronto Press, 2002); Peter H. Russell, *Recognizing Aboriginal Title: The Mabo Case and Indigenous Resistance to English-Settler Colonialism* (Toronto: University of Toronto Press, 2005).
43 *Haida Nation v. British Columbia (Ministry of Forests)*, [2004] 3 SCR 511, para. 19, 2004 SCC 73.
44 Ibid., para. 20.
45 *Mikisew Cree*, para. 32.
46 Ibid., 36–7.
47 Ibid., 45.
48 Ibid., 104, 140, 169.
49 Ibid., 78.
50 Ibid., 79.
51 Ibid., 93.
52 Gordon Christie, "A Colonial Reading of Recent Jurisprudence"; Veronica Potes, "The Duty to Accommodate Aboriginal Peoples Rights: Substantive Consultation?," *Journal of Environmental Law and Practice* 17, no. 1 (2006): 27–45; Minh Do, "Throughout Legitimacy and the Duty to Consult: The Limits of the Law to Produce Quality Interactions in British Columbia's EA Process," *Canadian Journal of Political Science* 53, no. 3 (2020): 577–95.
53 Nichols and Hamilton, "In Search of Honourable Crowns and Legitimate Constitutions," 356.
54 Alex Marland, *Whipped: Party Discipline in Canada* (Vancouver: UBC Press, 2020).

55 Russell Lawrence Barsh et al., "The Prairie Indian Vote in Canadian Politics 1965–1993: A Critical Case Study from Alberta," *Great Plains Research* 7, no. 1 (1997): 3–26; Anna Hunter, "Exploring the Issues of Aboriginal Representation in Federal Elections," *Electoral Insight* 5, no. 3 (2003): 27–33; Kiera Ladner and Michael McCrossan, *The Electoral Participation of Aboriginal People* (Ottawa: Elections Canada, 2007). It has been found that high Indigenous voter turnout corresponds with a higher proportion of Indigenous candidates, which suggests evidence that affinity voting may be taking place among this population. Therefore, the problem of low Indigenous participation in electoral politics may be tied to a lack of supply rather than demand for Indigenous political candidates. See Simon Dabin, Jean François Daoust, and Martin Papillon, "Indigenous Peoples and Affinity Voting in Canada," *Canadian Journal of Political Science* 52, no. 1 (2019): 39–53.

56 Glen Coulthard, *Red Skins, White Masks: Rejecting the Colonial Politics of Recognition* (Minnesota: University of Minnesota Press, 2014); Taiaiake Alfred, "Why Play the White Man's Game," *Wind Speaker* 17, no. 4 (1999): 4–5.

57 Meaghan Williams and Robert Schertzer, "Is Indigeneity like Ethnicity? Theorizing and Assessing Models of Indigenous Political Representation," *Canadian Journal of Political Science* 52, no. 4 (2019): 677–96.

58 Ibid., 684.

59 Sarah Maddison, "White Parliament, Black Politics: The Dilemmas of Indigenous Parliamentary Representation," *Australian Journal of Political Science* 45, no. 4 (2010): 663–80.

60 Royal Commission of Aboriginal Peoples, *Bridging the Cultural Divide: A Report on Aboriginal People and Criminal Justice in Canada*, vol. 2 (Ottawa: Government of Canada, 1996), 358.

61 Ibid., 358–9.

62 Ibid., 359; Michael Morden, "Indigenizing Parliament: Time to Re-Start a Conversation," *Canadian Parliamentary Review* 39, no. 2 (2016): 27.

63 Although this chapter is concerned with legislative rights review as an obligation flowing from section 35, it is conceivable that a House of First Peoples could also review all legislation passed in Parliament. However, Parliament's legitimacy deficit to balance section 35 rights makes the House of First Peoples' role more significant in the context of lawmaking that implicates the honour of the Crown.

64 Other actions taken by the executive that could affect Indigenous peoples, like amending regulations, can be done without parliamentary involvement. The duty to consult would likely be triggered in these contexts as the duty applies to strategic, high-level decisions taken by the executive. See *Rio Tinto Alcan v. Carrier Sekani Tribal Council*, [2010] 2 SCR 650, para. 44, 2010 SCC 43.

65 Jeff Corntassel, "Re-envisioning Resurgence: Indigenous Pathways to Decolonization and Sustainable Self-determination," *Decolonization: Indigeneity, Education & Society* 1, no. 1 (2012): 86–101.
66 Donald Smiley, "Federal-Provincial Conflict in Canada," *Publius* 4, no. 3 (1974): 7–24.
67 Richard Simeon, *Federal-Provincial Diplomacy: The Making of Recent Policy in Canada* (Toronto: University of Toronto Press, 2006).
68 Smiley, "Federal-Provincial Conflict," 17.
69 Morden, "Indigenizing Parliament."
70 Kiera Ladner, "Treaty Seven and Guaranteed Representation: How Treaty Rights can Evolve into Parliamentary Seats," *Great Plains Quarterly* 17, no. 2 (1997): 85–101.
71 *Calder et al. v. Attorney-General of British Columbia*, [1973] SCR 313, 329.
72 This observation also applies to reviewing legislation for federalism and the rights of provinces. See Wade Wright, "Against Privileging the Charter: The Case of Federal Pre-enactment Constitutional Review," *Review of Constitutional Studies* 25, no. 1 (2020–2021): 49–78.

3 Limiting Charter Rights: Judicial Review in the Administrative Context

G. ELIZABETH BERGMAN

The legitimacy of judicial review, and its effect on limiting rights, has been a point of contention in political-legal scholarship since the implementation of the Charter of Rights and Freedoms in 1982. This debate has centred on section 1 of the Charter, which "guarantees the rights and freedoms set out in it subject only to such reasonable limits prescribed by law as can be demonstrably justified in a free and democratic society."[1] As both a guarantee and a qualification of Charter rights, section 1 embodies this tension and debate between rights and limits.

Understanding that tension "is essential to understanding the political significance of the Charter."[2] As such, scholarship on section 1 has tended to emphasize the impact of the Charter on the Court-Parliament relationship.[3] Scholars such as Janet Hiebert, Peter Hogg and Allison Bushell (now Thornton), and Ted Morton and Rainer Knopff have deeply influenced the shape of Canadian constitutional scholarship. Early theories of judicial review – such as judicial activism and dialogue theory – were concerned about whether the Supreme Court of Canada would become too activist, or whether a "dialogue" was occurring that allowed for shared interpretive power between the Court and Parliament. Critically, however, many of these theories and findings have remained unaltered since they were first conceptualized in the late 1990s and early 2000s. The lack of theoretical development is concerning because it belies the dynamic nature of the Charter and its impact on our institutions.

This chapter does not reject this early scholarship, but instead challenges its exclusive focus on the Court-Parliament relationship. It argues that our theories of Charter review must be expanded to encompass a broader cross-section of political actors. In particular, administrative actors have come to play an increasingly important role in the Charter jurisprudence, and their decisions have come to represent "one of the principal manifestations of state power in the lives of Canadians."[4] Administrative actors are a highly diverse group, ranging from state actors – such as ministers – to the various boards and tribunals created by statute. These actors can be intimately connected to government or largely independent. They perform key functions within our institutions by implementing policy, adjudicating cases, imposing regulations, providing government oversight, and mediating conflicts. Incorporating administrative actors into our theories of judicial review of Charter complaints is vital for understanding how the Charter is interpreted – and who has authority over that interpretation.

The chapter begins by outlining the two most significant theories of judicial review in the Charter context: judicial activism and dialogue theory. I argue that these theories offer an incomplete picture of judicial review, and suggest that incorporating administrative actors into our theories of Charter review is necessary because of the important role they play in shaping how Charter rights are interpreted and applied by the courts. The next section turns to demonstrating how administrative law is transforming the Supreme Court of Canada's conception of its role as "guardian of the Constitution."[5] Finally, the last section examines how administrative law transforms the standards by which the courts evaluate rights infringements. In particular, the shift away from the *Oakes* test towards the *Doré* framework in the administrative law context impacts how the courts weigh competing interests under section 1 of the Charter. Administrative law does not raise new concerns for Charter interpretation. Rather, it raises old concerns about how rights should be limited, how competing values and interests should be weighed, and the extent to which the judiciary owes deference.

Theories of Judicial Review

The transformative impact of the Charter on the Canadian political-legal landscape is well-known. In early cases, the Court established itself as the "guardian of the Constitution," arguing that the Charter created new judicial responsibilities to review legislation in order to protect rights.[6] Extrajudicially, Justice Louis LeBel claimed that "[i]t is the duty of the judiciary, as 'the guardian of the constitution', to supervise state actors in their exercise of power to ensure they do not transgress the limits of their legal authority."[7] Justice Bertha Wilson, writing after her retirement from the bench, similarly argued that the Court did not "volunteer" to engage in constitutional review, but rather it was a role that was thrust upon the courts.[8]

The literature has reflected this understanding of the Charter as transformative. Notably, a full review of the nuances of Canadian Charter scholarship is beyond the scope of this chapter, and what follows is a simplification of that scholarly thinking. However, Dave Snow and Mark Harding have broadly outlined three waves within the literature.[9] The first wave they identified lasted until around 1997, and focused on the impact of the Charter on institutions and national unity, and on its ability to create social change. This wave was characterized by normative discussions of the impact of the Charter. The second wave, which lasted from 1997 to 2004, focused more intensely on how institutions responded to Charter rulings and how the Charter spurred institutional change.[10] This wave was more interested in public policy concerns and addressed the normative legitimacy of judicial review directly. Finally, the current wave, beginning in the early 2000s, has taken a more comparative and empirical turn, moving away from normative considerations in an attempt to understand how the Charter and the Canadian political-legal system compare globally.

The shift in the third wave towards a more empirical and comparative approach has meant that normative theories of judicial review have remained largely unchanged since the early to mid-2000s. As such, the two most prominent and lasting theories of judicial review arose out of what Snow and Harding identify as the second wave of Charter scholarship. The first theory argued that the judiciary has used the Charter to overstep its role and engage in "judicial activism";[11] the second challenged those theories of judicial activism and instead examined the extent to which the Court has engaged in "dialogue" with the legislature.[12]

Morton and Knopff's argument that there has been a "Charter revolution" is the most well-known iteration of the theory that the Charter ushered in an age of judicial activism.[13] While much scholarship has since followed, it was the work of Morton and Knopff that "set off a flurry of responses from social scientists and legal scholars."[14] The authors argued that the Court has used the Charter to increase its authority, and that the development of the "Court party" has led to the monopolizing of rights discussions by minority interest groups capitalizing on the courts as a way to avoid the democratic process. These authors suggest that constitutional/judicial supremacy has replaced parliamentary supremacy in Canada, and that "judges have abandoned the deference and self-restraint that characterized pre-*Charter* jurisprudence."[15]

While Morton and Knopff's argument is the most well-known iteration of judicial activism, they are not alone in their concern. For example, Thomas Bateman suggests that the Court is using its authority to impose a "thick" version of liberalism on religious minorities.[16] While Bateman avoids the hyperbolic language of Morton and Knopff, his argument suggests a similar concern that the Court is taking an overly active role in shaping Charter rights.

The second way the literature has responded to the transformative effect of the Charter has been to challenge the theory of judicial activism. Hiebert, for instance, argues that section 1 of the Charter could lead the Court to become too deferential in its willingness to accept the reasonableness of legislative objectives.[17] She was the first academic "to systematically examine the capacity of Parliament to respond to Charter decisions."[18] However, the most prominent theory pushing back against the claim of judicial activism has been Hogg and Bushell's (now Thornton's) "dialogue theory."[19] This theory argues that judicial review is not a threat to democracy because the judiciary does not have the final say when interpreting Charter rights.[20] Instead, judicial review sparks the beginning of a dialogic exchange between the legislatures and the courts about how best to balance rights with other interests. In other words, the two sides are engaged in a dialogue over interpretation. Because of mechanisms such as section 33 (the notwithstanding clause) and section 1 of the Charter, Parliament has meaningful opportunities to respond to judicial decisions with its own interpretation of rights.[21] As Christopher Manfredi and James Kelly note, "The functional essence of this dialogue is the ability of legislatures to reverse, modify, or avoid judicial nullification through the enactment of alternative statutes."[22]

These theories focus exclusively on the Court-Parliament relationship.[23] Given the relative nascence of the Charter, and its effect on our system of parliamentary sovereignty, this early focus on Parliament is understandable. However, subsequent developments in administrative law challenge the justifiability of that exclusive focus. For example, the Court's approach to the Charter under administrative law raises significant doubts about the claim that the judiciary has become unreservedly activist and, by implication, anti-democratic. As Justice LeBel notes, "Deference has been central to the Supreme Court's evolving view of the role of administrative bodies in a modern Canadian state" for almost twenty years.[24] Even with the introduction of the Charter, the Court has cultivated deference as a key feature of administrative law. Contrary to theories of judicial activism, the courts have become so deferential under the administrative law framework that legal scholars have expressed the opposite concern, arguing the developments in administrative law have resulted in Charter rights being *underprotected*.[25] In other words, there is strong evidence within the administrative law context to modulate the claim that the Charter has caused the judiciary to abandon deference and self-restraint.

Similarly, even while dialogue theory pushes back against judicial activism, its exclusive focus on the constitutionality of legislation fails to account for the importance of administrative actors. For example, Hogg and Thornton only find relevance for administrative action in those cases that resulted in legislative action, such as a law being struck down.[26] Likewise, Manfredi and Kelly make a point of emphasizing, in a response to Hogg and Thornton, that they "did not mean that they [Hogg and Thornton] should have included judicial review of executive action [in their study]."[27]

In spite of numerous critiques, dialogue theory remains the primary framework used for explaining the relationship between the judiciary and the government when it comes to the Charter. Yet, the prevailing assumptions behind the theory risk framing the judicial-government relationship too narrowly. Vuk Radmilovic, in his discussion of the impact of government interveners on judicial decision-making, notes:

> [B]y focusing solely on legislative replies enacted in the post-decision context, and by ignoring the extent to which governmental preferences expressed during litigation affect the Court's decision making, the dialogue theory also fails to fully capture the complexity of legislative-judicial relations ... its sole focus on legislative replies significantly *underestimates* the governmental capacity to constrain the policy-making influence of the Supreme Court.[28]

Although Radmilovic does not address the role of administrative actors, the thrust of his argument – that a broader understanding of how the political branches of government and the judiciary interact is critical to attaining a full understanding of the influences that shape judicial decisions – maintains a similar spirit to my own.

Dialogue theory and theories of judicial activism struggle to account for administrative actors and administrative law because they focus primarily on the effect of the Charter on Court-government relations. Both theories start from the premise that the Charter primarily operates to influence the legal and political world around it. I do not challenge those assertions. However, I suggest the Charter is also influenced by the legal and political world within which it exists. In this sense, the Charter is not only the subject influencing the Court's relationship with the governing branches; it is also the object being influenced and affected by the legal and political structures around it.

Guardians of the Constitution?

Judicial activism and dialogue theory were developed as direct responses to the Court's claim that it was the "guardian of the Constitution." Initially articulated in *Hunter et al. v. Southam Inc.*, this assertion continues to influence the Court's perception of itself.[29] The Court has often referred to itself as a "guardian," "umpire," and "referee," and within *Reference RE Supreme Court Act* alone described itself at points as "the 'final word' on matters of law, the 'final arbiter' of division of powers disputes, and the 'apex' of the legal system."[30]

However, under the administrative law framework, the Court seems to be reinterpreting its guardianship role. In particular, the Court's approach to the Charter under administrative law subverts assumptions of the supremacy of constitutional rights and turns aside the expectation that the state bears the burden of justifying exemptions to rights.[31] The evidence from the administrative law jurisprudence touching upon the Charter suggests that the Court is frequently willing to defer not only to the decisions and reasons of administrative actors, but to their interpretations of the Charter, as well.[32]

The tension between the Court's role as "guardian" and the drive towards deference under administrative law is rooted in a long-standing debate about what the Court's role should be in relation to administrative actors. The deferential trend in administrative law can be traced back to the late 1970s in *Nicholson v. Haldimand-Norfolk Regional Police Commissioners* and *CUPE v. N.B. Liquor Corporation*. In those decisions, the Court found that administrative actors should be partners in interpreting and shaping the law.[33]

The Court has struggled to balance its conflicting duties to uphold the "rule of law" (by providing rigorous oversight of administrative decisions) and to respect democratic choice (by deferring to Parliament's decision to delegate decision-making authority to administrative bodies). In *Dunsmuir v. New Brunswick* – one of the leading administrative law cases in Canada – the Justices held that judicial review is informed and shaped by the tensions between democracy and the rule of law.[34] This reference to the importance of democracy in administrative law is more than merely symbolic. The Court is deeply concerned with respecting the authority that has been invested in administrative actors by the legislature.[35] In other words, deference in administrative law is fundamentally rooted in a democratic impulse within the Court to "bring the Charter to the people."[36]

The deferential trend in administrative law was confirmed, at least in part, by the Court's decision in *Canada (Minister of Citizenship and*

Immigration) v. Vavilov. Vavilov is the most significant administrative law decision in recent history. The case was about whether a registrar's decision to revoke Alexander Vavilov's certificate of citizenship, on the basis that his parents were found to be Russian spies, was reasonable. In *Vavilov*, the majority reconsidered the structure of the administrative law framework in Canada and formalized the presumption of deference that since *Dunsmuir* had operated as an "unspoken rule."[37] The majority also held that the presumption of deference under the standard of reasonableness could only be rebutted in two ways: (1) where the legislature indicated a specific standard of review should be applied or where the legislation included an appeal mechanism in the legislation (in which case the Court would rely on appellate rather than administrative law standards of review);[38] and (2) where "the rule of law requires that the standard of correctness be applied."[39]

A full discussion of the impacts of *Vavilov* on administrative law in Canada is not necessary here.[40] Admittedly, some scholars have argued that the *Vavilov* framework may – contrary to its affirmation of deference as an analytical starting point – result in a more "robust" standard of reasonableness (deferential) review or even an influx of correctness (non-deferential) review of administrative decisions.[41] However, because *Vavilov* was not a Charter case, the majority declined to reconsider the application of the *Doré* framework to Charter questions (a point I will return to in the next section).[42] The Court has not yet made clear how, or to what extent, the broader changes *Vavilov* instigated will apply to or affect judicial review of administrative Charter decisions.[43] Moreover, even if those changes do apply, *Vavilov* nevertheless formalizes a presumption of deference to administrative actors and prohibits the courts from substituting their own reasons for those of an administrative decision-maker when evaluating the reasonableness of a decision.[44] While this could lead to more judicial oversight, it also suggests that the Court has maintained a certain level of tolerance for legal pluralism within the administrative context.[45]

Ultimately, administrative law changes how the Court views its role in relation to the Charter. Beth Bilson notes that "judges often remind us that their role in cases where the standard is one other than correctness is not to determine what interpretation is right and assess the interpretation reached by the administrative tribunal accordingly, but to defer to the tribunal and to accept their reading as long as it is reasonable."[46] There is a sense, then, that the Court does not consider itself the final authority on the Charter, but rather views itself as a "partner" to administrative actors. Glover similarly argues that the Court's approach to administrative actors has, for a long time, been a horizontal one in which interpretive authority is shared, rather than being a "static" and hierarchical relationship.[47]

On the surface, that declaration of partnership might seem to lend support to the principle thrust of dialogue theory. Certainly, the courts often draw upon Dyzenhaus's idea of "respectful deference" – a term meant to indicate "not submission but a respectful attention to the reasons offered or which could be offered in support of a decision."[48] However, there is a growing concern that the partnership has become unequal, and that the tip towards deference has become dangerous for the protection of rights. Some scholars have questioned whether the Court's deference is really "respectful," or whether it has come to look more like "submission."[49] Audrey Macklin, for instance, argues that deferential review risks "undervaluing the *Charter,*" with the result being that discretionary administrative decisions are "insulated from meaningful scrutiny."[50] While *Vavilov* has altered the administrative law framework in Canada, its uncertain impact on how the Charter will be interpreted and applied only solidifies the need for further research in this area.

While the Court has claimed for itself a guardianship role over the Charter in the legislative context, in the administrative context that guardianship role has been tempered by a desire to maintain a posture of deference.[51] As Mark Walters notes, "[T]here remains today a very powerful judicial commitment to the idea that administrative law represents a distinctive body of law, the integrity of which must be preserved. Even in cases where administrative discretion affects a constitutional right, the administrative law ethic – one that seems to be informed by functionalism and pluralism – must govern."[52] That commitment to the integrity of administrative law suggests a prioritization of administrative law principles that challenges both the primacy of the Charter and the Court's role as its overseer. In the administrative context, the Court seems more concerned with respecting democratic values and legislative intent than it does with maintaining control over the Charter or forwarding a holistic interpretation of it. As such, under administrative law, the Court's approach is directly at odds with, and perhaps represents a backing away from, its declared role as "guardian of the Constitution."

Section 1, *Oakes,* and the Rise of the *Doré* Framework

As noted above, the Court has tended to favour a deferential approach to administrative actors, even in the context of Charter complaints. The normative appropriateness of that deference has received substantial academic commentary, with some scholars arguing that judicial deference to administrative actors is a positive development,[53] while others are more cautious.[54]

Concerns about overt judicial deference are not new. Since the inception of the Charter – and especially in relation to section 1 and the implementation of the *Oakes* test – scholars have expressed unease about whether the courts would be too deferential. As early as the mid-1990s, Hiebert argued that, under the Charter, "the Court has become overwhelmingly deferential to governmental assertions about the importance and justification of the legislative objective, particularly in the context of social policy."[55] Her argument was that the Court tends to avoid challenging legislative objectives, and instead focuses its analysis on proportionality under the *Oakes* test.[56]

The *Oakes* test hinges on section 1 of the Charter, which entrenches within the Constitution the idea that rights are not absolute. And if rights are not absolute, then that inevitably requires the Court to establish a consistent and reliable way of balancing them against competing public interests. As such, the *Oakes* test solidifies the notion that some values outside of the Charter are equally worthy of protection as those contained within the Charter itself.[57]

The *Oakes* test has two steps. The first is to determine whether the objective of the legislation or the particular clause at issue is "pressing and substantial."[58] If it is, the Court then engages in a three-part proportionality test, to consider whether the means chosen to achieve the statutory objective impairs the Charter right as little as possible (within a range of reasonable options).

Until 2012, the *Oakes* test was the primary means for evaluating Charter complaints. However, the introduction of the *Doré* framework led the Court to abandon the *Oakes* test in the administrative context. In *Doré v. Barreau du Quebec*, Gilles Doré was reprimanded by the Barreau du Québec for an inappropriate letter he sent to a judge.[59] Doré argued that the reprimand violated his freedom of expression under section 2(b) of the Charter. The Court concluded that administrative law standards, rather than constitutional ones, should apply when reviewing the reasonableness of an administrator's decision – even if that decision resulted in a Charter complaint.

The *Doré* framework can be broken into three steps. The first step is to decide what Charter values are being raised and identify any potential impact on them by the administrative decision in question. The second step is to assess the overarching objective of the enabling statute or regulatory regime.[60] Finally, the last step is to assess "how the *Charter* value at issue will best be protected in view of the statutory objectives."[61]

The framework has faced strong criticisms from both scholars and judges. One of the primary criticisms levelled against *Doré* is that it is not clear who bears the evidentiary burden under the framework to prove (or not) a Charter violation.[62] *Doré* does not specify whether the onus is on the administrative actor to show its decision was reasonable, or on the complainant to show the administrative actor's decision was unreasonable. Without further clarity, litigants cannot know the level of evidence required to defend their cases. Moreover, depending on the approach chosen by the Court, different thresholds for rights protections could exist between administrative law and constitutional law cases, undermining the consistency in application that is meant to characterize Charter protections.

This is the fundamental weakness of the *Doré* framework: it is ill-defined and difficult to apply consistently. While individual judgments have commented on the burden of proof issue and on the difficulty in applying *Doré,* no majority judgment has confirmed which party bears the burden of proof.[63] And, since the justices in *Vavilov* expressly declined to comment on the *Doré* framework, these uncertainties in the law remain a live issue.[64]

Notably, the concern around who bears the onus of demonstrating the reasonableness (or lack thereof) of an administrative actor's decision under the *Doré* framework reflect the early debates from the 1980s about how section 1 of the Charter should be worded. An early draft read: "The *Canadian Charter of Rights and Freedoms* recognizes the following rights and freedoms subject only to such reasonable limits as are generally accepted in a free and democratic society with a parliamentary system of government."[65] There was strong opposition to this wording of section 1 because it was perceived as being too permissive in allowing limitations on rights. At the time, Walter Tarnopolsky was particularly outspoken.[66] His concern was that it imposed a significant burden on litigants to demonstrate that legislation was unreasonable because it "did not clearly determine where the onus should lie for demonstrating the reasonableness or unreasonableness of a limitation."[67] Tarnopolsky stressed that "the onus has to be upon the one who argues that there are restrictions, and that has to be put in terms of being either necessary or demonstrably justified or demonstrably necessary … and, which is important, it has to be prescribed by law."[68] Tarnopolsky's approach eventually won the day, as can be seen in the similarities between his suggestions and the final wording of section 1. Those concerns have also been addressed in how the Court framed the onus of proof under *Oakes*. However, the debate over who bears the onus to demonstrate reasonableness seems to have resurfaced under the guise of the *Doré* framework.

While the *Oakes* test is open to criticism,[69] it offers a more rigorous assessment of Charter violations than does *Doré*. Even with the risk of subjectivity in its application,[70] *Oakes* offers a more formal structure that allows for consistent application across cases, providing clear guidance to lower courts about how to address Charter complaints. By contrast, the loose structure of the *Doré* framework offers little consistency across cases and seems to provide minimal guidance to lower courts for how to address Charter complaints arising from different administrative contexts. And while courts have always shown a level of deference to legislative actors and how they define Charter values,[71] the difference is that legislation is the product of rigorous debate and has been subjected to public scrutiny. In contrast, administrative decisions often have little oversight, and often no written or explicit reasons are required to justify those decisions.[72] Where the *Oakes* test excels compared to the *Doré* framework is that, in general, it focuses on the normative question of what rights protections should look like and applies a structured, formal test that examines multiple angles of the problem and requires a series of thresholds to be passed in order for a rights infringement to be justified. *Oakes*, at a minimum, places the focus of the analysis squarely on the rights infringement; *Doré*, instead, emphasizes the statutory objective and whether the Charter can be accommodated within that objective.

Ultimately, the prioritization of administrative law standards of review has transformed the nature of judicial analysis from one based on proportionality under the *Oakes* test to one based on reasonableness under the *Doré* framework. Admittedly, there are similarities between proportionality and reasonableness, and the Court has argued that the *Doré* framework maintains "conceptual harmony" with the latter steps of the *Oakes* test.[73] The Court relies on this apparent similarity in *Doré* to find that "proportionality is simply an aspect of the standard of reasonableness – just more 'formulaic.'"[74] In particular, both methods of analysis are concerned with limiting rights infringements as little as possible and encouraging the weighing of different values to reach an "optimal" outcome.

Beyond those superficial similarities, however, there are important differences in the values and principles that inform these standards of review, including the willingness of the Court to engage in a probing review of rights infringements. As Iryna Ponomarenko notes, "[R]easonableness and proportionality are actually fairly distinct standards of review, not only in terms of their institutional and doctrinal effects, but also in terms of the implicit normative assumptions on which they operate."[75] Likewise, Walters argues that, under reasonableness, as long as administrative actors act in "good faith" and balance the relevant factors against their discretionary authority, they are largely free to weigh those factors however they wish.[76] By contrast, proportionality grants serious weight to the rights being evaluated and asserts that state objectives must "be shown to be pressing and substantial in a democratic society and the means adopted to secure them are rationally connected to the objective, impair rights as little as possible, and produce salutary results that are not outweighed by deleterious effects."[77] The difference, then, seems to lie in the level of robustness each evaluative standard requires. Under reasonableness, administrative actors have more freedom in how they balance the interests at play. By contrast, under proportionality, there exists a rigid series of thresholds that must be passed for an infringement to be considered justified.

Many scholars have questioned the ability of a reasonableness standard of review to sufficiently protect Charter rights.[78] In part, this is because the intensity of review under *Oakes* and *Doré* is different. The Court noted that the aim of the *Doré* framework was to ensure "that the decision interferes with the relevant *Charter* guarantee no more than is necessary *given the statutory objectives*."[79] This is a crucial distinction from a proportionality analysis, which "operates on the assumption that the scales are always tipped in favour of protecting constitutional rights."[80] To put the point differently, under a proportionality analysis, a Charter right is granted "normative priority,"[81] whereas under the *Doré* framework, it is the state objective that is given priority. While under a proportionality analysis there is an inherent assumption that the Court must reach the "right" decision, and the analysis tilts in favour of rights protections, under reasonableness review the framework favours the administrative actor and allows for more leeway in how rights claims can be resolved. In essence, the standard of reasonableness "is, by and large, 'the right to be wrong.'"[82]

For all the Court claims that reasonableness is informed by proportionality, and that the two standards are "harmonious," it is not clear the Court has been successful in defending that position. By not respecting the "primacy" of Charter rights in its analysis, and instead prioritizing statutory objectives, the *Doré* framework subverts a fundamental tenet of proportionality and undermines the purpose of having a bill of rights. Moreover, one of the key problems with the *Doré* framework is that reviewing courts are unable to challenge or reconsider the relative weight an administrative decision-maker has given to a right compared to other interests at play in a case.[83] Even if we were to accept that *Doré* harmonizes reasonableness and proportionality, that inability to reweigh the different rights and values in a case introduces a fundamental weakness into judicial review under the *Doré* framework that is not found under the *Oakes* test.[84] By requiring the Court to defer to the weighing conducted by administrative actors, reasonableness weakens rights protections because it limits the possibilities for review and lowers the threshold actors must meet to justify an infringement.

Admittedly, we should be careful about overstating the distinction between reasonableness and proportionality. Theoretical distinctions often become blurred in practice.[85] Nevertheless, even with some overlap in practice, in principle, reasonableness and proportionality are difficult to reconcile.[86] The fundamental goals of administrative law (reasonableness) and constitutional law (proportionality) are different; how they measure legitimacy, authority, and reason-giving are all based on different values and priorities that are difficult to combine into a single unified approach to rights.[87]

Proportionality pushes the government and administrative actors to justify their decisions and policy choices in ways that reasonableness review does not. Reasonableness review heavily focuses on the processes by which a decision was reached, with less attention given to the moral, political, or normative concerns of a case. Moreover, there is less consensus on how rights, values, and interests should be weighed under reasonableness than there is under proportionality, with the Court largely removing itself from the weighing process by deferring to the opinion of administrative actors. Reasonableness under the *Doré* framework does not resolve the issues raised by the *Oakes* test, but rather aggravates them. As such, the move from proportionality to reasonableness weakens, rather than strengthens or maintains, rights protections in Canada. All of this suggests that incorporating administrative actors and administrative law into our political theories about the Court-government relationship is critical for a full appreciation of how judicial review of the Charter has changed since the early days of its implementation.

Conclusion

The capacity for judges to comment on, critique, and even block legislation enacted by our elected representatives on the basis of rights claims has deep implications for our democracy and is worthy of serious attention. However, that focus on the development of legislation should not come at the expense of ignoring other categories of judicial review or changes that have occurred in the broader legal landscape. The decisions and regulations imposed by administrative actors have a substantial impact on the application of Charter rights in Canada. And because of this, they must be taken into account in our theories of judicial review. As Freya Kristjanson and Morgana Kellythorne note, the developing relationship between administrative law and the Charter "strikes at the heart of whether the *Charter* can be made 'meaningful to ordinary people.'"[88]

Scholars such as Hiebert, Hogg and Thornton, and Morton and Knopff have profoundly influenced the shape of Canadian political science scholarship. However, the law has changed substantially, and theories of judicial activism and dialogue theory no longer fully explain how the Court interacts with political actors when it comes to applying and limiting Charter rights. Examining how the Court responds to administrative actors is critical because the prioritization of judicial deference in the administrative context has changed the standards by which rights evaluations are made. The move from proportionality to reasonableness has not only weakened rights protections in Canada; it has also risked undermining constitutional law as the apex of our legal hierarchy and has diminished the Court's self-declared role as "guardian of the Constitution." Administrative law cases have much to tell us about how the Court understands its own role in relation to the governing branches. Many of the assumptions within the political-legal literature about the Court's relationship to the political branches of government require further nuancing, to better account for the multitudinous ways in which the Charter is applied and interpreted – and to account for the many actors to which the Court has granted interpretive authority.

NOTES

1 *Canadian Charter of Rights and Freedoms*, s. 7, Part I of the Constitution Act, 1982, being Schedule B to the Canada Act 1982 (UK), 1982, c11 at s. 1.

2 Janet L. Hiebert, *Limiting Rights: The Dilemma of Judicial Review* (Montreal: McGill-Queen's University Press, 1996), 6.

3 Ted Morton and Rainer Knopff, *The Charter Revolution & the Court Party* (Peterborough, ON: Broadview Press, 2000); Hiebert, *Limiting Rights*; Janet L. Hiebert, *Charter Conflicts: What Is Parliament's Role?* (Montreal: McGill-Queen's University Press, 2002); Mark Tushnet, *Weak Courts, Strong Rights: Judicial Review and Social Welfare Rights in Comparative Constitutional Law* (Princeton, NJ: Princeton University Press, 2008); Peter Hogg and Allison Bushell, "The Charter Dialogue Between Courts and Legislatures (or Perhaps the *Charter of Rights* Isn't Such a Bad Thing After All)," *Osgoode Hall Law Journal* 35, no. 1 (1997): 75–124; Christopher P. Manfredi

and James B. Kelly, "Six Degrees of Dialogue: A Response to Hogg and Bushell," *Osgoode Hall Law Journal* 37, no. 3 (1999): 513–27; Emmett Macfarlane, "Dialogue or Compliance? Measuring Legislatures' Policy Responses to Court Rulings on Rights," *International Political Science Review* 34, no. 1 (2012): 39–56.

4 *Canada (Minister of Citizenship and Immigration) v. Vavilov*, 2019 SCC 65 [*Vavilov*], at para. 4.

5 *Hunter et al. v. Southam Inc.*, [1984] 2 SCR 145, 11 DLR (4th) 641 [*Hunter, 1984*]; *Reference re Supreme Court Act, ss. 5 and 6*, 2014 SCC 21 [*Reference re Supreme Court Act*].

6 *Hunter*, 1984; *R. v. Therens*, [1985] 1 SCR 613, 18 DLR (4th) 655; *Singh v. Minister of Employment and Immigration*, [1985] 1 SCR 177, 17 DLR (4th) 422.

7 Louis LeBel, "Some Properly Deferential Thoughts on Deference," *Canadian Journal of Administrative Law & Practice* 21, no. 1 (2008): 3–4.

8 Bertha Wilson, "We Didn't Volunteer," *Policy Options* (April 1999): 9.

9 Dave Snow and Mark S. Harding, "From Normative Debates to Comparative Methodology: The Three Waves of Post-Charter Supreme Court Scholarship in Canada," *American Review of Canadian Studies* 45, no. 4 (2015): 451–66.

10 Snow and Harding, "From Normative Debates," 451–2.

11 Judicial activism is a porous term that can encompass a variety of meanings. In general, however, judicial activism refers to the frequency that courts interfere with the policy decisions of legislatures.

12 Hogg and Bushell, "Charter Dialogue."

13 Morton and Knopff, *Charter Revolution*.

14 Snow and Harding, "From Normative Debates," 455.

15 Morton and Knopff, *Charter Revolution*, 13.

16 Thomas M.J. Bateman, "The Supreme Court of Canada as Moral Tutor: Religious Freedom, Civil Society, and Charter Values," in *Liberal Education, Civic Education, and the Canadian Regime*, ed. David W. Livingstone (Montreal: McGill-Queen's University Press, 2015), 231–67.

17 Hiebert, *Limiting Rights*, 79.

18 Snow and Harding, "From Normative Debates," 456.

19 Hogg and Bushell, "Charter Dialogue."

20 Jamie Cameron, "Collateral Thoughts on Dialogue's Legacy as Metaphor and Theory: A Favorite from Canada," *University of Queensland Law Journal* 35, no. 1 (2016): 157.

21 Hogg and Bushell, "Charter Dialogue."

22 Manfredi and Kelly, "Six Degrees of Dialogue," 514.

23 See Macfarlane, "Dialogue or Compliance," as a more recent example.

24 LeBel, "Some Properly Deferential Thoughts," 4.

25 See Paul Daly, "Prescribing Greater Protection for Rights: Administrative Law and Section 1 of the Canadian Charter of Rights and Freedoms,"

Supreme Court Law Review 65, 2nd ser. (2014): 247–90; Matthew Horner, "Charter Values: The Uncanny Valley of Canadian Constitutionalism," *Supreme Court Law Review* 67, 2nd ser. (2014): 361–90; Mary Liston, "Administering the *Charter*, Proportioning Justice: Thirty-Five Years of Development in a Nutshell," *Canadian Journal of Administrative Law & Practice* 30, no. 2 (2017): 211–46; Audrey Macklin, "Charter Right or Charter-Lite? Administrative Discretion and the *Charter*," *Supreme Court Law Review* 67, 2nd ser. (2014): 561–88.

26 Peter W. Hogg and Allison A. Thornton, "Reply to 'Six Degrees of Dialogue,'" *Osgoode Hall Law Journal* 37, no. 3 (1999): 530–1.

27 Christopher P. Manfredi and James B. Kelly, "Dialogue, Deference, and Restraint: Judicial Independence and Trial Procedures," *Saskatchewan Law Review* 64 (2001): 327.

28 Vuk Radmilovic, "Governmental Interventions and Judicial Decision Making: The Supreme Court of Canada in the Age of the *Charter*," *Canadian Journal of Political Science* 46, no.2 (2013): 341.

29 *Hunter*, 1984.

30 Kate Glover, "The Supreme Court in Canada's Constitutional Order," *Review of Constitutional Studies* 21, no. 1 (2016): 152–3; *Reference re Supreme Court Act*, 2014.

31 See, for example, Hiebert, *Limiting Rights*, 44–5.

32 See, for example, *Law Society of British Columbia v. Trinity Western University*, 2018 SCC 32 [*TWU BC*]; *Ktunaxa Nation v. British Columbia (Forests, Lands and Natural Resource Operations)*, 2017 SCC 54 [*Ktunaxa*], where the Court largely deferred to the interpretations of the administrative decision-makers at the expense of a robust or probing proportionality analysis.

33 Matthew Lewans, "Administrative Law, Judicial Deference, and the Charter," *Constitutional Forum* 23, no. 2 (2014): 20; *CUPE v. NB Liquor Corporation*, [1979] 2 SCR 227, 97 DLR (3d) 417; *Nicholson v. Haldimand-Norfolk Regional Police Commissioners*, [1979] 1 SCR 311, 88 DLR (3d) 671.

34 *Dunsmuir v. New Brunswick*, 2008 SCC 9, at para. 27 [*Dunsmuir*].

35 *Pezim v. British Columbia (Superintendent of Brokers)*, [1994] 2 SCR 557, 114 DLR (4th) 385; *Canada (Director of Investigation and Research) v. Southam Inc.*, [1997] 1 SCR 748, 144 DLR (4th) 1; *Dunsmuir*, 2008; *Doré v. Barreau du Québec*, 2012 SCC 12 [*Doré*].

36 Macklin, "Charter Right or Charter-Lite," 563.

37 *Vavilov*, at para. 17.

38 Ibid.

39 Ibid.

40 For broader discussions of the impact of *Vavilov* on administrative law in Canada, see, for example, Daly, "The Vavilov Framework"; Paul Daly,

"Canadian Labour Law after Vavilov," *Canadian Labour & Employment Law Journal* 23, no. 1 (2021), 103–20; Paul Daly, "*Vavilov* and the Culture of Justification in Contemporary Administrative Law," *Supreme Court Law Review* 100 (2021): 279–307.

41 See, for example, David Mullan, "Reasonableness Review Post-*Vavilov:* An 'Encomium for Correctness' or Deference as Usual?" *Canadian Labour & Employment Law Journal* 23 (2021): 189–219; Paul Daly, "The *Vavilov* Framework and the Future of Canadian Administrative Law," *Canadian Journal of Administrative Law & Practice* 33 (2020): 111–44.

42 *Vavilov,* at para. 57. Note that the analysis in this chapter reflects the jurisprudence at the time of writing, in June of 2023. Since then, the Court has issued its decision in *Commission scolaire francophone des Territoires du Nord-Ouest v. Northwest Territories (Education, Culture and Employment),* 2023 SCC 31. While engagement with this case was not possible due to publication timelines, it is an important case to be aware of. The case affirms the continued applicability of the *Doré* framework in the post-*Vavilov* world and provides important guidance on the relationship between reasonableness and proportionality, the courts' role as guardian of the Constitution, and how the *Doré* framework should be applied.

43 Mark Mancini, "The Conceptual Gap between *Doré* and *Vavilov,*" *Dalhousie Law Journal* 43, no. 2 (2020): 793–834 *contra* Richard Stacey, "A Unified Model of Public Law: Charter Values and Reasonableness Review in Canada," *University of Toronto Law Journal* 71 (2021): 339–75.

44 *Vavilov,* at para. 96.

45 Edward Cottrill, "Administrative 'Determinations of Law' and the Limits of Legal Pluralism after *Vavilov,*" *Alberta Law Review* 58, no. 1 (2020): 153–86.

46 Beth Bilson, "The Voice from the Trenches: Administrative Tribunals and the Interpretation of the Charter," *Saskatchewan Law Review* 69, no. 1 (2006): 22.

47 Glover, "Canada's Constitutional Order," 158.

48 David Dyzenhaus, "The Politics of Deference: Judicial Review and Democracy," in *The Province of Administrative Law,* ed. Michael Taggart (Oxford: Oxford University Press, 1997), 279–307; *Baker v. Canada (Minister of Citizenship and Immigration),* [1999] 2 SCR 817, 174 DLR (4th) 193 at para. 65.

49 Mark D. Walters, "Respecting Deference as Respect: Rights, Reasonableness and Proportionality in Canadian Administrative Law," in *The Scope and Intensity of Substantive Review: Traversing Taggart's Rainbow,* ed. Mark Elliott and Hanna Wilberg (Oxford: Hart Publishing, 2015), 416–18.

50 Macklin, "Charter Right or Charter-Lite," 584.

51 Freya Kristjanson and Morgana Kellythorne, "Charter Cases Before Administrative Tribunals and on Judicial Review," *National Journal of Constitutional Law* 25 (2008): 229.

52 Walters, "Respecting Deference as Respect," 414.

53 LeBel, "Some Properly Deferential Thoughts"; Lewans, "Administrative Law, Judicial Deference"; Lorne Sossin and Mark Friedman, "Charter Values and Administrative Justice," *Supreme Court Law Review* 67, 2nd ser. (2014): 391–430.

54 Paul Daly, *A Theory of Deference in Administrative Law: Basis, Application and Scope* (Cambridge: Cambridge University Press, 2012); Paul Daly, "Prescribing Greater Protection for Rights"; Iryna Ponomarenko, "Tipping the Scales in the Reasonableness-Proportionality Debate in Canadian Administrative Law," *Appeal: Review of Current Law and Law Reform* 21 (2016): 125–44; Léonid Sirota, "Canadian Administrative Law and Good Governance," *Canadian Journal of Administrative Law & Practice* 31 (2018): 285–305.

55 Hiebert, *Limiting Rights,* 79.

56 Ibid., 80.

57 Ibid., 61.

58 *R. v. Oakes*, [1986] 1 SCR 103, 26 DLR (4th) 200 [*Oakes*] at para. 69.

59 *Doré.*

60 Christopher D. Bredt and Ewa Krajewska, "Doré: All that Glitters Is Not Gold," *Supreme Court Law Review* 67, 2nd ser. (2014): 348.

61 *Doré,* at para. 56.

62 Edward J. Cottrill, "Novel Uses of the *Charter* Following *Doré* and *Loyola*," *Alberta Law Review* 56, no. 1 (2018): 111.

63 See, for example, *TWU BC,* 2018.

64 *Vavilov.*

65 Hiebert, *Limiting Rights,* 21.

66 Ibid., 23.

67 Ibid.

68 Canada, Parliament, Senate and House of Commons, Special Joint Committee of the Senate and of the House of Commons on the Constitution of Canada, *Minutes of Proceedings,* 32nd Parliament, 1st session, Issue No. 7, 18 November 1980, at para. 7:10. Accessed 5 December 2024, https://primarydocuments.ca/wp-content/uploads/2018/02/SpecJointComConstitution71980Nov18.pdf.

69 See, for example, Richard Moon, "Limits of Constitutional Rights: The Marginal Role of Proportionality Analysis," *Israel Law Review* 50, no. 1 (2017): 49–68; Grégoire C.N. Webber, "Proportionality, Balancing, and the Cult of Constitutional Rights Scholarship," *Canadian Journal of Law and Jurisprudence* 23, no. 1 (2010): 179–202.

70 See, for example, Hiebert, *Limiting Rights,* 62; Dwight Newman, "The Limitation of Rights: A Comparative Evolution and Ideology of the *Oakes* and *Sparrow* Tests," *Saskatchewan Law Review* 62, no. 2 (1999): 547.

71 Hiebert, *Limiting Rights,* 151.
72 Though note that, under *Vavilov,* this may change somewhat. Greater attention to the reasons and justifications given for an administrative decision will be necessary for a court to find an administrative decision was reasonable.
73 *Doré,* at para. 57; *Loyola High School v. Quebec (Attorney General),* at para. 40; *TWU BC,* 2018, at para. 82.
74 Ponomarenko, "Tipping the Scales," 131–2.
75 Ibid., 127–8.
76 Walters, "Respecting Deference as Respect," 401.
77 Ibid.
78 See, for example, Daly, *Theory of Deference*; Macklin, "Charter Right or Charter-Lite"; Ponomarenko, "Tipping the Scales."
79 *Doré,* at para. 7, emphasis added.
80 Ponomarenko, "Tipping the Scales," 134.
81 Macklin, "Charter Right or Charter-Lite," 573.
82 Ponomarenko, "Tipping the Scales," 134, quoting Guy Régimbald, "Correctness, Reasonableness and Proportionality: A New Standard of Judicial Review," *Manitoba Law Journal* 31, no. 2 (2005): 254.
83 Gerald Heckman, "Developments in Administrative Law: The 2014–2015 Term," *Supreme Court Law Review* 72, 2nd ser. (2016): 51.
84 Macklin, "Charter Right or Charter-Lite," 581.
85 Walters, "Respecting Deference as Respect," 402.
86 Daly, *Theory of Deference;* Macklin, "Charter Right or Charter-Lite"; Ponomarenko, "Tipping the Scales."
87 Macklin, "Charter Right or Charter-Lite."
88 Kristjanson and Kellythorne, "Charter Cases Before Administrative Tribunals," 231.

4 Before We Go to War: Human Rights and the Prerogative Power

GEORGE WILLIAMS AND WINSOME HALL

The relationship between the executive and Parliament, especially in the realm of human rights protection, has been an area of significant contemporary interest. This has often focused on human rights instruments and their impact on government decision-making across nations such as Canada, the UK, and Australia.[1] The decision to go to war is an analogous area.[2] It raises important questions about the powers and responsibilities of the different arms of government, and how they should interact in making decisions with profound human rights implications.

This chapter examines the making of the decision to enter into armed conflict in Westminster systems of government in the United Kingdom, Canada, and Australia. The discussion begins with the current conception of the relationship between the executive and Parliament in the making of such a decision. In each jurisdiction, the power to enter an armed conflict is derived from the royal prerogative and has been exercisable by the executive without control or oversight by Parliament, or overt consideration of human rights. This has come under challenge. Since the Iraq War in 2003, public concern about countries' decisions to enter wars, and how and by whom that power is exercised, has increased. Of particular concern is the extent to which human rights considerations should influence, and be seen to influence through a deliberative process, the decision to go to war.

We examine how nations have responded by reshaping the relationship between the executive and Parliament in making the decision to enter an overseas conflict. In the UK and Canada it has become usual for a government considering entering an armed conflict to present its decision to Parliament before the exercise of the power. In Australia, the traditional relationship remains, although proposals have been put forward for parliamentary approval. The processes of reform in these nations are still underway, and so we set out where they should land. We propose that nations legislate to require parliamentary approval to enter an armed conflict. This process should engage with the international and domestic human rights implications of the decision.

The Prerogative

In the UK, Canada, and Australia, the commitment of Armed Forces to an overseas conflict is an exercise of the prerogative power by the executive with no legislated role for parliamentary oversight. The traditional conception of the relationship has been that the matter is one for the executive alone, with Parliament often playing little or no role in the making of the decision, other than being informed by the executive of developments. In this section, we discuss the nature and scope of the prerogative in this context.

Nature and Scope

The prerogative of the Crown in the UK, Canada, and Australia is an ancient and ill-defined set of powers held by each executive government. As a result, the nature and scope of the prerogative can be elusive. Albert V. Dicey's definition, commonly regarded as the standard definition of prerogative powers, holds that the prerogative is "both historically and as a matter of actual fact nothing else than the residue of discretionary or arbitrary authority, which at any given time is legally left in the hands of the Crown."[3] Other theorists and lawyers prefer William Blackstone's definition, which refers to a "special pre-eminence which the king hath, over and above all other persons, and out of the ordinary course of the common law, in right of his regal dignity."[4] As Noel Cox notes, these definitions are "significantly divergent, if not inconsistent,"[5] which – as he points out – presents a distinct difficulty for persons attempting to understand the nature and scope of the prerogative.

Canadian scholar Peter Hogg's definition of the prerogative refers to those "powers and privileges accorded by the common law to the Crown."[6] While this definition was recently critiqued by Alexander Bolt and Phillipe Lagassé, who proposed the alternative "powers and privileges of the Crown recognised at common law,"[7] these scholars urged jurists to prefer Hogg's to Dicey's definition.[8]

Regardless of the exact wording that one prefers in these contemporary definitions, they avoid the Diceyan use of words like "residue" and "arbitrary" which contain the assumption that prerogative powers are a "relic" that should give way to legislation.[9] Nonetheless, as a construct of the common law, it is accepted that the prerogative can be modified or displaced by legislation. Hence, in *R. (on the Application of Miller) v. Secretary of State for Exiting the European Union*[10] the United Kingdom Supreme Court held that "consistently with Parliamentary sovereignty, a prerogative power however well-established may be curtailed or abrogated by statute." Where this has occurred, the executive "can no longer rely on the prerogative power but must act in accordance with the statutory regime laid down by the parliament."[11]

Both the number and scope of prerogative powers is contested (a non-exhaustive list commonly includes the power to operate the machinery of government, enter treaties, grant mercy, or declare war). For the purposes of this chapter, we describe the prerogative power with which we are concerned as the "defence prerogative" and – as we discuss in the next section – consider its scope only in relation to formal declarations of war and in relation to the executive's power to enter into armed conflicts.

Source of the Prerogative Power to Enter Armed Conflicts

Discussion of the prerogative as it relates to national defence has historically focused on formal declarations of war. Declarations of war, however, no longer represent how states commonly enter into conflict. For example, Australia has not formally declared war since 1941 despite being involved in hostilities overseas on many occasions.[12] A better understanding is that the defence prerogative in modern times encompasses the deployment of armed forces overseas and the general conduct of military affairs. In each jurisdiction, a statute now governs *how* armed forces may be deployed, their operations, and their procedure. It is accepted in the UK, Canada, and Australia that it is a matter for the executive to answer these questions as doing so falls within the prerogative power.

In the UK, it is long-established that the executive has exclusive prerogative power over war.[13] This derives from the prerogative's status as an executive power (or, as David Kershaw puts it, "delegated powers from a parliamentary sovereign"[14]) as established by the political and constitutional events of 1688–9,[15] and the 1688 Bill of Rights in particular.[16] Exploring the full legal-historical complexity of these events and their effect on the prerogative is beyond the scope of this chapter; it is sufficient to say that they transferred certain powers to ministers that had previously been the sole purview of the monarch.[17]

The situation is different in other Commonwealth nations. In Canada, prerogative powers are declared to "continue" in section 9 of the

Canadian Constitution.[18] Section 15 vests in the monarch the power of commander in chief of Canada's Armed Forces (which the governor general is empowered to exercise as per the Letters Patent Constituting the Office of Governor General of Canada, 1947). The governor general, in accordance with the principle of responsible government, makes a decision to deploy the Armed Forces on the advice of his/her ministers. Under section 32 of the *National Defence Act*, Parliament must be convened within ten days to debate any deployment when the forces are placed on active service. However, in 1989 the governor in council issued an order placing the Canadian Armed Forces on active service at all times (for the purposes of complying with Canada's NATO obligations), which has rendered this parliamentary oversight mechanism irrelevant.[19]

In Australia, there is no explicit mechanism in the Constitution stating who can commit Australia to war or how that power is to be exercised. In 1941 the power to declare war was expressly delegated to the governor general of Australia by the king.[20] However, as discussed above, formal declarations of war are now uncommon. The silence in the Australian Constitution on how and when the defence prerogative can be exercised is unsurprising, given that at the time of its drafting, in the late nineteenth century, parliamentary or popular involvement in decisions about war was not contemplated.[21] At best, the Australian Constitution provides a starting point for considering the prerogative as it relates to decisions to enter armed conflict. Section 51, which sets out the legislative powers of Parliament, includes the power to pass laws in relation to "naval and military defence of the Commonwealth." Under section 68, the governor general as the king's representative is the commander in chief of Australia's naval and military forces (although, as a matter of practice, this is an honorific only as the governor general is understood to exercise authority over the Australian Defence Force on advice from the prime minister in accordance with the principles of responsible government). And section 61 provides a framework for understanding executive power, as power "vested in the Queen and … exercisable by the Governor-General as the Queen's representative [which] extends to the execution and maintenance of this Constitution, and the laws of the Commonwealth."[22]

The Rise of Human Rights Concerns

The Iraq War in 2003 elevated concerns in several countries about the unfettered capacity of governments to engage in armed conflict overseas. In a situation where there were serious misgivings about the legality of the entry of "the coalition of the willing" into Iraq, and widespread public sentiment against the war, the participation of the

UK and Australia in that conflict came under heavy scrutiny. Concerns about executive power to commit a nation to an armed conflict are long-standing. What was different about the events of 2003 was how wide-spread these concerns became, and how issues of international law and human rights came to the forefront of the discussion.

The traditional view in the UK, Canada, and Australia is that human rights concerns have no formal or public part to play in the decision to go to war. They may certainly be considered by the executive in exercising the prerogative power, but there is no requirement to do so. The conventional starting point, then, is that there is no intersection between human rights and political institutions with respect to the defence prerogative in these countries. This, however, lies at odds conceptually and legally with the development of international law since the Second World War. It is now the case that the entry of a state into an armed conflict engages a nexus of international law rules and obligations, many of which concern human rights.

Since the affirmation of individual human rights in the 1949 Geneva Conventions[23] and the adoption of the 1998 Rome Statute,[24] violations of certain fundamental rights can now be directly prosecuted via international tribunals without the interposition of national law. This is contrary to the traditional Westminster idea of rights protection where "rights," insofar as they are recognized, are protected by operation of the domestic law. The development of new international rules, and the assumption of obligations in relation to human rights in warfare by nations, will naturally bear upon the decision of those nations to engage in force overseas, and will raise questions about how such decisions are made. In particular, it raises questions about the appropriateness of vesting such a decision solely in the executive by way of the prerogative without a more significant opportunity to publicly deliberate in Parliament on the relevance of human rights and other international law factors to the decision.

Human rights violations have been raised repeatedly as part of governments' justifications for entering armed conflicts, as well as by Members of Parliament (MPs) concerned about the human rights implications of warfare.[25] As was argued in May 2003 by a member of the House of Lords in the context of the UK exercising its prerogative power to enter the Iraq conflict, "there should at least be a convention" that "where there is a substantial exercise involving sending people to kill and be killed on behalf of the country, then that should be with the consent, prior or at any rate immediate, of the House of Commons."[26] The gravity of the rights implications of the decision to go to war was implicitly recognized by this statement: killing or being killed engages with one of the most fundamental human rights, as expressed in Article 6(1) of the International Covenant on Civil and Political Rights.[27]

Current institutional practice in relation to the defence prerogative is also at odds with developments since 2003 that reinforce the significance of human rights concerns. For example, in 2018, Canada amended its arms export legislation to require the foreign minister to refuse to issue export permits if there was a substantial risk that equipment could be used to commit human rights violations.[28] Another example is that, because of certain alleged incidents during Australia's participation in the war in Afghanistan, the inspector-general of the Australian Defence Force published the *IGADF Afghanistan Inquiry Report* (the Brereton Report).[29] The report includes serious allegations of rights-violating conduct by members of the Australian Defence Force. Although the words "human rights" are not used in the unredacted sections of the Brereton Report (save in the glossary, within the acronym of "Afghan Independent Human Rights Commission"), the allegations as described in the report would likely, if proven, contravene non-derogable prohibitions in international human rights law. In Australia, the Brereton Report has prompted significant community concern with and discussion of the human rights implications of warfare.

The adoption of national human rights instruments in the UK and Canada has enabled legal challenges to the exercise of the defence prerogative on human rights grounds. In 2008 the families of two UK soldiers killed in Iraq in 2003 and 2004 sought to establish that the UK government had a duty, because of its human rights obligations, to have taken more thorough steps in deciding whether or not to enter that armed conflict.[30] The families contended that they had a right to a broad inquiry into the entry of the UK into Iraq in 2003, with a focus on the steps taken by the government to obtain advice on the legality of the invasion. This right was said to be derived from sections 1 and 2 of the *Human Rights Act 1998* (UK) and Article 2 of the European Convention on Human Rights (ECHR). It was argued that Article 2 of the ECHR imposed a duty on member states to protect life, which extends to the lives of soldiers. The families said that the UK government breached its Article 2 duty by failing to properly ascertain whether participating in the Iraq armed conflict would comply with international law. The families further argued that, had the UK obtained legal advice on this before invading Iraq in 2003, it would not have invaded and, had it not invaded, the young men would not have been killed.

The House of Lords in *R. (on the application of Gentle) v. The Prime Minister* unanimously rejected these arguments. First, and of critical importance to the questions considered in this chapter, the judges were not convinced that the ECHR provided a suitable framework for resolving questions about the resort to war. Lord Bingham noted that the courts have traditionally been restrained in ruling on "what has been called high policy – peace and war, the making of treaties, the conduct of foreign relations." Although he does not state this explicitly, these areas of "high policy" are traditionally part of the prerogative. Likewise, Lord Hope could not see the link between a duty on the government to hold an inquiry into its decision-making process to enter Iraq and the right under Article 2. He held that the guaranteed protection of life in Article 2 is not violated by deploying armed forces overseas into an armed conflict, even though there is an inherent risk they may be killed because they are deployed. Secondly, as several judges noted, there was a weakness in the causal argument linking the UK not taking further legal advice and not deciding to deploy soldiers in Iraq. As Lord Hoffman held, it was a weak argument to suggest that had the UK taken further legal advice at the time of deciding to enter Iraq there was a good chance it would not have taken part in the invasion (and that the soldiers would not have been killed). Although he emphasized that it was desirable for the government to take reasonable steps to discover whether or not it was about to act contrary to international law in entering a conflict, he held that Article 2 was not relevant as the government not doing this would not lead to noncompliance with that article.[31]

In Canada, the Supreme Court of Canada was clear in the case of *Operation Dismantle v. The Queen*[32] that the exercise of prerogative power could be reviewed for consistency with the Canadian Charter of Rights and Freedoms (the Charter). However, in *Blanco v. Canada,*[33] the difficulty of establishing a link between the exercise of the war prerogative and the violation of statutory rights arose. In February 2003, the plaintiff sought an injunction to restrain the sending of Canadian Armed Forces to war in Iraq without the consent of Parliament. The plaintiff's case centred on an argument that the *Act of Settlement 1701* (UK), as imported into Canadian law, required the executive to have the consent of Parliament before a declaration of war could be made to defend any territory not belonging to the English Crown. The plaintiff did not seek to challenge the decision based on a violation of the Charter. The trial division of the Federal Court of Canada refused to grant the injunction. In doing so, Justice Heneghan noted *Operation Dismantle* and concluded that the exercise of the prerogative was not justiciable in the absence of a Charter challenge.[34] Had the case been couched in terms of the Charter there may have been a basis for review of the exercise of the defence prerogative. However, as the experience of the United Kingdom in *Gentle* shows, cases seeking judicial review of an exercise of the defence prerogative on human rights grounds are likely to face significant causal and conceptual difficulties in making out these arguments.

Changing Relationship between Parliament and Executive

Recent years have seen change to the relationship between Parliament and the executive when it comes to the exercise of the defence prerogative, because pf factors such as those explored above. The most significant change to date has been to permit greater involvement by Parliament in the making and scrutiny of such decisions in certain jurisdictions, namely, the UK. This appears to have been influenced by ideas of accountability: that where lives are at stake, the executive should not make such a decision of its own motion. Although not always put in these terms, a prevailing theme of the pressure to require parliamentary scrutiny of the decision to go to war is recognition of the grave human rights implications of war; that killing or being killed, and other consequential deprivations of war, impact the human rights of those involved.

As an example, the latest Australian attempt to legislate for parliamentary approval of the decision to enter armed conflict, discussed below, included a statement of compatibility with human rights in its Explanatory Memorandum, which stated that the bill "enhances what many regard as a pre-eminent human right to peace, safety and stability and gives effect to the United Nations Declaration on the Right of Peoples to Peace" and, further, stated that "this Bill is compatible with human rights because it advances the protection of human rights."[35]

The UK has been a leader in this area. Since 2011 a convention has emerged that the House of Commons have an opportunity to debate, and since about 2013 to approve, the deployment of its Armed Forces overseas. In Canada, there are signs that a convention for Parliament to approve military action may emerge, but it is at an earlier stage of evolution than in the UK. In Australia no such convention yet exists. Even in the UK, where a convention has emerged, its scope remains contested and uncertain. As a practice yet not formalized in legislation, it is subject to change and interpretation.

United Kingdom

CONVENTION

In the UK a convention has developed that the House of Commons have the opportunity to debate and vote upon the deployment of military forces prior to the exercise of the prerogative. As described in the

Cabinet Manual, an authoritative source of laws, rules, and conventions of the UK government, the convention is said to be that "the House of Commons should have an opportunity to debate the matter" before troops were committed "except when there was an emergency and such action would not be appropriate."[36]

In 2018, a House of Commons briefing paper set out the threshold of the convention as follows:

> On the basis of the evidence, one could make the argument that, at the very least, prior parliamentary approval will be sought under the convention if any of the following applies:
>
> - The possibility of premeditated military action exists.
> - Military forces are to be deployed in an offensive capacity.
> - Deployments for training, humanitarian aid or logistical assistance would not meet these threshold criteria. However, should an existing non-combat operation evolve into one in which offensive action is envisaged (mission creep), then it could feasibly be expected that the threshold would be reached and fresh approval would have to be sought from Parliament.[37]

The briefing paper also stated that "[u]nder the Convention, as it has developed, it has been made clear that the Government would also come to the House retrospectively in emergency situations."[38]

On 18 March 2003, the UK Parliament voted on two substantive motions to authorize military action in Iraq. This was preceded by debate throughout November 2002, and a prior vote on 25 February 2003 on a motion calling upon Iraq to recognize its final opportunity to comply with its disarmament obligations. At that time, the Secretary of State noted that this motion was "not an endorsement of military action by United Kingdom forces" and that "we will put any decision on military action to the House."[39]

This critical moment came on 18 March 2003 when the government tabled a motion in the House of Commons to authorize the use of "all means necessary to ensure the disarmament of Iraq's weapons of mass destruction."[40] Before this motion was voted on an amendment was proposed, stating that the "case for war against Iraq has not yet been established, especially given the absence of specific United Nations authorisation." The vote to amend was held first. The amendment failed by 217–396 votes. The second vote, on the primary government motion, passed 412–149. This vote provided the approval of Parliament for entry into the Iraq conflict. Although the UK government had consulted Parliament on military actions since the Second World War, including debates in the House of Commons on military engagement and votes on substantive motions,[41] the votes marked the first example in modern times of prior parliamentary approval having been sought for deployment of force overseas. In the context of the growing public dissatisfaction with unilateral executive entry into war after 2003, discussed above, these votes came to be seen as a precedent for future decisions on military action.

The practice in the UK of Parliament voting on proposed entry into armed conflicts appeared to be cemented by David Cameron government's actions in 2013, in relation to the proposal that the UK join the US in military action in Syria. On 29 August 2013, Parliament rejected a government motion that "a strong humanitarian response is required from the international community and that this may, if necessary, require military action that is legal, proportionate and focused on saving lives by preventing and deterring further use of Syria's chemical weapons." The motion failed by 272–285 votes.[42]

After the motion, Labour MP Edward Miliband posed the question: "Will the Prime Minister confirm to the House that, given the will of the House that has been expressed tonight, he will not use the royal prerogative to order the UK to be part of military action before there has been another vote in the House of Commons?"[43] Prime Minister Cameron replied in the affirmative, stating: "I also believe in respecting the will of this House of Commons. It is very clear tonight that, while the House has not passed a motion, the British Parliament, reflecting the views of the British people, does not want to see British military action. I get that, and the Government will act accordingly."[44]

The defeat of the government's motion to undertake military action in Syria was widely viewed as confirming the changed relationship between Parliament and the executive in relation to this power, and an as an affirmation of parliamentary sovereignty. Apparent confirmation of this change in relationship come soon after with the Cameron government's decision to seek parliamentary approval for action against ISIS in September 2014 and December 2015 (votes which ultimately succeeded).[45]

By contrast, in April 2018, the Theresa May government conducted a series of airstrikes in Syria without parliamentary debate or consent. In a debate after the fact, Prime Minister May acknowledged the existence of the convention but provided reasons that the government believed this action did not fall within it.[46] May argued, on the basis of a 2016 statement by the then-defence secretary, that there was a broad exception to the convention wherein "[g]overnments can use their judgment about how best to protect the security and interests of the UK. In observing the convention, we must ensure that the ability of our armed forces to act quickly and decisively, and to maintain the security of their operations, is not compromised … If we were to attempt to clarify more precisely circumstances in which we would consult Parliament before taking military action, we would constrain the operational flexibility of the armed forces."[47] Given that the airstrikes appeared to be essentially the same kind of action contemplated in 2013, 2014, and 2015,[48] the refusal to consult Parliament in 2018 created significant uncertainty about the scope of the convention.

LEGISLATIVE PROPOSALS

In the face of ill-defined conventions that can be departed from by the will of the executive, a legislative solution appears attractive. There have been unsuccessful attempts in the UK to legislate a formal role for Parliament in overseeing the executive's war powers. These attempts span back to at least 1999 and include the Military Action Against Iraq (Parliamentary Approval) Bill 1999,[49] the Waging War (Parliament's Role and Responsibility) Bill 2006–7,[50] and the Armed Forces Deployment (Royal Prerogative) Bill 2016.[51]

In addition to attempted legislative reform, since 2003 there has been continued examination of Parliament's role in decisions to enter armed conflicts. A series of committee reports have recommended additional parliamentary oversight of the executive.[52] In 2007, the House of Commons debated and passed a motion welcoming "the precedents set by the Government in 2002 and 2003 in seeking and obtaining the approval of the House for its decisions in respect of military action against Iraq; is of the view that it is inconceivable that any Government would in practice depart from this precedent" and stating that "the time has come for Parliament's role to be made more explicit in approving, or otherwise, decisions of the Government relating to the major, or substantial, deployment of British forces overseas into actual, or potential, armed conflict."[53] Following this, several reports were published.[54] One of these, the Green Paper, stated:

> 26. The Government believes that [the exercise of the prerogative without formal parliamentary agreement] is now an outdated state of affairs in a modern democracy. On an issue of such fundamental importance to the nation, the Government should seek the approval of the representatives of the people in the House of Commons for significant, non-routine deployments of the Armed Forces into armed conflict, to the greatest extent possible. This needs to be done without prejudicing the Government's ability to take swift action to protect our national security, or undermining operational security or effectiveness.[55]

In 2011, the Political and Constitutional Reform Committee recommended that the convention of Parliament approving entry into armed conflict be included in the revised *Cabinet Manual*.[56] This was incorporated in the October 2011 revision of the *Cabinet Manual*.[57]

In 2013, the House of Lords Constitution Committee noted that, despite these changes, a lack of clarity remained over the role that Parliament should play in decisions to enter armed conflicts (in this case, in the context of the conflict in Syria). The report concluded that the existing convention was that "save in exceptional circumstances, the House of Commons is given the opportunity to debate and vote on the deployment of armed force overseas."[58]

In 2019, the Public Administration and Constitutional Affairs Committee recommended that the *Cabinet Manual* be updated again to clarify the convention on the use of the royal prerogative in relation to military action. The report noted that the evidence it received in relation to the non-consultation of Parliament before the 2018 Syrian airstrikes indicated uncertainty generated by the government's ability to alter the scope of the convention.[59]

Ultimately, the state of the relationship between Parliament and the executive in relation to the defence prerogative in the UK is that a convention of parliamentary approval before deployment of the it Armed Forces appears to have emerged. However, the boundaries of the convention continue to be uncertain because, in the absence of legislation modifying the prerogative, the executive can continue to assert broad exceptions to the convention and exert its power unilaterally to deploy the UK Armed Forces.

Canada

CONVENTION

It is unclear (but unlikely) that a convention to consult Parliament prior to deploying the Armed Forces has emerged in Canada. At certain times, the Canadian government has sought the approval of Parliament before making decisions about armed conflicts. In 2006, for example, the Canadian Parliament voted to extend the presence of its Armed Forces in Afghanistan, which had been slated to end in 2007 (although, notably, Prime Minister Harper stated that he would extend the mission for one year with or without the support of the House).[60] In 2008, parliamentary approval was again sought, and granted, for extending the deployment in Afghanistan, although the extension was given on the basis that there would be a withdrawal of Canadian Armed Forces in 2011.[61] This occurred in relation to other conflicts as well: in March

2011, Parliament passed a motion approving the deployment of Armed Forces to Libya, and in June and September 2011 voted on an extension of these operations; and in 2014, the Canadian House of Commons was again asked to vote to approve air strikes against ISIS in Syria.

Despite these examples, the executive's ability to act in relation to armed conflicts without a formal vote in Parliament continued. The government did not seek parliamentary approval for entry into Afghanistan in October 2001, with Prime Minister Chrétien simply announcing the deployment of Canadian Armed Forces.[62] Several days later, however, the House of Commons overwhelmingly passed a motion affirming its support for the deployment.[63] Likewise, further parliamentary approval was not sought by Prime Minister Harper in 2010 for an extension to deploy "military trainers" in Afghanistan.[64] The prime minister justified this on the basis that the deployment was a training mission, rather than the deployment of troops. Nor was a vote held in 2014 with regards to Canada's response to Russia's invasion of Ukraine, which included deploying fighter aircrafts to the region. In 2016, Prime Minister Trudeau announced changes to the Canadian mission in Iraq without a vote, although he pledged to consult Parliament.[65]

In Canada, any consultation of Parliament prior to entry into an armed conflict does not appear to rise to the level of a convention. Writing in 2017, Lagassé stated that the Canadian Parliament's role in decisions to deploy the military "remain[s] ambiguous,"[66] with the exercise of the defence prerogative being "unchecked by law or convention."[67] As Lagassé argues, political realities have meant that the executive in Canada has not faced the same pressures as the UK from opposition parties, parliamentary committees, and other stakeholders sufficient to form even a strong norm of parliamentary oversight.[68] Lagassé did, however, note that consultation with the House had been viewed as politically prudent[69] (quoting Hillmer and Lagassé's 2016 work which argues that Canada has a strong practice of holding parliamentary votes on decisions involving armed conflict).[70]

Likewise, Lagassé and Massie, writing in 2023, explored why Canadian governments frequently choose to involve Parliament in decisions to deploy the military despite there being no requirement to do so.[71] And there is evidence that the Canadian Parliament believes it is important that it is consulted before such a decision is made.[72] However, much of the political discussion in Canada seems to have framed parliamentary approval as a courtesy rather than a requirement. At best, it can be said that there is a supportive practice of parliamentary approval prior to entering armed conflicts that has yet to become a convention of the type recognized in the UK.

LEGISLATIVE PROPOSALS

There have been several attempts in Canada at legislative reform of the defence prerogative to provide parliamentary oversight. In 1994, the Reform Party introduced Bill C-295, which would have prevented the deployment of Canadian Armed Forces on peacekeeping operations without parliamentary approval.[73] The bill failed at second reading. In 1996 and 1998, motions were put forward (M-31[74] and M-380,[75] respectively) to require votes by Parliament on military deployments. These failed, despite gathering the support of most members of the opposition parties. The government, led by Prime Minister Chrétien during both periods, rejected the motions on the basis that such votes would unduly constrain the executive.[76] In 1999, the Bloc Québécois put forward a motion that the government allow Parliament to debate and vote on sending Canadian Armed Forces to the Yugoslavian conflict.[77]

There have also been a series of reports recommending legislative change. In 1994, the Special Joint Committee on Canada's Defence Policy recommended enhanced parliamentary oversight of the government's exercise of defence powers, as did the 1997 Commission of Inquiry into the Deployment of Canadian Forces to Somalia.[78] In 2000, the Standing Senate Committee on Foreign Affairs recommended that Parliament be required to vote on external military action.[79] None of these recommendations were adopted.

In 2004, members of the opposition stated that Parliament should vote on Canadian participation in armed conflicts.[80] The Conservative Party ran on an election platform in 2006 which included a promise to "make Parliament responsible for ... the commitment of Canadian forces to foreign operations."[81] To date this reform has not occurred.

Australia

CONVENTION

There has been no change to the traditional position in respect of executive exercise of the prerogative in Australia. In October 2001 no statement was made to Parliament when the Howard government announced Australia's commitment of sending its Defence Force to Afghanistan. The situation was slightly different in 2003 in relation to Iraq. Prime Minister John Howard made it clear that Parliament would be given the opportunity to debate the commitment of sending its Defence Force to Iraq.[82] On 20 March 2003, a motion that the Australian House of Representatives "endorses the government's decision to commit ADF elements to the international coalition of military forces" was resolved in the affirmative.[83] Ultimately, however, the tone of the debate made it clear that Members of Parliament understood that the decision had already been made and did not appear to think that the expression of their views against the commitment of the Australian Defence Force to Iraq would change that decision.[84] At the time there was not a strong precedent that Parliament be consulted,[85] a position that continues to date.

In September 2014, Australian the Defence Force was again deployed to the Middle East in response to a request for assistance by the United States. As in 2003, there was debate in the House of Representatives and in the Senate regarding the deployment. Once again, it was clear that Parliament was being informed rather than consulted.[86] In September 2015, Australia expanded its operation against ISIS into Syria. There was bipartisan support for both military engagements, though the then-shadow minister for foreign affairs and deputy leader of the opposition called upon Prime Minister Tony Abbott to address Parliament and "allow for appropriate parliamentary discussion."[87] There was discussion in the Senate, on 10 September 2015, during which then attorney general George Brandis responded to questions regarding the expanded operations,[88] and Greens Senator Di Natale criticized the government's refusal to allow a motion for parliamentary approval of the deployment.[89] However, there was no debate in the House of Representatives.

There continues to be a strong public interest in Australia in parliamentary oversight of decisions to enter armed conflicts.[90] This is driven by an understanding of the serious consequences that follow from entry into an armed conflict and the desire for robust debate and parliamentary – and thus representative – approval of such a decision. A number of parliamentary inquiries have been held into the issue, with the most recent by the Joint Standing Committee on Foreign Affairs, Defence and Trade.[91] Its report published in March 2023[92] did not recommend either a legislative role for Parliament in approving decisions to enter an armed conflict nor the development of a convention to that effect. However, the Joint Standing Committee stated that it was "firmly of the view that parliamentary engagement and oversight must be strengthened in relation to decisions by the Executive regarding international armed conflict and the subsequent ongoing conduct of such operations."[93] It made several recommendations, including that Parliament be recalled to advise after a decision had been made (Recommendation 3), that standing resolutions be introduced to both Houses of Parliament requiring that when "war or warlike operations" are occurring the prime minister make at least annual statements to both Houses of Parliament and facilitate debate (Recommendation 4), and that a Joint Statutory Defence Committee be set up to, amongst other things, exercise "general parliamentary oversight of war or warlike operations, including ongoing conflicts and involvement in significant non-conflict-related operations domestically and internationally" (Recommendation 6). Although these changes would be welcome, a legislative response is to be preferred for the reasons that we outline below.

LEGISLATIVE REFORM

There has been discussion in Australia for almost forty years regarding issues in relation to bypassing Parliament in the decision to go to war. This has spurred many attempts to introduce legislation requiring parliamentary approval of the exercise of the prerogative. Multiple bills have been introduced to allow oversight by Parliament of such decisions, all of which have failed to pass. In 1986, the Defence Amendment Bill 1985 was debated. A bill by the same name was introduced in 1988. The discussion was reignited by the Iraq War in 2003.[94] During the debates over entering Iraq, the Defence Amendment (Parliamentary Approval for Australian Involvement in Overseas Conflicts) Bill 2003 was proposed, which would have amended section 50C of the *Defence Act 1903* (Cth) requiring Parliament to approve the commitment of troops overseas. In February 2008, the Defence Amendment (Parliamentary Approval of Overseas Service) Bill 2008 was introduced, and a bill with the same name was introduced again in September 2008. In 2014, the Defence Legislation Amendment (Parliamentary Approval of Overseas Service) Bill 2014 was introduced.

The most recent legislative proposal would have amended the *Defence Act 1903* (Cth) to require parliamentary approval of overseas service by members of the Australian Defence Force (except in certain emergency situations). On 7 December 2020, Australian legislators introduced the Defence Amendment (Parliamentary Approval of Overseas Service) Bill 2020 (Cth).[95] In November 2021, the Senate Foreign Affairs, Defence and Trade Legislation Committee recommended that the Parliamentary Approval Bill not proceed.[96] The committee concluded that the "current checks and balances on executive power through the normal parliamentary processes" provide appropriate accountability to Parliament and the Australian people. This statement is questionable in light of the lessons learned in 2003 Iraq conflict and the growing prominence of human rights concerns to such decisions. The bill was not supported by the major parties and failed to pass the Senate on 29 March 2023.

The Way Forward

There are several difficulties with the status quo. First, as discussed above, the international obligations upon states involved in an armed conflict have changed but the prerogative power to enter armed conflict has not. The Australian Constitution, for example, was drafted four decades before Australia submitted to the UN Charter framework that currently governs its international obligations in respect of the use of force. This means that the use of force by Australia can raise issues than were not imagined at the time the Constitution was drafted. This has led to an incompatibility between public expectations of participation in decision-making – and public concerns about human rights – with the decision to enter into armed conflicts being made by the executive acting alone.

Second, there are a number of public policy arguments to be made in favour of parliamentary oversight of the decision to go to war, including: the gravity of the decision and inappropriateness of it being made a single figure (the prime minister) or a small group of persons (the prime minister and Cabinet); the lack of accountability of the executive to the community, a defect not shared by Parliament; and the lack of clarity and criteria for making the decision to go to war. This very point, that the power to commit a country to international obligations which may have far-reaching consequences is one that Parliament should oversee so that it can properly represent the views of the public, was recognized by the UK government in 2007.[97]

These factors mean that it has become increasingly recognized that the executive should not have an unfettered power to decide to deploy armed forces overseas. Its ability to do so based upon an ancient prerogative is increasingly ill-fitting for modern times. In particular, human rights, international law and other concerns have come to the fore in a way that demonstrate the need for parliamentary involvement. The strength of these considerations underpins the emergence of a convention requiring parliamentary involvement in the UK, and progress towards such a convention emerging in Canada.

The UK may be on the right path, but a convention is not by itself sufficient. The fact that the May government could so easily depart from the convention in its deployment of force in Syria in 2018 demonstrates the weakness of this approach. The response of that government also suggested a capacity to reinterpret the convention to provide significant latitude for it to be ignored.

A legislative response is needed. Parliament should assert its role in decision-making on whether to deploy troops overseas. This should not be left the discretion of the executive by way of a convention, and instead should be formalized in legislation. Legislation will also provide the opportunity to set out the scope of parliamentary involvement with greater precision that can take account of the need for emergency action. In such a case, it is reasonable that the executive be able to act unilaterally while also being required to retrospectively seek parliamentary endorsement.

A legislative framework will also permit careful attention to be given to how Parliament will, or will not, access intelligence and other information held by the government that may be important to assessing military action. In essence, a legislative approach has the benefits of providing a more secure framework for parliamentary involvement that reflects human rights and other concerns, while also ensuring the framework is supported by an appropriate process and tailored to the many circumstances in which force may be deployed overseas.

Conclusion

Going to war is one of the gravest decisions a government can make. Concerns about the exercise of this power are not new, but they have reached a new level in the years since the Iraq War in 2003. The major factors driving reform include a desire by the public for a say in these decisions by way of their representatives in Parliament. The Iraq War also elevated the prominence of human rights and international law considerations when decisions of this kind are made.

In a world in which states' international human rights obligations have increased in complexity, there is all the more reason for reform. As Justice Hans-Peter Kaul stated, "[W]ar making [and] armed conflicts … are the deadliest threat to human rights."[98] Parliamentary oversight of the decision to go to war will not mean that human rights violations and tragedies do not occur in wars approved by Parliament. However, it will mean that decisions with such momentous rights consequences will at least be made after public deliberation by elected representatives. This offers an opportunity for better decision-making and for greater public confidence in such decisions.

The strength of these arguments is reflected in the emergence of a convention requiring parliamentary approval in the UK. Such a convention may yet emerge in Canada, and Australia would also do well to follow this path. However, the convention is not by itself sufficient. Conventions have value, but they are political constructs subject to being ignored or reinterpreted when it suits the interests of the government of the day. The importance of this area, and the need to move beyond an ancient prerogative that vests decision-making solely in the executive, means that legislative reform is required. If Parliament is to play a greater role in deliberating on the use of force overseas, it needs to assert such a role through its lawmaking function.

NOTES

1 Janet L. Hiebert has had a profound influence on academic discussion of these issues. For example, see, Janet L. Hiebert, "The Human Rights Act: Ambiguity about Parliamentary Sovereignty," *German Law Journal* 14, no. 12 (2019): 2253–74; Janet L. Hiebert, "Parliamentary Bills of Rights. Do They Alter the Norms of Legislative Decision-Making?," in *Comparative Constitutional Theory*, ed. Gary Jacobson and Miguel Schor (London: Edward Elgar Publishing, 2018), 123–43; Janet L. Hiebert, "Parliamentary Bills of Rights: An Alternative Model?," *Modern Law Review* 69, no. 1 (2006): 7–28; and Janet L. Hiebert, "Parliament and the Human Rights Act: Can the JCHR Help Facilitate a Culture of Rights?," *International Journal of Constitutional Law* 4, no. 1 (2006): 1–38.

2 George Williams, "The Power to Go to War: Australia in Iraq," *Public Law Review* 15, no. 1 (2004): 5–9; Anne Twomey, "The Prerogative and the Courts in Australia," *Journal of Commonwealth Law* 3, no. 1 (2021): 55–101, https://www.journalofcommonwealthlaw.org/article/24261-the-prerogative-and-the-courts-in-australia; Alexander Braden, "Decision Instruments of the Federal Cabinet: Legally Exercising the 'War Prerogative,'" *Journal of Commonwealth Law* 3, no. 1 (2021): 157–217, https://www.journalofcommonwealthlaw.org/article/24255-decision-instruments-of-the-federal-cabinet-legally-exercising-the-war-prerogative; Tanzil Chowdhury, "Taming the UK's War Prerogative: The Rationale for Reform," *Legal Studies* 38 (2018): 500–13.

3 Albert V. Dicey, *Introduction to the Study of the Law of the Constitution* (London: Macmillan, 1959), 424–5.

4 Sir William Blackstone, *Commentaries on the Laws of England*, book 1 (London: Edward Christian, 1803), 245.

5 Noel Cox, *The Royal Prerogative and Constitutional Law: A Search for the Quintessence of Executive Power* (New York: Routledge, 2021), 4.

6 Peter Hogg, *Constitutional Law of Canada*, vol. 1 (Scarborough, ON: Thomson Carswell, 2007), 9.

7 Alexander Bolt and Philippe Lagassé, "Beyond Dicey: Executive Authorities in Canada," *Journal of Commonwealth Law* 3, no. 1 (2021): 24, https://www.journalofcommonwealthlaw.org/article/23701-beyond-dicey-executive-authorities-in-canada.

8 Ibid., 23.
9 Alexander Braden, "Decision Instruments of the Federal Cabinet: Legally Exercising the 'War Prerogative,'" *Journal of Commonwealth Law* 3, no. 1 (2021): 157, https://www.journalofcommonwealthlaw.org/article/24255-decision-instruments-of-the-federal-cabinet-legally-exercising-the-war-prerogative.
10 [2017] 1 All ER 593, 615.
11 *Re Residential Tenancies Tribunal (NSW); Ex parte Defence Housing Authority* (1997) 190 CLR 410 at 459 (per McHugh J) citing the principle in *Attorney-General v. De Keyser's Royal Hotel* [1920] AC 508.
12 "Proclamation," *Commonwealth Gazette*, vol. 251, 8 December 1941, https://trove.nla.gov.au/newspaper/article/232130502?searchTerm=war.
13 Joseph Chitty, *A Treatise on the Law of the Prerogative Powers of the Crown* (London: Butterworth, 1820), chap. 4.
14 David Kershaw, "Revolutionary Amnesia and the Nature of Prerogative Power," *International Journal of Constitutional Law* 20, no. 3 (2022): 1071–1102, https://academic.oup.com/icon/article/20/3/1071/6845527.
15 Ibid., 1097–8.
16 *Bill of Rights 1688* (Eng), Ch 2, 1 Will and Mar Sess 2, https://www.legislation.gov.uk/aep/WillandMarSess2/1/2/introduction.
17 UK House of Lords Select Committee on Constitution, Fifteenth Report, *Waging War: Parliament's Role and Responsibility*, (July 2006), chap. 1, https://publications.parliament.uk/pa/ld200506/ldselect/ldconst/236/23603.htm.
18 *Constitution Act 1867* (UK), s. 9.
19 Order Placing Members of the Canadian Forces on Active Service for the Purpose of Fulfilling Canada's Obligations under the North Atlantic Treaty, SI/89–103, https://laws-lois.justice.gc.ca/eng/regulations/si-89-103/FullText.html.
20 Anne Twomey, "The Prerogative and the Courts in Australia," *Journal of Commonwealth Law* 3, no. 1 (2021): 55, https://www.journalofcommonwealthlaw.org/article/24261-the-prerogative-and-the-courts-in-australia.
21 Williams, "The Power to Go to War."
22 Australian Constitution, section 51(vi), section 68, and section 61.
23 Geneva Conventions of 1949, Common Article 6/6/6/7.
24 UN General Assembly, Rome Statute of the International Criminal Court, 17 July 1998.
25 For information about Australia during the 2003 Iraq debates, Australian House of Representatives, *Hansard Parliamentary Debates*, 40th Parl., First Sess., 20 March 2003, 13127 (Hon. Nicola Roxon), https://parlinfo.aph.gov.au/parlInfo/search/display/display.w3p;db=CHAMBER;id=chamber%2Fhansardr%2F2003-03-20%2F0025;query=Id%3A%22chamber%2Fhansa

rdr%2F2003-03-20%2F0000%22; in the UK context, during the 2018 Syria debates, see Sir Vince Cable, House of Commons, *Hansard Parliamentary Debates*, 57th Parl., 2017-19 Sess., 17 April 2018, Column 221 (Hon. Sir Vince Cable), https://hansard.parliament.uk/Commons/2018-04-17/debates/EF164C0A-E0F5-40B6-A718-DD8693A2490C/MilitaryActionOverseasParliamentaryApproval?highlight=%22the%20white%20helmets%2C%20the%20syrian%20human%20rights%20organisation%2C%20has%20come%20up%20with%20the%20figure%20of%20213%20in%20the%20last%20five%20years%22#contribution-B29C381B-9A14-4E32-BB97-CA0018FA0150.

26 Inquiry into Ministerial Powers and the Prerogative, Lord Hurd of Westwell, Question 54, https://publications.parliament.uk/pa/cm200203/cmselect/cmpubadm/uc642-ii/uc64202.htm.

27 UN General Assembly, International Covenant on Civil and Political Rights, 16 December 1966, United Nations, Treaty Series, vol. 999.

28 *An Act to amend the Export and Import Permits Act and the Criminal Code (amendments permitting the accession to the Arms Trade Treaty and other amendments*, S.C. 2018, c. 26, section 7.4. See also section 7.3(1).

29 Inspector-General of the Australian Defence Force, *IGADF Afghanistan Inquiry Report*, 10 November 2020, https://web.archive.org/web/20201120203636/https://afghanistaninquiry.defence.gov.au/sites/default/files/2020-11/IGADF-Afghanistan-Inquiry-Public-Release-Version.pdf.

30 *R. (on the application of Gentle) v. The Prime Minister* [2008] UKHL 20; [2008] 1 AC 1356 ("Gentle").

31 *R. (on the application of Gentle) v. The Prime Minister* [2008] UKHL 20; [2008] 1 AC 1356, 16.

32 [1985] 1 SCR 441.

33 (2003) 231 FTR 3 (TD).

34 *Blanco v. Canada* (2003) 231 FTR 3 (TD), 17, per Heneghan J.

35 Defence Amendment (Parliamentary Approval of Overseas Service) Bill 2020, Explanatory Memorandum, 6, https://parlinfo.aph.gov.au/parlInfo/download/legislation/ems/s1281_ems_1c042b23-54d8-4de2-b398-0485f41f8a74/upload_pdf/20S20em.pdf;fileType=application%2Fpdf.

36 United Kingdom Cabinet Office, *The Cabinet Manual*, October 2011, section 5.36, at 44. https://assets.publishing.service.gov.uk/media/5a79d5d7e5274a18ba50f2b6/cabinet-manual.pdf.

37 Claire Mills, House of Commons Briefing Paper CBP 7166, "Parliamentary Approval for Military Action," 8 May 2018, https://researchbriefings.files.parliament.uk/documents/CBP-7166/CBP-7166.pdf.

38 Ibid.

39 United Kingdom House of Commons, Hansard Parliamentary Debates, 53rd Parl., 2002-03 Sess., 26 February 2003, Column 265, https://hansard

.parliament.uk/Commons/2003-02-26/debates/63bdd199-49c8-406d-a87a-e8b192a1066f/Iraq.

40 United Kingdom House of Commons, Hansard Parliamentary Debates, 53rd Parl., 2002-03 Sess., 18 March 2003, Column 902, https://hansard.parliament.uk/Commons/2003-03-18/debates/987bf3ff-3fb4-4014-9ba3-4d99782aa2bf/Iraq.

41 United Kingdom House of Commons, Public Administration and Constitutional Affairs Committee, "The Role of Parliament in the UK Constitution: Authorising the Use of Military Force," Twentieth Report of Session 2017–19, HC 1891, 6 August 2019, 15–16, https://publications.parliament.uk/pa/cm201719/cmselect/cmpubadm/1891/189102.htm.

42 United Kingdom House of Commons, Hansard Parliamentary Debates, 55th Parl., 2012-13 Sess., 29 August 2013, https://hansard.parliament.uk/commons/2013-08-29/debates/1308298000001/SyriaAndTheUseOfChemicalWeapons.

43 United Kingdom House of Commons, Hansard Parliamentary Debates, 55th Parl., 2012-13 Sess., 29 August 2013, https://hansard.parliament.uk/commons/2013-08-29/debates/1308298000001/SyriaAndTheUseOfChemicalWeapons.

44 United Kingdom House of Commons, Hansard Parliamentary Debates, 55th[h] Parl., 2012-13 Sess., 29 August 2013, https://hansard.parliament.uk/commons/2013-08-29/debates/1308298000001/SyriaAndTheUseOfChemicalWeapons.

45 See, for example, Prime Minister Cameron's statement in the House of Commons Debate on 26 September 2014, which acknowledges the role of the convention that the House of Commons be properly consulted and a motion be put to a vote (with reservation of the power to act immediately in certain emergency circumstances): United Kingdom House of Commons, Hansard Parliamentary Debates, 55th Parl., 2014-15 Sess., 26 September 2014, Column 1265, https://publications.parliament.uk/pa/cm201415/cmhansrd/cm140926/debtext/140926-0001.htm.

46 United Kingdom House of Commons, Hansard Parliamentary Debates, 57th Parl., 2017-19 Sess., 17 April, 2018, Columns 205–8, https://hansard.parliament.uk/Commons/2018-04-17/debates/bcddb216-4a57-413a-9f5a-e4440a8023c8/CommonsChamber.

47 Michael Fallon, Secretary of State for Defence, "Armed Forces Update," United Kingdom House of Commons, Hansard Parliamentary Debates, 56th Parl., 2015-16 Sess., 18 April 2016, Vol. 608, Column 11WS, https://hansard.parliament.uk/Commons/2016-04-18/debates/1604181000010/ArmedForcesUpdate.

48 Public Administration and Constitutional Affairs Committee, "Inquiry into The Role of Parliament in the UK Constitution: Authorising the Use of

Military Force," March 2019, 63, https://publications.parliament.uk/pa/cm201719/cmselect/cmpubadm/1891/1891.pdf.

49 Military Action Against Iraq (Parliamentary Approval) Bill 1999 (UK), https://www.publications.parliament.uk/pa/cm199899/cmbills/035/1999035.htm.

50 Waging War (Parliament's Role and Responsibility) Bill 2006–7 (UK), https://publications.parliament.uk/pa/pabills/200607/waging_war_parliaments_role.htm.

51 Armed Forces Deployment (Royal Prerogative) Bill 2016 (UK), https://bills.parliament.uk/bills/1783. The intervening bills are the Armed Forces (Parliamentary Approval for Participation in Armed Conflict) Bill 2004–5, https://publications.parliament.uk/pa/cm200405/cmbills/031/05031.i-i.html; the Armed Forces (Parliamentary Approval for Participation in Armed Conflict) Bill 2005–6, https://www.publications.parliament.uk/pa/cm200506/cmbills/016/06016.i-i.html; the Constitutional Reform (Prerogative Powers and Civil Service) Bill 2006, https://www.publications.parliament.uk/pa/cm200506/cmbills/222/2006222.pdf; the Armed Forces Deployment (Royal Prerogative) Bill 2014, https://www.publications.parliament.uk/pa/bills/lbill/2014-2015/0017/15017.pdf; and the Armed Forces Deployment (Royal Prerogative) Bill 2015, https://www.publications.parliament.uk/pa/bills/lbill/2015-2016/0034/16034.pdf.

52 Public Administration and Constitutional Affairs Committee, "The Role of Parliament in the UK Constitution: Authorising the Use of Military Force," Annexure 1, https://publications.parliament.uk/pa/cm201719/cmselect/cmpubadm/1891/189110.htm.

53 United Kingdom House of Commons, Hansard Parliamentary Debates, 54th Parl., 2006-07 Sess., 15 May 2007, Column 481–583, https://hansard.parliament.uk/commons/2007-05-15/debates/07051555000001/ArmedConflict(ParliamentaryApproval) .

54 Ministry of Justice, "The Governance of Britain," July 2007, Policy Paper, CM7170, https://assets.publishing.service.gov.uk/government/uploads/system/uploads/attachment_data/file/228834/7170.pdf; Ministry of Justice, "The Governance of Britain: War powers and treaties: Limiting Executive Powers," 25 October 2007, Consultation Paper, CM7239, https://assets.publishing.service.gov.uk/government/uploads/system/uploads/attachment_data/file/243164/7239.pdf; Ministry of Justice, "The Governance of Britain – Constitutional Renewal," March 2008, White Paper, CM 7342-I, https://assets.publishing.service.gov.uk/government/uploads/system/uploads/attachment_data/file/250803/7342_i.pdf; Ministry of Justice, "The Governance of Britain: Review of the Executive Royal Prerogative Powers: Final Report," October 2009, http://data.parliament.uk/DepositedPapers/Files/DEP2009-2493/DEP2009-2493.pdf.

55 Ministry of Justice, "The Governance of Britain," July 2007, Policy Paper, CM7170, 26, https://assets.publishing.service.gov.uk/government/uploads/system/uploads/attachment_data/file/228834/7170.pdf.

56 Political and Constitutional Reform Committee, "Constitutional Implications of the Cabinet Manual," Sixth Report of the Session 2010–12, HC 734, 61, https://publications.parliament.uk/pa/cm201011/cmselect/cmpolcon/734/734.pdf.

57 United Kingdom Cabinet Office, *The Cabinet Manual*, October 2011, at section 5.38, at 44, https://assets.publishing.service.gov.uk/media/5a79d5d7e5274a18ba50f2b6/cabinet-manual.pdf.

58 House of Lords Constitution Committee, "Constitutional Arrangements for the Use of Armed Force," Second Report of Session 2013–14, HL 46, 4, https://publications.parliament.uk/pa/ld201314/ldselect/ldconst/46/46.pdf.

59 Public Administration and Constitutional Affairs Committee, "The Role of Parliament in the UK Constitution: Authorising the Use of Military Force," Twentieth Report of Session 2017–19, 63, https://publications.parliament.uk/pa/cm201719/cmselect/cmpubadm/1891/189106.htm#_idTextAnchor019.

60 Canadian House of Commons, Hansard Parliamentary Debates, 39th Parl., First Sess., 17 May 2006, 1610, https://www.ourcommons.ca/DocumentViewer/en/39-1/house/sitting-25/hansard.

61 Canadian House of Commons, Hansard Parliamentary Debates, 39th Parl., Second Sess., 13 March 2008, https://www.ourcommons.ca/DocumentViewer/en/39-2/house/sitting-66/hansard. The text of the 13 March 2008 motion may be found in Canadian House of Commons, Report of Standing Committee on Foreign Affairs and International Development, Kevin Sorenson MP, "Canada in Afghanistan," July 2008, Appendix I, 115–17.

62 Prime Minister Jean Chrétien, "An Address to the Nation Concerning the International Campaign against Terrorism," 7 October 2001, https://epe.lac-bac.gc.ca/100/205/301/prime_minister-ef/jean_chretien/2003-12-08/stagingpm_3a8080/default.asp@language=e&page=newsroom&sub=speeches&doc=nationterrorism.20011007_e.htm.

63 Canadian House of Commons, Hansard Parliamentary Debates, 37th Parl., First Sess., 15 October 2001, 708–9, https://www.ourcommons.ca/DocumentViewer/en/37-1/house/sitting-94/journals.

64 BBC News, "Canada PM Says No Vote Needed to Extend Afghan Mission," *BBC News*, 12 November 2010, https://www.bbc.com/news/world-us-canada-11748277.

65 Philippe Lagassé, "Parliament and the War Prerogative in the United Kingdom and Canada: Explaining Variations in Institutional Change and Legislative Control," *Parliamentary Affairs* 70 (2017): 281, quoting the Prime Minister's Office (PMO), "Talking Points for Prime Minister Trudeau: New

Approach to Address the Ongoing Crises in Iraq and Syria," 8 February 2016.

66 Ibid., 296.

67 Ibid., 298.

68 Ibid., 280–300.

69 Ibid., 298.

70 Norman Hillmer and Phillippe Lagassé, "Parliament Will Decide: An Interplay of Politics and Principle," *International Journal* 71, no. 2 (2016): 336.

71 Philippe Lagassé and Justin Massie, "ParliamentarizingWar: Explaining Legislative Votes on Canadian Military Deployments" *International Relations* (2023), https://journals.sagepub.com/doi/full/10.1177/00471178231151904.

72 "The Liberal government did not provide elected parliamentarians the opportunity to debate and vote on this overseas mission in the House of Commons as is customary. Operation PRESENCE was undertaken with no parliamentary debate or public discussion which calls into question the legitimacy of the manner in which our Canadian Armed Forces were committed to a complex conflict zone with improper parliamentary oversight," although note that this (1) was contained in one of the dissenting opinions, and (2) related to a commitment of forces to a peacekeeping mission rather than an armed conflict. House of Commons, Standing Committee on National Defence, "Canada's Role in International Peace Operations and Conflict Resolution," May 2019, 16th Report, 42nd Parl., 1st Sess., https://www.ourcommons.ca/DocumentViewer/en/42-1/NDDN/report-16/page-ToC.

73 Bill C-295, "An Act to provide for the control of Canadian peacekeeping activities by Parliament…," https://parl.ca/Content/Bills/351/Private/c-295/c-295_1/351231bE.html.

74 Canadian House of Commons, Hansard Parliamentary Debates, 35th Parl., Sec. Sess., 23 October 1996, 1805, https://www.ourcommons.ca/DocumentViewer/en/35-2/house/sitting-89/hansard.

75 Canadian House of Commons, Hansard Parliamentary Debates, 36th Parl., First Sess., 29 October 1998, 1750, https://www.ourcommons.ca/DocumentViewer/en/36-1/house/sitting-145/hansard.

76 Canadian House of Commons, Hansard Parliamentary Debates, 36th Parl., First Sess., 10 June 1998, 1825–30, https://www.ourcommons.ca/DocumentViewer/en/36-1/house/sitting-119/hansard, quoted in Michael Dewing and Corinne McDonald, *International Deployment of Canadian Forces: Parliament's Role* (Ottawa: Library of Parliament, 2006).

77 Canadian House of Commons, Hansard Parliamentary Debates, 19 April 1999, 1205, quoted in Dewing and McDonald, *International Deployment of Canadian Forces: Parliament's Role.*

78 Dewing and McDonald, *International Deployment of Canadian Forces*, 6.

79 Standing Senate Committee on Foreign Affairs, "The New NATO and the Evolution of Peacekeeping: Implications for Canada," April 2000, quoted in Dewing and McDonald, *International Deployment of Canadian Forces*, 74.

80 Conservative Party of Canada, Press Release, "Harper, Duceppe and Layton Propose Changes to the Standing Orders of the House," 9 September 2004, quoted in Dewing and McDonald, *International Deployment of Canadian Forces: Parliament's Role*.

81 Conservative Party of Canada, "Stand Up for Canada – Federal Election Platform" (2006), 45, https://www.poltext.org/sites/poltext.org/files/plateformesV2/Canada/CAN_PL_2006_PC_en.pdf.

82 Prime Minister John Howard, Press Conference on Iraq, 17 March 2003, Parliament House, Canberra, https://parlinfo.aph.gov.au/parlInfo/search/display/display.w3p;query=Id:%22media/pressrel/U8T86%22.

83 Australian House of Representatives, Hansard Parliamentary Debates, 40th Parl., First Sess., 20 March 2003, 13159, https://parlinfo.aph.gov.au/parlInfo/search/display/display.w3p;db=CHAMBER;id=chamber%2Fhansardr%2F2003-03-20%2F0068;query=Id%3A%22chamber%2Fhansardr%2F2003-03-20%2F0000%22.

84 See, for example, Anna Burke MP, Australian House of Representatives, Hansard Parliamentary Debates, 40th Parl., First Sess., 20 March 2003, 13090, https://parlinfo.aph.gov.au/parlInfo/search/display/display.w3p;db=CHAMBER;id=chamber%2Fhansardr%2F2003-03-20%2F0005;query=Id%3A%22chamber%2Fhansardr%2F2003-03-20%2F0000%22; Anthony Albanese MP, Australian House of Representatives, Hansard Parliamentary Debates, 40th Parl., First Sess., 20 March 2003, 13124, https://parlinfo.aph.gov.au/parlInfo/search/display/display.w3p;db=CHAMBER;id=chamber%2Fhansardr%2F2003-03-20%2F0023;query=Id%3A%22chamber%2Fhansardr%2F2003-03-20%2F0000%22.

85 Greg Jennet interview with George Williams, "The World Today: International law Implications of Iraq Attack," *Australian Broadcasting Corporation*, 29 January 2003, https://www.abc.net.au/worldtoday/stories/s772210.htm.

86 Australian Senate, Hansard Parliamentary Debates, 44th Parl., First Sess., 1 September 2014, https://www.aph.gov.au/Parliamentary_Business/Hansard/Hansard_Display?bid=chamber/hansards/49cdeae9-b762-449e-9e05-7239b8940f5f/&sid=0038. After deployment, there was criticism in the Senate for the lack of parliamentary approval: Australian Senate, Hansard Parliamentary Debates, 44th Parl., First Sess., 30 September 2014, https://www.aph.gov.au/Parliamentary_Business/Hansard/Hansard_Display?bid=chamber/hansards/f7c86505-3e24-4599-8943-0a55f6f94ca3/&sid=0004.

87 Tanya Plibersek, MP, "Security and Military Engagement in Uncertain Times," Australian Strategic Policy Institute, 10 September 2015, https://

www.aspi.org.au/video/security-and-military-engagement-uncertain-times-tanya-plibersek-aspi.

88 George Brandis, "Answer to Question without Notice: Syria," Australian Senate, Hansard Parliamentary *Debates*, 44th Parl., First Sess., 10 September 2015, 6553, https://parlinfo.aph.gov.au/parlInfo/search/display/display.w3p;query=Id:%22chamber/hansards/6fa0f283-325b-4c20-bd6d-2d626f5c8ef1/0105%22.

89 Senator Di Natale, Australian Senate, Hansard Parliamentary Debates, 44th Parl., First Sess., 10 September 2015, 6586, https://parlinfo.aph.gov.au/parlInfo/search/display/display.w3p;query=Id:%22chamber/hansards/6fa0f283-325b-4c20-bd6d-2d626f5c8ef1/0138%22.

90 See, for example, Malcolm Fraser and Paul Barratt, "Going to War is a Matter for Parliament," *The Australian*, 8 September 2014; Kim Landers interview with Peter Leahy, "World Today: Australia's Decisions to Go to War Should Be Made in Parliament: Former Army Chief," *Australian Broadcasting Corporation*, 7 July 2016, https://www.abc.net.au/worldtoday/content/2016/s4496208.htm.

91 Parliament of Australia, "Committee to Review International Armed Conflict Decision Making," media release, 30 September 2022, https://www.aph.gov.au/About_Parliament/House_of_Representatives/About_the_House_News/Media_Releases/Committee_to_review_international_armed_conflict_decision_making.

92 Joint Standing Committee on Foreign Affairs, Defence and Trade, Inquiry into armed conflict decision making report, March 2023, https://www.aph.gov.au/Parliamentary_Business/Committees/Joint/Foreign_Affairs_Defence_and_Trade/Armedconflict/Report.

93 Joint Standing Committee on Foreign Affairs, Defence and Trade, Inquiry into armed conflict decision making report, March 2023, 3.51, https://www.aph.gov.au/Parliamentary_Business/Committees/Joint/Foreign_Affairs_Defence_and_Trade/Armedconflict/Report.

94 Williams, "The Power to Go to War."; Landers, "Australia's Decisions to Go to War"; Cameron Leckie, "Parliament Should Decide if Australia Goes to War," *The Canberra Times*, 5 January 2022, https://www.canberratimes.com.au/story/7569952/parliament-should-decide-if-australia-goes-to-war/.

95 Defence Amendment (Parliamentary Approval of Overseas Service) Bill 2020 (Cth), https://www.aph.gov.au/Parliamentary_Business/Bills_Legislation/Bills_Search_Results/Result?bId=s1281.

96 Senate, Foreign Affairs, Defence and Trade Legislation Committee, *Defence Amendment (Parliamentary Approval of Overseas Service) Bill 2020*, November 2021, 10, https://parlinfo.aph.gov.au/parlInfo/download/committees/reportsen/024793/toc_pdf/DefenceAmendment(ParliamentaryApprovalofOverseasService)Bill2020.pdf;fileType=application%2Fpdf.

97 Ministry of Justice, "The Governance of Britain: War Powers and Treaties: Limiting Executive Powers," 25 October 2007, Consultation Paper, CM7239, https://assets.publishing.service.gov.uk/government/uploads/system/uploads/attachment_data/file/243164/7239.pdf.

98 Justice Hans-Peter Kaul, "Human Rights and the International Criminal Court," *The Protection of Human Rights through the International Criminal Court as a Contribution to Constitutionalization and Nation-Building*, 21 January 2011, https://www.icc-cpi.int/NR/rdonlyres/2C496E38-8E14-4ECD-9CC9-5E0D2A0B3FA2/282947/FINAL_Speech_Panel1_HumanRightsandtheInternational.pdf.

5 A Culture of Rights or Governing like Judges? Assessing the Trudeau Government's Use of Charter Statements

BRENDAN DELL AND MARK S. HARDING

Beginning in 2016, with the legislative response to the Supreme Court of Canada's decision in *Carter v. Canada*,[1] Minister of Justice and Attorney General Jody Wilson-Raybould began issuing publicly available "Charter Statements" when new bills were introduced into Parliament. This process was formalized and made mandatory through Bill C-51 in 2019. The government's aim for these statements is to ensure that Charter rights are considered throughout the policymaking process with the goal to increase public awareness and understanding of the Charter of Rights and Freedoms.[2] While ensuring that proposed legislation is consistent with the Charter has always been a mandatory practice, Charter Statements make explicit what was once implicit: that the minister has considered the Charter implications for a proposed law and is communicating to the House (or Senate) and to the public the minister's confidence in its constitutionality.

The origins of Charter Statements are one part of the Justin Trudeau-led Liberal Party's efforts to brand itself closely with the Charter and minority rights.[3] In addition to emphasizing the Charter in its political messaging, once in government, the Liberals initiated reforms to further incorporate the Charter into the political process. Prime Minister Trudeau's mandate letter to the minister of justice after the 2015 federal election stated that government initiatives should "respect the Constitution of Canada, court decisions, and [should keep] with our proudest legal traditions."[4] On policymaking and the Charter, the mandate letter stressed: "You are expected to ensure that the rights of Canadians are protected, that our work demonstrates the greatest possible commitment to respecting the Charter of Rights and Freedoms, and that our government seeks to fulfill our policy goals with the least interference with the rights and privacy of Canadians as possible."[5] Under Minister Wilson-Raybould, the government pursued a number Charter-related initiatives, including re-establishing the Court Challenges Program, repealing laws declared unconstitutional by the Supreme Court of Canada, and tabling a Charter Statement for every proposed government bill to speak to its compliance with the Charter.

At the time of writing, ministers of justice have issued statements on over one hundred pieces of proposed legislation. This political initiative of issuing Charter Statements raises theoretical and empirical questions about rights and Canadian political institutions: Do these statements contain substantive Charter analysis or are they political window dressing? How do the statements engage with the Supreme Court of Canada's jurisprudence? Do any use "independent interpretation"[6] of the Charter or do they parrot the judicial construction of rights? The objective of this chapter is to examine the above questions. We begin by exploring the political context behind Charter Statements, and then situate the government's use of these statements within the literature on legislating with the Charter in Canada. Based on an original dataset of all the statements issued under the Trudeau government, this chapter focuses on the legalization of cannabis (Bills C-45 and C-46) and legislative amendments tackling gender-based violence (Bills C-51 and C-28), each of which were prominent in the Liberal Party's campaign platforms from the 2015, 2019, and 2021 federal election campaigns. We find that the government's Charter Statements have made use of Charter analysis in summarizing proposed legislation. In a limited sense, the government has achieved its objective of encouraging a culture of rights. However, we find when the Charter Statements do reference the Supreme Court's jurisprudence, they either do not engage the rights-based analysis with much substance or simply mimic what the Court said previously. In short, Charter Statements have yet to provide much of a complementary parliamentary perspective to rights, but have mainly reinforced the dominant assumptions about the judicial role in defining Charter rights.

Rights Construction: Political, Judicial, or Both?

Early in Wilson-Raybould's tenure as minister of justice, she appointed Grégoire Webber to serve as her legal affairs adviser. Webber, a prominent constitutional theorist, had written numerous works on inter-institutional dialogue and the legislative role in protecting rights.[7] A few months before joining the government, Webber praised the Trudeau government's commitment to enhancing Parliament's role in taking rights seriously.[8] This praise is consistent with Webber's scholarship of theorizing about the prospects (and limits) of the idea of a political rather than a legal constitution.[9] Indeed, Charter Statements can be viewed as facilitating some "political constitutionalism" by enhancing the participation of all three branches of government over rights-issues. The statements are initiated by the *executive* through the minister of justice as part of the process of assuring the *legislature* that the executive's proposed actions are constitutionally sound. The executive's statement often relies on the *judiciary's* past decisions to bolters its case. What motivates this chapter, in part, is to probe whether Charter Statements can provide a venue where more *political* rather than *judicial* constructions of rights can occur.

In his book, *The New Commonwealth Model of Constitutionalism,* Stephen Gardbaum distinguishes between three venues where rights can be considered.[10] First, "political rights review" happens within the legislative process. After a law is enacted, it can be subject to "judicial rights review" by the courts. Finally, if the law is invalidated by a judicial decision, there is an opportunity for the non-judicial branches to engage in "post-judicial rights review" and enact a new law addressing the rights-based defects identified by the court. Gardbaum argues that by mixing political and legal interpretations of rights and political and legal modes of accountability, the new Commonwealth model provides an effective answer to how rights should be protected in a democracy.[11]

Gardbaum's new commonwealth model identifies many of the same dynamics identified earlier by Janet Hiebert. In her influential book *Charter Conflicts: What Is Parliament's Role?*, Hiebert outlines this debate between two camps: one side that views favouring political judgment on rights ("Charter skeptics"), and one that stresses the primacy of judicial framing of rights as most appropriate ("fundamental-rights scholars").[12] As Hiebert notes, there is also a middle-ground approach, which holds that neither the judiciary nor the legislature should be primarily responsible for constructing and interpreting rights.[13] This approach is called the "coordinate" or "relational" approach to rights interpretation. Hiebert argues persuasively for a shared role between the institutions.[14] Hiebert's relational approach assumes that both the legislature and the judiciary have "valid insights into how legislative objectives should reflect and respect the Charter's normative values."[15] Together, the insight from both institutions on the interpretation of the Constitution and rights is valuable.[16]

Finally, discussions concerning blending judicial and legislative inputs to rights is often associated with scholarly debate over the "dialogue" metaphor. The concept of dialogue championed by Peter Hogg and Allison Bushell has been influential in Canada and abroad.[17] The term has attracted substantial criticism along the way, specifically concerning the concepts usefulness and difficulty to conceptualize and operationalize.[18] Our concern and interest is whether Charter Statements, like the promise of dialogue, has also become a mechanism that promises the possibility of coordinate construction but in practice reinforces judicial interpretative finality over the meaning of rights.

Governing with Rights in Canada

Canada has been a pioneer of parliamentary-based approaches to rights-protection. In 1960, John Diefenbaker's government adopted the Canadian Bill of Rights to place codified rights at the forefront of assessing the legitimacy of legislation. The "Diefenbaker Bill of Rights" is associated as much with its flaws as its successes.[19] Instead of relying on judicial review, the Bill of Rights placed the responsibility of ensuring rights consistent legislation in the hands of Parliament. Courts still reviewed laws, but the Supreme Court of Canada only once declared a law inoperative under the Bill of Rights; thus, rights consistency was generally assumed to be left to Parliament.[20] The Bill of Rights used two mechanisms we now associate with political rights protection: (1) a statutory reporting requirement for the minister of justice to notify Parliament when a bill being introduced in Parliament was inconsistent with rights set out in the Bill of Rights, and (2) a new practice for bureaucratic assessments of proposed legislation's consistency with rights.[21] These new changes under the Bill of Rights were expected to create a new culture of rights within the federal government.[22]

The adoption of the Canadian Charter of Rights and Freedoms in 1982 began a transition from parliamentary to a more judicially oriented approach to rights. However, there is still a parliamentary role regarding rights judgments set out in both the "reasonable limits" clause and the "notwithstanding" clause in section 33 of the Charter.[23] This model envisaged a role for both the representative institutions and the judiciary to have responsibility regarding making judgments about rights.[24] This environment in which laws are drafted in line with the Charter is understood as "political" or "legislative" rights review.[25] As highlighted in further detail in this volume (see Dell and Puddister), this process occurs in two venues: the bureaucratic venue (within the executive) and the parliamentary venue (within Parliament).[26]

Bureaucratic rights review is particularly developed in Canada due to the strength of the Prime Minister's Office and related central agencies of government.[27] Rights review in the bureaucratic venue occurs in these two separate streams that originated from the Bill of Rights:

(1) an advisory stream for policy development, where the Department of Justice, in partnership with other departments, thoroughly assesses the risk of rights infringement, and (2) the statutory reporting obligation, situated in the *Department of Justice Act*, for legislation inconsistent with provisions in the Charter.[28] By contrast, within the parliamentary venue, opposition parliamentarians and committees question and scrutinize proposed laws on Charter grounds. This is especially weak and ineffective in Canada due to aspects of our Westminster system such as strong majority governments, party discipline, and executive dominance of the legislative process.[29]

The introduction of Charter Statements is a new, and potentially significant, development within legislative rights review in Canada. These statements fit under the second "stream" of bureaucratic rights review where the minister of justice is obligated to report any inconsistencies of proposed legislation with any provisions of the Charter. The Charter Statements issued by the minister of justice is another mechanism (alongside the reporting duty under section 4.1(1) of the *Department of Justice Act*, discussed below) to ensure that rights are considered by the executive in the policymaking process.

Judicial Influence: Consistency with the Charter

James Kelly argues that judicial power and influence exists in two dimensions: (1) where judicial review is established and courts can require governments to uphold the Constitution, and (2) where judicial values and processes are internalized within the legislative institutions.[30] This second dimension of judicial power is particularly relevant to how Canadian governments legislate. Elsewhere, Hiebert notes that the Charter's potential to encourage stronger political scrutiny of proposed legislation is due to the threat that judicial review poses, because legislation may be struck down if found to conflict with provisions of the Charter.[31] This judicial influence on the policymaking process can go so far as governments appearing to "govern like judges" as if "judges were in the corridors of power at the time legislation is being developed."[32] However, Hiebert argues that neither the risk of invalidation nor the introduction of section 4.1(1) of the *Department of Justice Act* has led to Canadian governments "governing like judges."[33] Yet there is considerable evidence of judicial influence in the Canadian system. In fact, the fear that a judicial ruling against government legislation could have substantial costs, alongside high expectations to comply with judicial rulings, has had a greater influence on legislation in Canada than in the United Kingdom and New Zealand.[34]

Although not explicitly required by the Charter or the *Department of Justice Act*, consistency with case law is considered an essential element of claiming compatibility with the Charter.[35] Pre-introduction review of legislation focuses heavily on whether these proposed legislative initiatives will satisfy the courts' interpretations of "proportionality," leading to a significant judicial influence in the bureaucratic stage of policymaking.[36] Given what we know about how governments legislate with rights, and the judicial influence of that process, the introduction of Charter Statements provides us with another avenue to analyse this process in practice. Below, we focus on three significant case studies using Charter Statements that (a) engage with or respond to Supreme Court of Canada jurisprudence to some degree and (b) concern proposed legislation that are salient to the Trudeau government's legislative agenda. These case studies concern the legalization of cannabis and two laws concerning gender-based violence (sexual assault and extreme intoxication), issues featured in the Liberal Party's recent campaign platforms.[37] They are also broadly emblematic of the style and substance of the government's Charter Statements to date. As we discuss below, some of these statements are cursory and do not engage Charter rights in a substantive way. These are to be contrasted with those instances where the government should be lauded for its thoughtful construction of robust Charter Statements.[38] We employ the following criteria in assessing substantive Charter Statements: First, the statement should be detailed about which provisions of the bill will engage specific Charter rights. Second, the minister's statement should address how the bill seeks to enhance (rather than violate) Charter rights. Third, the statement should state why the minister believes specific provisions of the proposed law are ultimately constitutional. Finally, citing a Supreme Court case on its own, does not in our view, amount to substantive engagement with Charter rights. It is just one way the minister can justify a proposed law.

Charter Statements: By the Numbers

All Charter Statements begin with the same "Explanatory Note" that outlines the purpose, which is to "help inform public and Parliamentary debate on a government bill," by "sharing some of the key considerations that informed the review of a bill for consistency with the Charter." The explanatory note describes how the statements achieve this by identifying "Charter rights and freedoms that may be potentially engaged by a bill and [by providing] a brief explanation of the nature of any engagement, in light of the measures being proposed." Further, this note explains that these statements identify "potential justifications for any limits a bill may impose" on rights and freedoms. Finally, the explanatory note concludes with a qualifier that these statements are not intended to be a comprehensive overview of all Charter considerations, and are not legal opinions on the constitutionality of proposed bills. Following the explanatory note, Charter Statements sometimes – but do not always – provide brief context behind the details or objectives of the proposed bills before outlining any Charter considerations the minister of justice has for the proposed bills.

The first Charter Statement by Minister Wilson-Raybould was issued early in Trudeau's first ministry when the government introduced its legislative response to the Supreme Court of Canada's decision on assisted dying in *Carter*.[39] Since then, Ministers Wilson-Raybould (until January 2019) and David Lametti (since January 2019) have issued 105 Charter Statements. Over a third of these (n = 36 or 34.2 per cent) pertained to laws regarding the criminal justice system (including criminal offences) and public safety, compared with 28.5 per cent (n = 30) on budgetary matters or spending. Other areas of law included COVID-19 (n = 11), Indigenous issues (n = 6), and international relations (n = 5).[40]

Of the 105 statements issued under the Trudeau government, 66 (or 62.9 per cent) engaged substantively with Charter rights, whereas the other 39 statements (or 37.1 per cent) did not.[41] For the latter bills, the Charter Statements featured a sentence stating that in reviewing the bill, the minister of justice did not identify any potential effects on the Charter. Of the 66 statements that did substantively engage with Charter rights, 13 featured a response or direct engagement with a specific Supreme Court of Canada decision. We now turn to our three case studies.

Legalization of Cannabis (Bill C-45 and C-46)

Cannabis legalization was a key aspect of the Liberal Party's campaign platform for the 2015 federal election. The government argued that cannabis prohibition had been unsuccessful: It had not kept the drug out of the hands of young people; it was a financial burden on the criminal justice system; and, as a result, there were too many Canadians with a criminal record for minor non-violent drug offences. The platform pledged to legalize, regulate, and restrict access to cannabis in Canada.[42] After the election, the government introduced two bills to Parliament in April of 2017: Bill C-45 (*Cannabis Act*) and Bill C-46.

The *Cannabis Act* legalized recreational cannabis use, making Canada the second country in the world to do so. The act focused on amendments to criminal offences regarding cannabis, restrictions on promotion, packaging, and labelling, among other amendments. As identified by the minister of justice in the Charter Statement for Bill C-45, areas of the bill engaged numerous sections of the Charter (sections 2(b), 7, 8, 11(d), and 15).[43]

Bill C-45 created new criminal offences that replaced existing offences for cannabis possession, distribution, and production in the *Controlled Drugs and Substances Act*. The Charter Statement for Bill C-45 identified sections 7 and 15 Charter rights as potentially engaged by these offences. After providing a general description of section 7 of the Charter, the minister stated that the offences in the bill were consistent with section 7 of the Charter.[44] In doing so, the minister cited decisions by the Supreme Court of Canada in *R. v. Malmo-Levine*[45] and *R. v. Clay*,[46] which upheld the complete prohibition of recreational cannabis. However, according to the minister:

> As compared to the existing law, the proposed narrowed offences would promote liberty and autonomy by creating a zone of lawful conduct in relation to cannabis. The Bill would retain the overarching purposes of the existing law – the protection of public health and public safety – while adding a number of more specific purposes, including in relation to the protection of the health of young persons and the reduction of illegal activities in relation to cannabis ... As such, they reflect a tailored approach to the legislative objectives.[47]

However, the Charter Statement did not engage with *Malmo-Levine* or *Clay* or the Court's construction of section 7 regarding the prohibition of recreational cannabis use. Instead, it provided a justification for the new offences by arguing that the "overarching purposes of the existing law" were retained while the new offences reflected a "tailored approach to the legislative objectives" and were, thus, in line with section 7 of the Charter.[48]

On the promotion, packaging, and labelling of cannabis (and accessories), the minister identified that such restrictions engaged, but were consistent with section 2(b) of the Charter (freedom of expression).[49] In doing so, the statement explained that such restrictions were modelled on the approach taken in the *Tobacco Act*, which was upheld by the Supreme Court as a reasonable limit on freedom of expression in *Canada (A.G.) v. JTI-MacDonald*.[50] Thus, the minister justified the bill's potential engagement with section 2(b) by relying on the Court's interpretation of the section and subsequent ruling that such restrictions are a reasonable limit on those rights.[51]

Bill C-46, a companion bill introduced alongside Bill C-45, was concerned with amending impaired driving offences and increasing police powers related to impaired driving. In this Charter Statement, the minister identified that sections 7, 8, and 11(d) rights in the Charter may be engaged by proposed amendments in this bill.[52] In the statement's section on section 11(d) – the right to be presumed innocent until proven guilty – regarding proof of blood alcohol concentration (BAC) using "approved instrument tests," the minister relied on *R. v. St-Onge Lamoureux*,[53] a Supreme Court decision on impaired driving provisions, to justify the amendments in the bill. In *St-Onge Lamoureux*, the Court struck down impaired driving provisions on the basis that they violated section 11(d) of the Charter. The Court held that the statutory presumption of accuracy of the blood alcohol level tests violated the right to be presumed innocent if its effect was that an accused person could be convicted even though the judge had reasonable doubt.[54]

The changes in Bill C-46 regarding this provision reflected the procedure the Court recommended. In the Charter Statement for Bill C-46, the government ensured that section 11(d) was upheld in the new law by following the recommended procedure and making sure the onus remained on the Crown to prove the offence beyond a reasonable doubt.[55] Specifically, language in this section of the Charter Statement was almost directly taken from the majority's decision in *St-Onge Lamoureux* regarding section 11(d) at paragraphs 25–7. For this specific provision in Bill C-46, it appeared that the government simply followed the Court ruling and construction of section 11(d) rights regarding proof of BAC using approved instrument tests.

Sexual Assault Reforms (Bill C-51)

In recent campaigns, the Liberals emphasized justice for victims of gender-based violence. In 2015, they proposed a comprehensive federal gender violence strategy along with an action plan to support survivors of domestic violence, sexual assault, and sexual harassment.[56] These efforts concerning sexual assault, gender-based violence, and intimidate partner violence were also reflected in the 2019 and 2021 Liberal Party campaign platforms. Once elected, the Trudeau government introduced multiple bills to advance these issues.

Bill C-51, passed in 2018, sought to clarify "the sexual assault provisions of the *Criminal Code* to reinforce protections for sexual assault complainants throughout the trial process, while preserving trial fairness for the accused."[57] The Charter Statement for Bill C-51 focused on three areas of sexual assault reform: consent and the defence of mistaken belief in consent, a revised rape shield law, and third-party records. Each of these areas of sexual assault reform engaged with the Supreme Court's jurisprudence and Charter rights (sections 7, 11(d), and 15). Regarding consent, the statement reiterated that the clauses in this bill *enhanced* the Charter rights of complainants, specifically under sections 7 and 15(1).[58] However, the Charter Statement did not substantively engage with these rights in principle. Instead, it described the amendments to the consent provisions by engaging with relevant Supreme Court decisions on consent. For example, it amended the definition in section 273.1 of the Criminal Code to clarify that an unconscious person was not capable of consent, making it consistent with the Court's decision in *R. v. J.A.*,[59] which held that the consent requires "ongoing, conscious agreement [of sexual activity] while it is occurring."[60] Regarding the defence's mistaken belief of consent, the government amended section 273.2 of the Criminal Code to "clarify that an accused cannot rely on this defence if their mistake is based on a mistake of law or if their belief is based on the complainant's passivity," bringing it in line with the Court's decision in *R. v. Ewanchuk*.[61] The statement concluded by stating that the above amendments "promote" sections 7 and 15(1) of the Charter that identify the rights of complainants.[62]

The Charter Statement also explained that amendments to sections 276 of the Criminal Code (known as a "rape shield" law) may engage sections 7 and 11(d) of the Charter due to measures limiting the types of evidence that may be admitted at trial. Bill C-51 amended section 276 to clarify that evidence of past sexual activity could never be admitted to support one of the discriminatory myths about victims of sexual violence.[63] Specifically, the bill amended this section to clarify that "evidence of past sexual activity" includes "communications made for a sexual purpose or whose content is of a sexual nature" – this includes text messages, emails, or video recordings.[64] The statement also argued that the proposed amendments were consistent with the Charter and that the Supreme Court upheld the rape shield law as complying with the Charter in the *R. v. Darrach* decision, specifically finding that these provisions enhanced the fairness of trials by excluding misleading evidence.[65] Again, without substantively engaging with section 11(d) of the Charter, the statement defended the proposed amendments by stating that they would "preserve the features of the law that allow the accused to present evidence relevant to their defence."[66] Much like language used to frame reforms around consent, the section concludes by stating that the proposed amendments "promote core values that underpin the *Charter*, including equality, security of the person, and privacy rights of sexual assault complainants."[67]

Finally, regarding third-party records, of which the existing law has created a procedure to be followed if the accused wishes to obtain access to complainants' private records, the bill establishes a process to determine whether such records can be admitted as evidence by the accused at trial. Here again, the minister identified that the process has the potential to engage sections 7 and 11(d) of the Charter regarding "the right of an accused to make full answer and defence."[68] As in the other statement, it did not substantively engage with these rights when justifying the proposed amendments, rather, it stated that the Court upheld the existing third-party record regime as complying with the Charter in *R. v. Mills*.[69] It further noted that the proposed amendments preserve features of that law by allowing "the accused to present evidence relevant to their defence" and continuing to promote the equality, security of the person, and privacy rights of sexual assault complainants.[70] Overall, while the Charter Statement for Bill C-51 did identify relevant Charter sections that may be engaged by these amendments, the statement did not substantively engage with these rights or use independent construction of these rights. Instead, it relied on past Supreme Court rulings to justify the proposed amendments.

Self-Induced Extreme Intoxication Defence

In May 2022, the Supreme Court rendered its judgment on *R. v. Brown*, a case concerned with the constitutionality of section 33.1 of the Criminal Code, which prevented an accused from raising the common law defence of self-induced intoxication akin to automatism.[71] This specific law was enacted in response to the Supreme Court's decision in *R. v. Daviault*, which had confirmed the common law rule that intoxication is not a defence to crimes of general intent. A majority of the justices in *Daviault* recognized that the Charter mandated an exception where intoxication is so extreme that an accused falls into a condition akin to automatism and is incapable of voluntarily committing a guilty act or of having a guilty mind.[72] Following *Daviault*, Parliament enacted section 33.1 of the Criminal Code to block the defence of automatism for designated general intent crimes, including aggravated assault and sexual assault. The accused in *Brown* had challenged the constitutionality of section 33.1 on the basis that it violated sections 7 and 11(d) of the Charter.[73] The Court ruled that section 33.1 breached section 7 of the Charter by allowing a conviction without proof of *mens rea* or proof of voluntariness and violated section 11(d) of the Charter.[74] These Charter infringements could not be saved as reasonable limits under section 1 of the Charter and were invalidated.

A month after the decision in *Brown*, the government promptly tabled a legislative response in Bill C-28. The Charter Statement summarized *Brown* and how the Court ruled on each implicated Charter right. The statement then described the proposed amendments to section 33.1 of the Criminal Code, which would provide that "a person who, as the result of self-induced extreme intoxication, lacks the general intent or voluntariness normally required to commit a violent offence still can be found criminally responsible for that offence if the person is criminally negligent in consuming intoxicants."[75] Thus, the proposed amendments in the bill would "integrate the act and fault of negligent extreme self-induced intoxication as elements of the violent offences subject to s. 33.1 for cases where a defence of extreme intoxication is raised."[76] The Charter Statement then stated that the amendments responded to the reasons given in *Brown* and were consistent with the Charter. However, the statement did not provide any engagement with the specific rights identified earlier in the statement (sections 7 and 11(d)), nor did it engage at all with how the proposed amendments may impact those specific rights. The extent to which rights were discussed is as follows:

> The incorporation of a criminal negligence standard in s. 33.1 would ensure that any rights impairment in relation to the accused would be minimal and that any limit on rights would be proportionate overall to the objectives of the measure because criminal liability would be sufficiently connected to underlying criminal fault to justify conviction for the offences themselves.[77]

While the statement did mention limits on rights (section 1) – something that is uncommon in Charter Statements – the statement failed to substantively identify how the relevant rights may (still) be implicated by the amendments, or not.

Conclusion

Overall, these case studies demonstrate that Charter Statements do feature some degree of Charter analysis regarding specific provisions of proposed bills. In this manner, Charter Statements accomplish what they set out to do: identifying potential effects that a bill may have on rights and freedoms, and explaining the considerations that support the constitutionality of a proposed bill. However, the statements rarely substantively explain *how* certain provisions of bills may directly impact (or enhance) certain rights. For example, in Bill C-51, the Charter Statement raised section 11(d) when discussing rape shield laws and changes regarding third-party records, but did not directly engage with the potential implications that the law may have on the accused's section 11(d) rights. Nor did it explain the constitutionality of the provisions that potentially implicate section 11(d). In Bill C-28, on the extreme intoxication defence, the statement identified sections 7 and 11(d) from *Brown*, yet did not directly engage with these rights when discussing the proposed amendments in the law. Given that the minister of justice had the Court's reasoning from *Daviault* and *Brown*, an opportunity was lost by not engaging in a more sustained expression of Charter rights. The controversial subject matter of Bill C-28 and the speed of the legislative response were likely contributing factors. This fits a pattern of the government's view of the Charter as primarily one of risk management, a matter we address in more detail below.

While the statements have often engaged with the Supreme Court of Canada's jurisprudence, they have featured little independent consideration of Charter rights. Thus, when Supreme Court decisions were engaged with, the statements often relied upon the judicial construction of rights. In Bill C-46, the statement used nearly identical language from the Court's decision in *St-Onge Lamoureux* regarding the bill's implications on section 11(d) of the Charter. Further, these Supreme Court decisions were often used as justifications for proposed amendments that may engage certain rights. In Bill C-45, regarding the restrictions on the promotion, packaging, and labelling of cannabis, the statement used the Supreme Court's ruling in *Canada (A.G.) v. JTI-MacDonald* (on advertising and promotion of tobacco products) as justification for engaging (and potentially infringing) section 2(b) of the Charter.

These findings suggest that, as viewed through Charter Statements, the Trudeau government and its ministers of justice may have been "governing like judges" in regard to the construction and interpretation of rights. As Hiebert notes, under bills of rights, executives are cautious and may refrain from advancing legislation that may be considered inconsistent with judicial decisions.[78] Hiebert and other scholars would not be surprised to hear that the Trudeau government is producing "legalistic legislation," as if "judges were in the corridors of power at the time legislation is being developed."[79]

What is driving this process? Recall that the Trudeau government branded itself as the defender of the Charter and minority rights.[80] Specifically, the Liberal Party's 2015 platform and Trudeau's mandate letter to the minister of justice emphasized restoring dignity to the relationship between the government and the Supreme Court, and respecting the Constitution *and* court decisions.[81] That emphasis can be viewed as a deliberate restoration of what might have been lost in the previous

Harper era regarding the relationship between the government and the Supreme Court.[82] Relatedly, given the general popularity of the Charter and the high public regard for the Supreme Court, Hiebert notes that governments have strong incentives to avoid introducing legislation that will be characterized as violating rights.[83] Put differently, we can see "judicialization from within" on display through these statements as judicial values and processes become internalized. Arguably, the incorporation of judicial norms into the policy process has emerged as a form of risk management by the minister of justice and the government. In *Charter Conflicts*, Hiebert warns of the unintended consequences resulting from the overreliance of "judicial perspectives" on rights.[84] "My focus and concerns," Hiebert writes, "are directed toward Parliament," as they can be overly "influenced by the adverse implications for governing that may stem from an excessive reliance on judicial wisdom to resolve contentious social conflicts."[85] If taken too far, Hiebert warns, it could "negate governmental responsibility" to address pressing matters of social policies.[86]

It is important to consider what can be lost if governments rely too heavily on past judicial constructions of rights when deliberating the merits of proposed legislation. If only the Supreme Court's view of the Charter is considered, it will lower the horizons of politics. Hiebert is attuned to how the dominant assumption of the judiciary is that it has the exclusive prerogative to interpret the Charter.[87] To not challenge that assumption is to give up on the idea of parliamentary-based approaches to rights. In Hiebert and Kelly's framing, the idea of a "parliamentary bills of rights" was premised on the idea of "judicial power that is consistent with the principle of parliamentary sovereignty."[88] The use of Charter Statements in a way that reinforces judicial supremacy might also lower the horizons on a wider variety of policy options within Canada. As one former provincial attorney general states:

> In my experience, Charter compliance in the legislative process is inherently reactive, rather than proactive, as it requires government to approach policy-making from the perspective of risk analysis rather than from the perspective of broader social and economic priorities or the balancing of different societal interests. In other words, although the question "is this legislation Charter-compliant?" often leads to a different answer than the question "is this legislation good public-policy?," the former question often takes precedence in public policy analysis. As a result, risk management becomes the driver of the analysis.[89]

To be clear, Charter Statements have not been a wholly negative development. The introduction of this practice should be welcomed as promoting some level of transparency at this stage of the policymaking process. Moreover, the fact that the minister of justice adopts the Supreme Court's interpretation of rights is not always an undesirable outcome. We are critical, however, of the use of Charter Statements to date, insofar as they have yielded little independent construction or interpretation of Charter rights.

Our analysis does demonstrate that Charter Statements are worthy of further scholarly exploration. As this chapter is solely focused on statements that engaged with Supreme Court jurisprudence and were central to the Trudeau government's legislative agenda, we still need a better overall picture of all the Charter Statements issued. Therefore, an exhaustive examination of all Charter Statements should be explored. Additionally, we have only seen these statements issued under the Trudeau government, which introduced and formalized this process. Will future governments – and ones that may potentially be more willing to diverge from the Court's construction of rights – use these statements? Will they persist as a feature of the policymaking process, or will they suffer a similar fate as the reporting requirement under section 4.1(1) of the *Department of Justice Act*, which has not served as a check on the executive's legislative agenda? Relatedly, future research could further investigate the impact that these statements have on (a) the effectiveness (or lack thereof) of parliamentary rights review in Canada[90] and (b) judicial decisions interpreting relevant legislation.[91]

Finally, future research should look at how this new development within pre-legislative rights review in Canada functions in relation to Canada's Commonwealth cousins in New Zealand and the Australian State of Victoria, which issue similar statements upon tabling proposed legislation. Addressing questions like these will give us a better sense of whether Charter Statements can foster a culture of rights or are just another way that judges govern from the bench.

NOTES

1 *Carter v. Canada (Attorney General)*, [2015] 1 SCR 331.

2 For a full list of statements, see Government of Canada, "Charter Statements," 13 December 2019, https://www.justice.gc.ca/eng/csj-sjc/pl/charter-charte/index.html.

3 Alex Marland, *Brand Command: Canadian Politics and Democracy in the Age of Message Control* (Vancouver: UBC Press, 2016), 390.

4 Canada, Parliament, Office of the Prime Minister, "Minister of Justice and Attorney General of Canada Mandate Letter," 12 November 2015, https://

pm.gc.ca/en/mandate-letters/2015/11/12/archived-minister-justice-and-attorney-general-canada-mandate-letter

5 Ibid.

6 Emmett Macfarlane, "Dialogue or Compliance? Measuring Legislatures' Policy Responses to Court Rulings on Rights," *International Political Science Review* 34 (2013): 39–56.

7 Geoffrey Sigalet and Joanna Baron, "The 'Charter Party's' New Dance with the Judiciary," *Policy Options*, 8 September 2016, https://policyoptions.irpp.org/magazines/september-2016/the-charter-partys-new-dance-with-the-judiciary/; Grégoire C.N. Webber, *The Negotiable Constitution: On the Limitation of Rights* (Cambridge: Cambridge University Press, 2009).

8 Grégoire Webber, "The Charter Party and the Work of Parliament," *Policy Options*, 27 January 2016, https://policyoptions.irpp.org/2016/01/the-charter-party-and-the-work-of-parliament/.

9 Graham Gee and Grégoire C.N. Webber, "What Is a Political Constitution?" *Oxford Journal of Legal Studies* 30, no. 2 (2010): 273–99.

10 Stephen Gardbaum, *The New Commonwealth Model of Constitutionalism Theory and Practice* (Cambridge: Cambridge University Press, 2013).

11 Ibid., 25.

12 Janet Hiebert, *Charter Conflicts: What Is Parliament's Role?* (Montreal: McGill-Queen's University Press, 2002).

13 Ibid., 43.

14 Ibid., 28–33.

15 Ibid., 52.

16 Ibid. See also Dennis Baker, *Not Quite Supreme: The Courts and Coordinate Constitutional Interpretation* (Montreal: McGill-Queen's University Press, 2010).

17 Peter Hogg and Allison Bushell, "The Charter Dialogue between Courts and Legislatures (or Perhaps the Charter of Rights Isn't Such a Bad Thing after All," *Osgoode Hall Law Journal* 35, no. 1 (1997): 75–124.

18 Christopher P. Manfredi and James B. Kelly, "Six Degrees of Dialogue: A Response to Hogg and Bushell," *Osgoode Hall Law Journal* 37, no. 3 (1999): 513–27; Emmett Macfarlane, "Conceptual Precision and Parliamentary Systems of Rights: Disambiguating 'Dialogue,'" *Review of Constitutional Studies* 17, no. 2 (2012): 73–100; Macfarlane, "Dialogue or Compliance?"

19 It was a federal statute and therefore did not apply to provincial laws. It was not superior to other statutes, which made it difficult for the judiciary to issue a remedy between equal parliamentary acts.

20 *The Queen v. Drybones* [1970], SCR 282.

21 Janet Hiebert, "Parliamentary Engagement with the Charter: Rethinking the Idea of Legislative Rights Review," *The Supreme Court Law Review* 58, no. 1 (2012): 87–107.

22 Ibid., 89.
23 Hiebert, *Charter Conflicts*, 47–8.
24 Ibid. See also Janet Hiebert, "New Constitutional Ideas: Can New Parliamentary Models Resist Judicial Dominance When Interpreting Rights," *Texas Law Review* 82, no. 7 (2004): 1963–88.
25 Gardbaum, *The New Commonwealth Model of Constitutionalism*, 25; Janet L. Hiebert, "Interpreting a Bill of Rights: The Importance of Legislative Rights Review," *British Journal of Political Science* 35, no. 2 (2005): 235–55.
26 James B. Kelly, *Governing with the Charter: Legislative and Judicial Activism and Framers' Intent* (Vancouver: UBC Press, 2005).
27 Ibid., 42. See also Donald J. Savoie, *Governing from the Centre: The Concentration of Power in Canadian Politics* (Toronto: University of Toronto Press, 1999).
28 Janet Hiebert, "The Charter, Policy, and Political Judgment," in *Policy Change, Courts, and the Canadian Constitution*, ed. Emmett Macfarlane (Toronto: University of Toronto Press, 2018), 81–102; Kelly, *Governing with the Charter*.
29 Hiebert, "The Charter, Policy, and Political Judgment"; Savoie, *Governing from the Centre*.
30 Kelly, *Governing with the Charter*, 26–7.
31 Hiebert, *Charter Conflicts*, 4.
32 Janet Hiebert, "Governing like Judges?" in *The Legal Protection of Human Rights: Sceptical Essays*, ed. Tom Campbell, K.D. Ewing, and Adam Tomkins (Oxford: Oxford University Press, 2011), 40–65.
33 Hiebert, "The Charter, Policy, and Political Judgment," 95.
34 Hiebert, "Governing like Judges?" 42.
35 Ibid., 49.
36 Ibid., 50.
37 Liberal Party of Canada, *Real Change: A New Plan for a Strong Middle Class* (Ottawa: Liberal Party of Canada, 2015), https://liberal.ca/wp-content/uploads/sites/292/2020/09/New-plan-for-a-strong-middle-class.pdf; Liberal Party of Canada, *Forward: A Real Plan for the Middle Class* (Ottawa: Liberal Party of Canada, 2019), https://2019.liberal.ca/wp-content/uploads/sites/292/2019/09/Forward-A-real-plan-for-the-middle-class.pdf.
38 See the Charter Statement for Bill C-14 (medical assistance in dying) for an example of a strong statement with substantive engagement with Charter rights at https://www.justice.gc.ca/eng/rp-pr/other-autre/adra-amsr/p4.html#p4.
39 *Carter v. Canada (Attorney General).*
40 Before Charter Statements became a statutory obligation, it was a voluntary initiative within the Department of Justice; therefore, there exists

a possible overrepresentation of bills initiated by the DOJ, which would be primarily criminal law or related to public safety.

41 Section 8 was identified the most (42), followed by section 2(b)(36), section 7(36), section 15(32), section 11(d)(14), section 12(10), and section 11(10) identified under five times.

42 Liberal Party of Canada, *Real Change*, 55.

43 Government of Canada, Charter Statements, "Bill C-45: An Act respecting cannabis and to amend the Controlled Drugs and Substances Act, the Criminal Code and other Acts," 29 May 2017, https://www.justice.gc.ca/eng/csj-sjc/pl/charter-charte/c45.html.

44 Ibid.

45 *R. v. Malmo-Levine*, [2003] 3 SCR 571.

46 *R. v. Clay*, [2003] 3 SCR 735.

47 Government of Canada, "Bill C-45."

48 Ibid.

49 Ibid.

50 *Canada (Attorney General) v. JTI-Macdonald Corp.*, [2007] 2 SCR 610.

51 Government of Canada, "Bill C-45."

52 Government of Canada, Charter Statements, "Bill C-46: An Act to amend the Criminal Code (offences relating to conveyances) and to make consequential amendments to other Acts," 11 May 2017, https://www.justice.gc.ca/eng/csj-sjc/pl/charter-charte/c46.html.

53 *R. v. St-Onge Lamoureux*, [2012] 3 SCR 187.

54 Ibid., para. 85.

55 Government of Canada, "Bill C-46."

56 Liberal Party of Canada, *Real Change*, 52.

57 Government of Canada, Charter Statements, "Bill C-51: An Act to amend the Criminal Code and the Department of Justice Act and to make consequential amendments to another Act," 6 June 2017, https://www.justice.gc.ca/eng/csj-sjc/pl/charter-charte/c51.html. Bill C-51 also formalized the practice of issuing Charter Statements.

58 Ibid.

59 *R. v. J.A.*, [2011] 2 SCR 440.

60 Ibid., para. 3.

61 *R. v. Ewanchuk*, [1999] 1 SCR 330.

62 Government of Canada, "Bill C-51."

63 These "twin myths" are (1) that past sexual experience makes them more likely to have consented to the sexual activity in question, and (2) that past sexual experience makes complainants less worthy of belief.

64 Government of Canada, "Bill C-51."

65 *R. v. Darrach*, [2000] 2 SCR 443.

66 Government of Canada, "Bill C-51."

67 Ibid.
68 Ibid.
69 *R. v. Mills*, [1999] 3 SCR 668.
70 Government of Canada, "Bill C-51."
71 *R. v. Brown*, [2022] SCC 18.
72 *R. v. Daviault*, [1994] 3 SCR 63.
73 *R. v. Brown*.
74 Ibid.
75 Government of Canada, Charter Statements, "Bill C-28: An Act to amend the Criminal Code (self-induced extreme intoxication)," 17 June 2022, https://www.justice.gc.ca/eng/csj-sjc/pl/charter-charte/c28_1.html.
76 Ibid.
77 Ibid.
78 Hiebert, "Governing like Judges?" 56.
79 Ibid., 40.
80 Marland, *Brand Command*, 390.
81 Liberal Party of Canada, *Real Change*, 31.
82 Matthew A. Hennigar, "Unreasonable Disagreement?: Judicial-Executive Exchanges about Charter Reasonableness in the Harper Era," *Osgoode Hall Law Journal* 54 (2017): 1245–73; Emmett Macfarlane, "'You Can't Always Get What You Want': Regime Politics, the Supreme Court of Canada, and the Harper Government," *Canadian Journal of Political Science* 51, no. 1 (2018): 1–21.
83 Hiebert, "New Constitutional Ideas"; Hiebert, "Governing like Judges?" 56.
84 Hiebert, *Charter Conflicts*, xii.
85 Ibid.
86 Ibid.
87 Ibid., 117.
88 Janet Hiebert and James B. Kelly, *Parliamentary Bills of Rights: The Experiences of New Zealand and the United Kingdom* (Cambridge: Cambridge University Press, 2015), 3.
89 Geoffrey Plant, quoted in Thomas M.J. Bateman, Janet Hiebert, Rainer Knopff, and Peter H. Russell, *The Court and the Charter: Leading Cases*, 2nd ed. (Toronto: Emond Publishing, 2017), 21.
90 For preliminary observations on parliamentary use of Charter Statements, see Charlie Feldman, "Preliminary Observations on Parliamentary and Judicial Use of *Charter* Statements," *Journal of Parliamentary and Political Law* 13 (2020): 587–601.
91 An initial search on CanLII reveals limited engagement with Charter Statements by lower courts in Canada.

6 The Notwithstanding Clause and National Unity in a Time of Interculturalism

ANDREW MCDOUGALL*

The objective of this chapter is to assess the role of the notwithstanding clause in preserving national unity after Quebec's strong turn towards interculturalism. Its contention is that Quebec politics has now started to move away from the American-inspired liberal nationalism that persisted at the time of the patriation and has now been replaced by a new conception of the Quebec "model" of accommodation – interculturalism – which raises much deeper questions about rights, national unity, and Quebec's place in Canada. The passage of *An Act Regarding the Laïcité of the State*, C.Q.L.R. c L-0.3 (Bill 21) and to a lesser extent *An Act Respecting French, the Official and Common Language of Quebec*, S.Q. 2022, c 14 (Bill 96), was jarring for many and brought these questions to the surface. Of course, the role of the notwithstanding clause in accommodating diversity is not new, it has always served this function to a degree.[1] Even so, the clause has mostly been triggered during debates between legislatures and the judiciary over specific legally entrenched guarantees.[2] That section 33 could serve to reconcile broader cultural differences and approaches has been less well appreciated, except in Quebec. This characteristic of the override mechanism has been steadily receiving more solid theoretical treatment, and this line of literature sees the notwithstanding mechanism as a device to allow deep cultural pluralism in a multinational state.[3] While Canadians are well accustomed to the challenges of federalism, the question remains: How far do the limits of tolerance go?

The introduction of interculturalism as a defining state characteristic means that section 33's growing use in Quebec is no longer a question of reconciling different visions of rights, but really about navigating the tensions arising out of a new cultural vision that has arisen since the Bouchard-Taylor Commission in 2008. This mostly European-inspired philosophy is at odds with the liberal view of rights taken in the Charter of Rights and Freedoms and, but for section 33, an interculturalist agenda would likely be found unconstitutional. Still, state secularism appears to be very popular in Quebec and very unpopular in the rest of the country, and it creates a new dynamic in Quebec-Canada relations.[4] Interestingly, this is happening at a moment in which separation is actually off the agenda. It therefore forces us to reflect on the meaning of diversity and toleration in modern Canada, and whether the Constitution more broadly is successfully balancing individual freedoms alongside the demands of a multinational state.

This chapter will proceed as follows. It will begin by exploring the historical underpinnings of section 33 as a national unity mechanism to suggest that while it can play this role it has never been its dominant purpose. From there it will argue that this role has become more important in light of recent events in light of Bill 21 and Bill 96 and the overall drop in separatist sentiment. It will argue that the challenge interculturalism presents is different from that seen in national unity crises of previous decades because there has been a real change in the vision of how Quebec accommodates outsiders. At the end of the day, the use of the clause to defend state secularism is what Janet Hiebert has termed a "federalist" use of the clause, one that allows for a cultural community to define itself in a way that would otherwise be precluded by judicial intervention.[5] However much the rest of the country may disagree with the constraints of interculturalism, the use of the clause to defend the project is likely serving to avoid a broader clash between Quebec and Canada.

Section 33 and National Unity

Despite being recognized as a mechanism to preserve national unity, that has never been the main purpose of section 33 or the focus of the scholarship around it. In fact, to some degree that role has been an afterthought, certainly in English Canada.[6] Early writing focused squarely on how the clause changed the balance of power between courts and legislatures, and on how it might resolve the "counter-majoritarian difficulty."[7] But section 33's role as a mechanism of resolving differences between Quebec and Canada has been more ambiguous, and its origins prior to 1982 cannot be traced to concerns over national unity. Section 33's antecedent in the Bill of Rights, 1960 predated what is normally thought to be the "mega constitutional era," and in that instance it was passed with the clear objective to preserve some level of parliamentary control over the definition of rights.[8] While the Bill of Rights was not a success, the precedent of the *non-obstante* clauses proved useful during the patriation process as a template for a section that would both offer legislatures some room to define rights alongside the judiciary and as a concession to Quebec to ensure its cultural distinctiveness.[9] Hiebert has written that it was used as a bargaining chip as part of the "provincial resistance strategy" late in the patriation process against adopting the strongest form of judicial review.[10]

Still, it is undeniable that national unity was at least part of the reason section 33 was included. Much of the urgency for patriation was the sense that that a constitutional update was needed to keep Quebec in Canada, which was growing detached from the status quo in Canadian federalism.[11] There was a particular concern that Bill 101, or the Charter of the French Language, would be struck down if the Charter were enacted. Bill 101 was controversial and of dubious legality under any Charter scenario, but retaining it was seen as an absolute necessity if Quebec was to remain in the country. And section 33 has indeed played a role in defending language legislation over the years. The clause was triggered to protect a new version of the Charter of the French Language in 1988 after parts of it were struck down for being more than "minimally impairing" of the Charter's section 2(b) in *Ford v. Quebec (A.G.)* [1988] 2 S.C.R. 712, although it was not renewed.[12] Beyond this, section 33 has played a symbolic role in demonstrating Quebec's distinctness in Canada, and was enacted to insulate all legislation in the 1980s as a protest to the constitution being patriated without Quebec's consent (although that application of the clause also lapsed). But otherwise, the uses of the clause both inside and outside of Quebec tended to be focused on individual rights disputes and could be quite eclectic in the extent to which it was used.[13]

Perhaps unsurprisingly, the awareness of the need for the notwithstanding clause as a national unity mechanism has been most acute in Quebec.[14] For some it is best seen as a "steam release valve" for when conflicts with the rest of the country grow out of control. A more nuanced take holds that the notwithstanding clause is a method to protect community and cultural rights, stemming from the principle of parliamentary supremacy. This view holds that section 33 should not be seen as "overriding" the judiciary but rather as a reflection of the pre-existing democratic tradition in both Canada and in Quebec. Section 33 preserves democracy, and by extension cultural uniqueness, rather than threatening it. In Quebec it has been increasingly used proactively, failing to give the judiciary any chance to rule at all before the law is enacted under the legislative shield. But this is fine, if one adheres to the view that section 33 defends democratic values:

> [E]ven prior to a judicial ruling invalidating a law on Charter grounds, using the notwithstanding clause can be justified in the name of democracy

> and parliamentary sovereignty. This is especially true when made in order to protect Quebec's distinctive identity or to push forward social progress, issues concerned with matters of collective rights and interests that may, in some circumstances, be more important than some individual liberties, in a way not contrary to the human rights principles recognized by international law.[15]

Of course, despite the more positive reception the clause has seen in Quebec, there are those, especially in English Canada, who see section 33 playing a destructive, rather than constructive, role in resolving national unity questions. Its use in the early years by Quebec governments of different partisan backgrounds may have made subsequent efforts to come to a political settlement with Quebec in the 1980s and 1990s much more difficult than they needed to be. Section 33's association with separatism and nationalism, cemented in particular after the application of the clause following the *Ford* decision, gave it a negative connotation for many in Canada and left many Canadians with a dim view of Quebec and its politics.[16] Writing after the collapse of the Meech Lake Accord, Patrick Monahan argued that the framers failed to see the destabilizing role section 33 could play for national unity. The mere presence of the "safety valve" meant that, in a case like *Ford*, it had to be used simply because it was there, and to fail to use it would leave any Quebec premier vulnerable to an attack of being soft on language.[17] Without the clause, thorny rights decisions would have to be respected leaving politicians with the "easy out" of blaming the courts and reducing the chance of linguistic tensions spilling out into the open.

Even so, most of the times that the clause has been triggered in Quebec have been more about discrete rights disputes rather than statements of identity.[18] Although section 33's use to curb English was controversial and was justified in the name of protecting Quebec's culture, other early uses of the clause were not particularly problematic for English Canada.

What *Does* Quebec Want?

In fact, at the time section 33 was adopted, Quebec was, if anything, becoming *more* like the rest of the country than at any time in its history by adopting an increasingly liberal, globalized outlook. Emerging out of the Quiet Revolution, Quebec had made a clear choice that it would move away from the conservative, Catholic traditions that had defined its culture up to that point and move into a modern and liberal future. That evolution brought it more into line with contemporary Western modernity – there was a focus on education, social investment, and gender equality, with far less time for the intervention of religious authorities.[19] The shift led to a blossoming of the new Quebec nationalism, which was both modern while also unabashedly committed to the promotion of the French fact in North America. Quebec shared with the rest of the country the same post-material shift in values that had been tracked in many places since the 1960s, and which had been documented by scholars such as Ronald Inglehart and Neil Nevitte.[20] The Quebec public had become much more sceptical of traditional institutions like the Church, more individualistic on matters of rights (with the exception of French language rights), and much more concerned with gender equality. It was similarly taken up with newer causes such as environmentalism and social justice, which were of growing concern everywhere. The economy progressed rapidly, through a process that was explicitly designed to catch up with the rest of the world (*rattrapage*) and conducted through social programs and institutions that were among the most advanced anywhere, such as the Quebec Pension Plan and the Caisse de dépôt et placement du Québec.[21] The result was a new Quebec by the middle of the 1970s, much more educated and integrated into the Canadian and, later, the North American economies.

That left the question of how this modern, post–Quiet Revolution Quebec really differed from the rest of the country in ways that the Constitution could not already accommodate. Outside of the French fact, it was not always clear how the province was different from Ontario or, for that matter, New York or Vermont. In an era of globalization and cultural homogenization, Quebec was hardly alone in struggling to define how it was different from other places. When the question arose in the mega constitutional era, "What does Quebec want?," nobody really knew, including those inside of Quebec. Perhaps the best articulation of the answer to that question was in the Meech Lake Accord, when Quebec stated a set of five conditions under which it would sign the Constitution. These included recognition as a distinct society, more control over immigration, a role in the selection of the Quebec's three Supreme Court and Senate seats, stronger veto protections for Quebec, and money for opting out of federal programs to run provincial equivalents.[22] But while each of these conditions would protect the autonomy of Quebec, and offer latitude for the internal development of the province's social programs, they actually said little about what the cultural content of Quebec was to the extent that it was different from the rest of Canada. And there were many inside Quebec who pointed this out. In 1978 the political scientist André Bernard of the Université de Montréal wrote in *What Does Quebec Want?* that while survival of the French language, cultural protection, and economic development were high priorities, the reforms sought were as much about changing the political *process* to empower Quebec than they were about substantive cultural demands.[23]

This situation broadly kept until the turn of the century and the arrival of interculturalism. Arising out of the politics of accommodation, and borrowing heavily from the experiences that have driven politics in Europe, there is a clearer sense about how Quebec culture differs in many respects from that of English Canada on the question of cultural boundaries and accommodation.

Interculturalism and the Challenge to Canada

Interculturalism's arrival marked an important shift in the identity debate in Quebec that is still being explored.[24] Although the concept of state secularism had been widely debated in France and had previously had some traction in Quebec, the early 2000s marked a moment in Quebec politics in which the politics of identity and accommodation began to take up more of the political agenda. Much of this was driven by a sense that there was a crisis in the ability of the province to accommodate immigrants who came from non-Christian backgrounds. Notable events included the request by Orthodox Jews to a YMCA to frost its windows so that men could not see women swimming, an incident where two ambulance drivers were asked to eat a non-kosher lunch somewhere other than the cafeteria of Montreal's Jewish General Hospital, along with other incidents.[25] Events made international headlines when the town of Hérouxville announced that it was passing a municipal ordnance that banned "barbaric cultural practices" such as the stoning of women even though no such events had taken place and there were no Muslims who lived in the city to begin with.[26] Nationalist politicians were eager to seize on these events to suggest that the requests that were being made were unreasonable, and that it was the immigrant community, not the majority, who needed to adapt.[27]

Although there was a "ripped from the headlines" component to the crisis, it arose out of the long-standing anxieties that Canadian multiculturalism has long engendered in Quebec. For many reasons, multiculturalism has been viewed with suspicion in the province, due in no small part to the origins of the program in the denationalizing vision of Pierre Trudeau. More than anyone else, Trudeau is credited with his efforts to create a civic, national identity in Canada, albeit alongside state bilingualism, that played down local identities. His efforts to push this project often brought him into collision with other Canadian leaders who saw little in the project but an effort to dilute their own identities. Notable events included the infamous "White Paper" that proposed eliminating the *Indian Act* as well Trudeau's resistance to any special status for Quebec.[28]

In response to the sense that there was a crisis, in 2007 Premier Jean Charest announced the formation of the Bouchard-Taylor Commission (named after the academics who served as commissioners, Gérard Bouchard and Charles Taylor) and which was tasked with developing a framework for the reasonable accommodations of new immigrants. Their solution, "interculturalism," was essentially a form of state neutrality towards religion that took its departure from the French model of *laïcité*. Under the French model, there is a "public" and "private" sphere, the former of which is subject to strict regulation by the state to ensure the equality and integration of all citizens and which has been an offshoot of immigration policy.[29] French *laïcité* has emerged out of a view of civic republicanism that squared the openness implied by individual "equality" and "liberty" with that of the communal value of "fraternity"; an effort to build a common commitment of citizens to one another within an identity framework.[30] To a real degree, this has made France comparatively open from the perspective of immigration and accommodation, but it has not come without tensions and is in conflict with other approaches to integration. By far the most fraught politics have arisen in France around the Muslim community and the perception of their failure to successfully integrate, and led to high-profile controversies around how women can dress.[31]

Interculturalism as expressed in the Bouchard-Taylor Commission was milder than how it was eventually expressed in legislation. The commission accepted the basic ideas behind interculturalism – for example, that there was a public and private sphere and that there could be some legitimate regulation of the former in order to guarantee community cohesion and a sense of common citizenship. To the extent that the public sphere had any real substance, it was defined by the need to speak French, which had traditionally been the sine qua non of Quebec's cultural difference compared to that of English Canada or broader North America. Although there has been an alleged ethnic component to *Québécois* identity in the past, Quebec nationalism was more often expressed in civic terms by leaders such as Robert Bourassa or René Lévesque. It was in this vein that Commissioners Bouchard and Taylor saw Quebec society, and to that end they prescribed a weaker form of "*laïcité overte*" or "open secularism" that defended the use of French in the public sphere but stopped short of fully embracing the French model which they felt went too far.[32] In the view of the commissioners, the reach of the interculturalist model extended only to the institutions of Quebec, which should maintain a strict division on neutrality. But this need not extend to the people who worked for them or to other citizens in Quebec, who should, they felt, be free to express themselves however they liked. To the extent that the commissioners felt that there were justifiable limitations that could be put on religious headgear, it was when those limitations interfered with their job. A teacher would therefore be free to wear a headscarf but not a burqa, as the latter would get in the way of the person's ability to teach.[33] They also went further to suggest that it was time to remove the more ostentatious signs of Catholicism in much of Quebec's public life, most notably the crucifix in the National Assembly. The crucifix, first hung in the Assembly in the 1930s, was seen as too close to being an endorsement of one religion over others and ran afoul of their vision of open secularism.[34]

After the commission's report was released, both its authors and the governing Liberals appeared to think that it would be the end of the debate on reasonable accommodations. One commissioner felt that it was time to "move on" from the question.[35] Both commissioners felt that the debate was overblown, that Quebec was a tolerant society by any measure and that drastic steps were not needed. This also seemed to be the feeling of the premier at the time, and Jean Charest did nothing initially to implement the report.[36] Subsequent political developments showed, however, the extent to which the idea of state secularism began to take root in Quebec and shape a new approach to both as religious accommodation and arguably as a defining characteristic of Québécois culture. Despite this early disinterest in the project from Charest, it began to play a larger role in Quebec identity politics. After the Liberals lost power to the Parti Québécois in 2012, state secularism was endorsed as the basis for a new identity program of the PQ, which culminated in 2013 in Bill 60 as the proposed Quebec "Charter of Values."[37] The bill went much further than the Bouchard-Taylor report, and would have restricted wearing ostentatious religious clothing in the public sphere when giving or receiving state services. Although it was widely criticized for being an illiberal attack on minorities and Islamophobic, given the disproportionate impact it had on Muslim women, it still polled well with the public.

Indeed, it polled so well that eventually the Liberals gravitated in the same direction, offering a more moderate vision of state secularism under the new Liberal Premier Phillipe Couillard who took over from the PQ in 2014.[38] That year, Quebec's Intergovernmental Affairs Minister Jean-Marc Fournier made it clear that interculturalism was more than just an immigration policy, but basic to the way Quebecers saw themselves and their place in Canada. He raised interculturalism in the context of a speech about possibly amending the Canadian Constitution, to recognize that Quebec was a "nation" along the lines of what had been recognized by Stephen Harper in the Quebec "nation" motion of 2008. "The Quebec of the future is already visible," Fournier said, "a nation within a federation. With one language, one culture, civil law, and distinct social values. It is a pluralistic society that long ago opted for an interculturalism approach. This choice of interculturalism is also part of Quebec's specificity."[39] The chances that his call would result in the rest of the country agreeing to reopen the Constitution were of course minimal, but as the constitutional position that Quebec was taking to the rest of the country, it was important. It made it clear not just that Quebec was a nation, it fleshed out *what that nation was all about*, and in particular how it defined what counted and what did not. It also suggested more precisely how Quebec's culture and values differed from the rest of the country beyond the necessity to speak French.

The eventual bill the Liberals passed was watered down from the PQ version. Known as Bill 62, it provided that public servants who were providing or receiving public services – including in libraries, transit, or going to the doctor – must have their faces uncovered.[40] This was a break from the previous Liberal attitude towards state secularism, in which they essentially adhered to the view that interculturalism really meant nothing more than an open and tolerant society where there was a common agreement that the language of the public sphere was French. The decision to limit what people could wear on religious grounds was new for them, and ran into the same issues that the PQ had faced around enforceability and consistency. It was also demonstrably not what the original authors of the Bouchard-Taylor report had in mind, who joined in the criticism of the bill as incoherent.[41] It was not clear who, if anyone, was going to enforce the law. The fact that the bill would have left the crucifix in the National Assembly intact seemed only to add insult to injury to the whole idea of state religious neutrality. For his part, Charles Taylor described the Liberal effort as a "dog's breakfast."[42]

The Liberals were being pushed, however, from political currents that were too strong to ignore. Not only was the popularity of the interculturalist approach undeniable, but the Liberals were facing similar projects being advanced by the other parties. After losing the election in 2018, the controversy around interculturalism became much larger with the election of the Coalition Avenir Quebec (CAQ) on 1 October 2018. Under the new premier, François Legault, the CAQ made identity politics more central, and introduced a series of bills that embraced state secularism more aggressively than the Liberals. The first, Bill 21, had much more in common with the PQ's original "Charter of Values" bill than with the more moderate bill of the Liberals. The bill did a number of things, the most important of which was to make interculturalism foundational to the identity of the state. In section 1 it declared that the "State of Quebec is a lay state" and, in section 2, it went on to declare that this principle rested on the religious neutrality of the state, the separation of church and state, the equality of all citizens, as well as the principle of conscience and religion.[43] Chapter 5 also amended the Quebec Charter of Human Rights and Freedoms, C.Q.L.R. c C-12, to entrench state secularism in a number of places in that law as well. But it also expanded on the approach the Liberals had taken to restrict religious clothing in the public sphere, when either giving or receiving public services. The bill was subject to a number of legal challenges, not the least of which was the Canadian Civil Liberties Association, which argued that it was a violation of the Canadian Charter's provisions around freedom of expression, but because it was passed pursuant to the notwithstanding clause and had to be challenged on more tenuous legal arguments, the chances of success were dim. At this point, Charles Taylor broke with the interculturalism project and his role in it completely, admitting that he was "naïve" about how interculturalism would end up being implemented.[44] He went so far as to say "I made a mistake" in writing the report, arguing that integration begins in the workplace and that the proposed legislation would make it harder, not easier to accommodate immigrants.[45] He felt that Bill 21 encouraged Islamophobia, much of it originating in the United States, and that the proposed law was making the situation worse, not better. For his part, Gérard Bouchard also felt the bill went too far, given the lack of clarity that existed on how it would be enforced. In addition, he felt the pre-emptive use of the notwithstanding clause was putting Quebec on a "dangerous path."[46]

Regardless, Legault later expanded on Bill 21 in Bill 96, which was aimed at strengthening the French language guarantees, and again making use of the notwithstanding clause pre-emptively.[47] In many ways, it was a continuation of the approach that had long been adopted in Quebec around the Charter of the French Language, C.Q.L.R. c C-11. English was even more limited in public and commercial life. Although it was strenuously criticized by English rights groups, there was little doubt that the bill was valid provincial legislation and that the government had the right to enact the notwithstanding clause pre-emptively. Additionally, although the link to interculturalism was far less obvious, it was rolled out alongside a new call for the constitutional recognition of Quebec as a nation – something that had long been linked to interculturalism. Unexpectedly, and what became the subject of much controversy, Legault announced that he could do it unilaterally, although the majority of experts did not accept that. The assertion was in keeping with those made by previous governments of the desirability of having Quebec constitutionally recognized as a nation in the Constitution, and was in keeping with the previous Liberal government's assertion that interculturalism is essential to how the Quebec nation is defined.

Quebec's turn has caused much concern in the rest of the country. It has raised the question of what obligations the rest of the country have, if any, to citizens whose rights may be suppressed in the name of protecting majority Québécois culture. Bill 21 and the use of the notwithstanding clause is a clear example of local norms clashing with more entrenched norms of justice and individual rights in Canada and under the Charter.[48] Indeed, it is very much seen as being a debate over religion that pits the "rest of Canada" against Quebec.[49] But to date, no federal or provincial leader has taken any meaningful action to challenge Quebec's legislation. And many thinkers would likely argue that this approach is the correct approach in a multinational state, in keeping with the value of respecting "deep diversity," multiculturalism, and the need to accommodate.[50]

The rest of the country has been left to contemplate the limits of the Canadian Constitution, and what, if anything can (or should) be done in a case like this. The short answer is, of course, not much. But the political reaction of the rest of the country has also been telling; while it is clear that the rest of the country is dissatisfied with the interculturalist project, the use of the clause is taken as dispositive. Politically there has been little appetite to engage in a confrontation over rights; rather, the embrace of state secularism is viewed as an internal Quebec affair. Had section 33 not been available, it is questionable whether the federal government would have been able to resist calls to get involved, in particular given the ideological orientation of the current government of Justin Trudeau, which has made the embrace of Charter rights central to its message. Instead, both the federal government, as well as other provincial leaders, have accepted that letting the matter drop is the preferable choice. While this is deeply troubling from a rights perspective, the shield that the notwithstanding clause provides has made a direct confrontation between Quebec and the rest of the country through the federal system similar to that which occurred during the "mega constitutional era" very unlikely, along with any return of the destabilizing constitutional politics that was the hallmark of the period.

In 2019, Hiebert asked the provocative question of whether or not the notwithstanding clause could accommodate federalism.[51] She distinguished between "democratic" and "federalist" uses of the clause, with the latter defined by the motivation to protect cultural rights and provincial autonomy rather than defending legislation that may be popular but would be surely struck down by the courts.[52] The use of the clause to defend an interculturalist project is an example of a federalist use of the clause, and is legally a completely legitimate use of the provision, however offensive some may find it. Still, to the degree that it is serving as a mechanism to allow for major cultural differences between Quebec and Canada to be channeled and managed, it is likely serving to avoid another national unity crisis. Had the interculturalist turn happened in Quebec and the clause had been unavailable, it may have given rise to a new period of tension in federal-provincial relations.

Conclusion

Interculturalism is something new in Canada, and is now gaining full expression through the use of the notwithstanding clause. It is an approach to the accommodation of minorities that is a direct challenge to the Canadian concept of multiculturalism and would almost certainly not be accepted by the courts. To a degree, this shift gives further, meaningful content in the ways that Quebec is fundamentally *different* from the rest of the country beyond the fact that it simply speaks a different majority language. Interestingly, it is also happening at a time when national unity concerns have reached a new low, with little prospect of an outright split between Canada and Quebec. Section 33 may be going some ways to demonstrate Quebec actually does have the cultural security it has sought through constitutional amendments but never found, and it may be serving an important role of keeping the secessionist genie in the bottle.

This "federalist" use of the clause will strike many outside of Quebec as unacceptable on rights grounds, however. The turn towards interculturalism will test the ability of the Canadian Constitution to reconcile diversity with equality, and it is unlikely that many Canadians will be satisfied with the results. Still, they will have to balance their displeasure with the counterfact of a Quebec finding itself unable to express its values fully in our constitutional arrangements. If history is any guide, that could lead to serious problems on its own.

NOTES

* The author would like to thank Charlie Buck, a doctoral student in the Department of Political Science at the University of Toronto, for his excellent work as a research assistant.

1 Peter H. Russell, "Standing Up for Notwithstanding," *Alberta Law Review* 29, no. 2 (1991): 305.

2 Tsvi Kahana, "Understanding the Notwithstanding Mechanism," *The University of Toronto Law Journal* 52, no. 2 (2002): 223–4; see also Paul C. Weiler, "Of Judges and Rights, or Should Canada Have a Constitutional Bill of Rights?," *Dalhousie Review* 60, no. 2 (1980): 205–37; Brian Slattery, "A Theory of the Charter," *Osgoode Hall Law Journal* 25, no. 4 (1987): 701–47; Lorraine Weinrib, "Learning to Live with the Override," *McGill Law Journal* 35, no. 3 (1990): 541–71.

3 Guillaume Rousseau and François Côté, "A Distinctive Quebec Theory and Practice of the Notwithstanding Clause: When Collective Interests Outweigh Individual Rights," *Revue Générale de Droit* 47, no. 2 (2017): 360.

4 CTV News Staff, "Majority of Quebecers Support Proposed Bill Banning Religious Clothing: Poll," *CTV News*, 26 August 2013, https://www.ctvnews.ca/canada/majority-of-quebecers-support-proposed-bill-banning-religious-clothing-poll-1.1427098; CTV News, "New Online Poll Claims 66% Support in Quebec for Values Charter," *CTV News*, 10 September 2014, http://www.ctvnews.ca/canada/new-online-poll-claims-66-support-in-quebec-for-values-charter-1.1448791; Philip Authier, "Majority of Canadians Disapprove of Bill 21, but Quebecers Are in Favour: Poll," *The Gazette*, 6 August 2019, https://montrealgazette.com/news/quebec/majority-of-canadians-disapprove-of-bill-21-but-quebecers-are-in-favour-poll. It should also be noted that conceptually, state secularism or *laïcité* and interculturalism are slightly different, as state secularism is about the presence or absence of religion in the public sphere while interculturalism is a reaction to multiculturalism that requires integration to a dominant culture rather than acceptance of deeper pluralism, they are often used interchangeably. I thank the anonymous reviewer of the piece for pointing out the need to make the distinction.

5 Janet Hiebert, "Notwithstanding the Charter: Does Section 33 Accommodate Federalism?," in *Canada: The State of the Federation 2017*, ed. Kyle Hanniman and Elizabeth Goodyear-Grant (Montreal: McGill-Queen's University Press, 2019), 65.

6 Ibid., 63.

7 John D. Whyte, "On Not Standing for Notwithstanding," *Alberta Law Review* 28, no. 2 (1990): 347–57; Russell, "Standing Up for Notwithstanding"; Janet Hiebert, *Charter Conflicts : What Is Parliament's Role?* (Montreal: McGill-Queen's University Press, 2002); Janet Hiebert, *Limiting Rights: The Dilemma of Judicial Review* (Montreal: McGill-Queen's University Press, 1996); Tsvi Kahana, "The Notwithstanding Mechanism and Public Discussion: Lessons from the Ignored Practice of Section 33 of the Charter," *Canadian Public Administration* 44, no. 3 (2001): 255–91;

Kahana, "Understanding the Notwithstanding Mechanism"; David Snow, "Notwithstanding the Override: Path Dependence, Section 33, and the Charter," *Innovations: A Journal of Politics* 8 (2008): 1–15; see also the literature on dialogue theory inspired by Peter W. Hogg and Allison A. Bushell, "The Charter Dialogue between Courts and Legislatures (or Perhaps the Charter of Rights Isn't Such a Bad Thing after All)," *Osgoode Hall Law Journal* 35, no. 1 (1997): 75–124, and the importance of the notwithstanding clause for those purposes.

8 Mark Carter, "Diefenbaker's Bill of Rights and the Counter-Majoritarian Difficulty: The Notwithstanding Clause and Fundamental Justice as Touchstones for the Charter Debate," *Saskatchewan Law Review* 82, no. 2 (2019): 136.

9 Rousseau and Côté, "A Distinctive Quebec Theory," 471.

10 Janet Hiebert, "The Notwithstanding Clause: Why Non-Use Does Not Necessarily Equate with Abiding by Judicial Norms," in *The Oxford Handbook of the Canadian Constitution*, ed. Peter Oliver, Patrick Macklem, and Nathalie Des Rosiers, online ed. (Oxford: Oxford Academic), 695–714, https://doi.org/10.1093/law/9780190664817.003.0033; Carter, "Diefenbaker's Bill of Rights and the Counter-Majoritarian Difficulty," 136.

11 See Weiler, "Of Judges and Rights," 207, for an early, pre-Charter articulation of the fear.

12 Rousseau and Côté, "A Distinctive Quebec Theory," 404.

13 Kahana, "The Notwithstanding Mechanism and Public Discussion"; Kahana, "Understanding the Notwithstanding Mechanism."

14 See Rousseau and Côté, "A Distinctive Quebec Theory," for an excellent analysis and summary of the literature.

15 Ibid.

16 For example, Dennis Baker, *Not Quite Supreme: The Courts and Coordinate Constitutional Interpretation* (Montreal: McGill-Queen's University Press, 2010), 116; Adam Dodek, "The Canadian Override: Constitutional Model or Bête Noire of Constitutional Politics?," *Israel Law Review* 49, no. 1 (2016): 60–1.

17 Patrick Monahan, *Meech Lake: The Inside Story* (Toronto: University of Toronto Press, 1991), 166–7.

18 Rousseau and Côté, "A Distinctive Quebec Theory," 379.

19 See Michael D. Behiels, *Prelude to Quebec's Quiet Revolution: Liberalism Versus Neo-Nationalism, 1945–1960* (Montreal: McGill-Queen's University Press, 1985); Alain-G. Gagnon, *Minority Nations in the Age of Uncertainty: New Paths to National Emancipation and Empowerment* (Toronto: University of Toronto Press, 2014).

20 Ronald Inglehart, *The Silent Revolution: Changing Values and Political Styles among Western Publics* (Princeton, NJ: Princeton University Press, 1977);

Ronald Inglehart, "Post-Materialism in an Environment of Insecurity," *The American Political Science Review* 75, no. 4 (1981): 880–900; Ronald Inglehart, "Cultural Change in Advanced Industrial Societies: Postmaterialist Values and Their Consequences," *International Review of Sociology Series 1* 2, no. 3 (1988): 77–99; Ronald Inglehart, *Culture Shift in Advanced Industrial Society* (Princeton, NJ: Princeton University Press, 1990); Ronald Inglehart, "Changing Values among Western Publics from 1970 to 2006," *West European Politics* 31, no. 1–2 (2008): 130–46; Peter Miller, "Postmaterialism and Social Movements," in *The Wiley-Blackwell Encyclopedia of Social and Political Movements*, ed. Donatella della Porta, Bert Klandermans, Doug McAdam, and David A. Snow (New York: John Wiley & Sons, 2013); Neil Nevitte, *The Decline of Deference: Canadian Value Change in Cross-National Perspective* (Peterborough, ON: Broadview Press, 1996).

21 Rodney Haddow, *Comparing Quebec and Ontario: Political Economy and Public Policy at the Turn of the Millennium* (Toronto: University of Toronto Press, 2014), 46.

22 Pierre Fournier, *A Meech Lake Post-Mortem: Is Quebec Sovereignty Inevitable?* (Montreal: McGill-Queen's University Press, 1991), 17–26.

23 André Bernard, *What Does Quebec Want?* (Toronto: James Lorimer & Company, 1978).

24 Geneviève Zubrzycki, *Beheading the Saint: Nationalism, Religion, and Secularism in Quebec* (Chicago: University of Chicago Press, 2016), see generally chap. 5.

25 Ibid., 149.

26 Ibid., 151.

27 Ibid. Mario Dumont was particularly key in drawing attention to what he saw as the crisis in reasonable accommodations.

28 Michael Morden, "Theorizing the Resilience of the Indian Act," *Canadian Public Administration* 59, no. 1 (2016): 116; see also Kenneth McRoberts, *Misconceiving Canada: The Struggle for National Unity* (Toronto: Oxford University Press, 1997), for the canonical take on Trudeau's rejection of the dualist approach to Canada.

29 Emily Laxer, *Unveiling the Nation: The Politics of Secularism in France and Quebec* (Montreal: McGill-Queen's University Press, 2019), 20–2.

30 Ibid., 21.

31 Ibid.

32 Zubrzycki, *Beheading the Saint*, 154.

33 Ibid., 154–5.

34 Ibid., 155.

35 CBC News, "Let's Move on, Says Quebec Accommodation Commission," *CBC News*, 5 May 2008, https://www.cbc.ca/news/canada/montreal/let-s-move-on-says-quebec-accommodation-commission-1.709976.

36 Zubrzycki, *Beheading the Saint*, 157.
37 National Assembly of Quebec, "Bill 60 Charter Affirming the Values of State Secularism and Religious Neutrality and of Equality between Women and Men, and Providing a Framework for Accommodation Requests" (2013), http://www.assnat.qc.ca/en/travaux-parlementaires/projets-loi/projet-loi-60-40-1.html.
38 CTV Montreal, "Quebec Liberals Working on 'Moderate' Charter of Values," *CTV News*, 17 September 2014, http://montreal.ctvnews.ca/quebec-liberals-working-on-moderate-charter-of-values-1.2011365.
39 Quoted in Don Macpherson, "Don Macpherson: The Couillard Government's 'One Language, One Culture' Idea of Quebec," *The Gazette*, 24 October 2014, https://montrealgazette.com/opinion/columnists/don-macpherson-the-couillard-governments-one-language-one-culture-idea-of-quebec.
40 Benjamin Shingler, "Quebec Face-Covering Law Called a 'Dog's Breakfast' by Author of Landmark Report," *CBC News*, 20 October 2017, https://www.cbc.ca/news/canada/montreal/quebec-bill-62-bouchard-taylor-1.4362278.
41 Ibid.
42 Ibid.
43 Quebec, "An Act Respecting the Laïcité of the State," S.Q. L-0.3 (2019), http://legisquebec.gouv.qc.ca/en/showdoc/cs/L-0.3, section 1 and 2.
44 Philip Authier, "Bill 21 Hearings: 'We Were Very Naive' about Impact of Report, Charles Taylor Says," *The Gazette*, 7 May 2019, https://montrealgazette.com/news/quebec/expect-sparks-to-fly-as-bill-21-hearings-are-launched-tuesday.
45 Giuseppe Valiante, "Charles Taylor: Decade since Reasonable Accommodation Report Proof 'I Made a Mistake,'" *CTV News*, 8 May 2019, https://montreal.ctvnews.ca/charles-taylor-decade-since-reasonable-accommodation-report-proof-i-made-a-mistake-1.4411311.
46 Ibid.
47 Jacob Serebin, "Quebec's Use of Notwithstanding Clause in Language Law Opens Constitutional Debate," *CBC News*, 29 May 2022, https://www.cbc.ca/news/canada/montreal/quebec-notwithstanding-clause-constitutional-debate-1.6470091.
48 Frédéric Mégret, "Ban on Religious Symbols in the Public Service: Quebec's Bill 21 in a Global Pluralist Perspective," *Global Constitutionalism* 11, no. 2 (2022): 217–48.
49 Mario Polèse, "Quebec's Bill 21: Is There Room for More than One View of Religion in Canada?," *Policy Options*, 4 August 2021, https://policyoptions.irpp.org/magazines/august-2021/quebecs-bill-21-is-there-room-for-more-than-one-view-of-religion-in-canada/.

50 Gagnon, *Minority Nations in the Age of Uncertainty*; Alain-G Gagnon, *Le Choc Des Légitimités* (Montreal: Presses de L'Université Laval, 2021); Will Kymlicka and Bashir Bashir, *The Politics of Reconciliation in Multicultural Societies* (Oxford: Oxford University Press, 2008).

51 Hiebert, "Notwithstanding the Charter."

52 Ibid., 65–6.

7 Rights Talk and the COVID-19 Pandemic

NANCY HILLS AND EMMETT MACFARLANE

The impact of the Charter of Rights and Freedoms on political discourse has been subject to less study than its effects on public policy, but it is widely agreed that the Charter has increasingly encouraged Canadians to frame political demands in terms of rights.[1] Rights talk is understood as the "increasing tendency to speak of what is most important to us in terms of rights and to frame nearly every social controversy as a clash of rights."[2] While the positive benefits of rights claiming seem obvious, a number of commentators have raised the dangers of rights talk. In their view, rights talk tends to frame rights in absolutist terms, diminishing opportunities for political compromise, increasing tensions in pluralistic societies, and creating a winner-takes-all approach to politics. This view is most substantively advanced in the United States context by Mary Ann Glendon, who argues that rights talk presupposes a claim that overrides other considerations, such as values or alternative policy objectives. This poses a problem in part because of the inherent contestation over rights themselves, and disagreement over what needs, interests, or values comprise rights.[3] To invoke a right is to attempt to play a trump card, ultimately stifling room for consensus and substantive or principled political debate. In Glendon's view, rights talk also increases the chances for political and societal conflict.[4]

Glendon's thesis suggests that the detrimental aspects of rights talk are unique to the United States context, and she specifically points to Canada as curbing its absolutist tendencies by virtue of the presence in the Charter of section 1's limitation clause and section 33's notwithstanding clause, which allows legislatures to temporarily immunize legislation from the effects of judicial review in respect of certain sections of the Charter. She notes that, "like most postwar constitutions, the Charter has avoided hard-edged, American-style proclamations of individual rights."[5]

However, empirical study of rights talk in the Canadian context calls this assertion into question. Emmett Macfarlane's study of media coverage of major Charter decisions finds that limits on rights are rarely reflected to Canadians and that rights talk in Canada is not so distinct from the American version described by Glendon.[6] He finds that "Canadian newspapers do little to indicate to readers that most Charter decisions involve extensive limitations analysis, and discourse surrounding the notwithstanding clause only aggravates [an absolutist] conception of rights."[7] Further, Macfarlane finds that "[a]ll rights claims are usually presented as holding equal weight, regardless of how central or marginal the circumstances might otherwise indicate." This in turn "makes it difficult for politicians to articulate support for legislative policies that come up against rights-based claims."[8]

Macfarlane's finding accords with the conclusion of other scholars that Canadian rights talk presents challenges for political discourse and compromise. Janet Hiebert writes that the predominant view of the Charter fails to recognize the role of section 1 in accommodating values not entrenched in its provisions, and that an "unbridled enthusiasm for the Charter has generated a propensity to assume a 'rights must be paramount' view of Canadian politics which affords little scope for s.1."[9] Numerous other commentators make similar claims about the Canadian experience.[10]

This chapter contributes to the empirical literature on rights talk by exploring Canadian rights discourse in the context of the COVID-19 pandemic. We believe the pandemic provides a rich and interesting context for examining rights talk because the basis for limits on rights during public health emergencies is especially pronounced. In short, pandemic measures enacted to protect individuals and the broader health care system from transmission of a serious illness should put discussion of reasonable limits at the fore. If an absolutist conception of rights talk remains prominent in this context, it would provide particularly strong support for the general thesis advanced by scholars like Hiebert and Glendon, and would further illuminate the extent to which political discourse around rights presents problems not only for the quality of debate and for our ability to arrive at consensus over policy solutions but also for the general welfare in the midst of an ongoing emergency.

We analyze rights talk from three distinct sources. First, we present a content analysis of news media reporting on pandemic restrictions to explore how the rights issues implicated by them are framed. Traditional media platforms, such as newspapers, are important elements in communicating to the public social and political problems.

Currently, traditional media are still the most common source that Canadians use in order to obtain political information.[11] As a result, it is important to look to these platforms to assess their rights discourse in relation to pandemic health mandates and determine whether they are acknowledging the limits that can be placed upon rights. Second, we present a content analysis of social media posts, specifically tweets from Twitter (now X), on how Canadian users are discussing pandemic restrictions in relation to their rights. Scholars have suggested that information sharing via newspapers has the ability to influence news conversations on different mediums, including social media.[12] By analyzing tweets posted on Twitter, we provide an understanding of another source of rights discourse Canadian users employ when viewing and discussing their rights. Finally, we present an analysis of elite level discourse by politicians engaged in debate in the Legislative Assembly of Ontario. Understanding how political elites frame and debate rights, and to what extent they engage in discussion of reasonable limits on rights, offers another way in which rights frames inform the broader public.

Our findings confirm that, even in the context of a global emergency like the pandemic, rights talk of the absolutist kind exists and, in some contexts, flourishes in Canada. Newspaper coverage usually fails to convey an understanding that there are limits on rights, and even when constitutional rights are discussed, the idea that those rights are subject to reasonable limits analysis often goes unmentioned. Simplistic and absolutist rights talk is especially pervasive online, as our analysis of discourse on Twitter around pandemic measures reveals rights talk in pronounced form, with virtually no acknowledgment of limits or the legitimate need for measures to protect the health and safety of people to combat the pandemic. By contrast, the debate in the Legislative Assembly of Ontario routinely offered a balanced recognition of limits on rights and the policy objectives at stake with respect to pandemic measures. Absolutist rights talk generally emerged from members of the legislature who had been removed from the government caucus for their extreme anti-mandate perspectives. At the elite level of elected representatives, then, we find a potential disciplining effect on members' statements around the pandemic, as the government had implemented measures (sometimes partially, with some resistance) that were supported (pushed for) by the opposition parties. This dynamic mitigated the overall extent to which rights were invoked in debate on the assembly floor. Overall, our findings generally confirm the arguments of scholars who warn about the likelihood that rights talk is prevalent in Canada.

Approach to Examining Rights Talk within News Media

To investigate how pandemic restrictions were discussed in Canadian newspaper coverage, a content analysis was conducted on two English-speaking newspapers: the *Globe and Mail* and *National Post.* These two newspapers were selected as they are, nominally, the two national newspapers in Canada. While this selection does not provide for robust regional comparison, previous studies have relied on analyses limited to these two newspapers to provide a general snapshot of how media coverage operates.[13]

The data from the *Globe and Mail* and *National Post* were collected using the database Canadian Newsstream. Specific keywords were used such as "COVID" and "Coronavirus" to search for articles and then each article was reviewed and collected based on whether it discussed a COVID-19 public health mandate in Canada and made a reference to rights.

In total, 74 articles were collected and examined based on their coverage of rights and the discussion of six COVID-19 pandemic health measures: mandatory wearing of masks, social distancing, quarantining, travel restrictions, lockdowns, and vaccine mandates. The articles were collected between the timeframe of June 2021 to October 2021, as by this point of the pandemic all six measures had been implemented and enforced throughout the country. The dataset was comprised of 49 (66.2%) news articles and 25 (33.8%) editorials/op-eds.

Analysis and Results of News Media

Our analysis is divided into three categories. The first is how and to what level of detail rights were discussed in relation to pandemic health measures. The nature of how rights were discussed is examined along three codes: a specific reference to a right, a close reference to a right, or a broad discussion of a right. A newspaper article was coded as a specific discussion of rights when the user referenced a section or the exact name of the right within the Charter. An article was coded as a close reference to a right when the author did not state a specific right but rather a similar variation. For example, "freedom of speech" is considered a close reference as the specific right is "freedom of expression." Lastly, a newspaper article was coded as a broad discussion of rights when the author discussed rights in a general or far-reaching manner.

The second category investigates the tone surrounding the discussion of rights in order to determine whether or not the discussion was implying or explicitly stating a rights violation in relation to pandemic health measures. Three codes were created: a positive discussion of the rights implications at stake, a negative discussion of the rights implications at stake, or a neutral discussion. A positive discussion occurred when the author stated that rights were either protected or not violated by the measures or quoted sources that made such arguments. A newspaper article was coded as a negative discussion if the author stated that their right had been violated/infringed, if they used language that insinuated the idea that their rights had been violated (i.e., discussion of tyranny, Nazi Germany, discrimination, segregation, etc.), or if they only quoted individuals that made such arguments. The discussion of rights was coded as neutral when the author did not make a statement regarding whether a right had been infringed or if the author had included a balanced discussion of the topic containing both sides of the argument. For example, an article in this category contained quotes discussing both how the public health measures did violate their rights and did not violate their rights.

The third category investigates the types of limitations discussed in relation to the pandemic health restrictions. This was a particularly important category as it seeks to determine whether Glendon's view of Canada's discussion of rights differs from America's due to our inclusion of these limitations within the Charter or if the results are similar to Macfarlane's findings of absolutist rights talk. The discussion of limitations was coded in three ways: the reasonable limits clause (section 1), the notwithstanding clause (section 33), or a broad discussion of limits. An article was coded as discussing the reasonable limits clause or the notwithstanding clause if it mentioned its specific name or the relevant section of the Charter. An article was coded as a broad discussion of limits when the article stated that rights were not absolute or discussed the fact that rights have limits, without specifically mentioning section 1 or section 33.

The results show that only a small percentage of newspaper articles discussed a specific right when referring to pandemic health measures. Specifically, out of the 74 articles, only 11 (14.9 per cent) contained a specific discussion of rights. An example of a specific discussion of rights would be (emphasis added):

> One reason for this hesitancy is the worry that a mandatory vaccination requirement might violate *Section 7 of the Canadian Charter of Rights and Freedoms*.[14]

Eighteen articles (24.3 per cent) contained a close reference to a right. A few examples of rights that were considered a close reference include freedom of choice, privacy rights, and hate speech. Lastly, the results show that a strong majority of newspaper articles discussed rights in a broad manner, with 45 newspaper articles (60.8 per cent). The following is an example that would be considered a broad discussion (emphasis added):

> Premier Jason Kenney doesn't believe in mandates, presumably because they are an *infringement on people's civil rights*.[15]

The tone surrounding the discussion of rights throughout the newspaper articles was fairly even in its distribution regarding the newspaper articles that discussed rights implications positively, negatively, or in a neutral manner. Specifically, 24 articles (32.5 per cent) discussed rights implications positively, 19 (25.7 per cent) discussed rights implications negatively, and 30 (40.5 per cent) discussed rights implications in a neutral manner. One newspaper article was coded as "other" as the discussion around rights was complex and difficult to code.[16]

An example of a positive discussion of rights would be:

> When I hear leaders say they don't want to interfere with "rights" by imposing vaccine mandates, I am genuinely confused. Civil liberties fundamentalists – and I count myself as one – can distinguish between the state bursting into their homes and the state drawing lines to protect everyone else.[17]

An example of a newspaper article containing a negative discussion of rights would be:

> As a result, the vaccine passports in Canada, as they currently exist, are discriminatory and likely violate Canadians' charter right not to be discriminated against on the basis of a disability.[18]

The idea that limitations can be placed on rights were discussed in just under one-third of articles (32.4 per cent or 24 articles). Of the articles that mentioned limitations of rights, there were 17 articles (50 per cent) that contained a broad discussion of limits on rights, 7 articles (20.6 per cent) that mentioned the reasonable limits clause (section 1), and one article (1.4 per cent) that discussed the notwithstanding clause (section 33). It should be noted that one article discussed section 1 and section 33, and was therefore coded under both, which is why there are 24 articles that discussed limitations, but 25 total mentions.

These findings reflect the conclusions made by other scholars that suggest rights talk in Canada often fails to acknowledge that limits can be reasonably placed on rights. Even when compared to earlier findings made by Macfarlane, this study suggests that while discussing pandemic restrictions, Canadian newspapers made note of the limits on rights less frequently. For example, Macfarlane found that 25.2 per cent of articles mentioned the notwithstanding clause, with only 18 per cent of articles actually discussing the potential use of it, whereas within this study only one newspaper article (1.4 per cent) discussed the notwithstanding clause. Both studies had similar results regarding the newspapers discussion of the reasonable limits clause and an acknowledgment of the general limitation on rights.

This is concerning as scholars have stressed that failing to acknowledge such limits can result in Canadians having an inaccurate view of their rights and what they entail. By not recognizing the reasonable limits clause, it enforces the idea that rights are absolute within Canada and override all policy initiatives, values, and considerations. This view of rights prevents negotiation and compromise from taking place within social justice or, in this case, health issues and can make it difficult for politicians to gain support on legislative policies that may be subject to rights-based claims.

Approach to Examining Rights Talk within Social Media

To investigate how pandemic restrictions were discussed by Canadians on social media, a content analysis was conducted of posts on Twitter. Twitter was selected for this study as it is a commonly used forum in Canada that has a diverse group of users. It was selected over other social media platforms as Twitter's primary purpose is to allow for its users to share their thoughts with a large audience.[19]

In order to find tweets that are related to rights talk and COVID-19 pandemic measures, five hashtags related to the health measures were selected (#nomorelockdowns, #vaccinemandate, #novaccinepassportsanywhere, #wearelivingalie, #nomaskmandate) and paired with search terms of Canadian locations that ranged from Canada to a specific province, such as Ontario or Alberta. These hashtags were selected as they were the most commonly used hashtags for discussing pandemic health mandates and rights. Other general hashtags, such as #COVID19, were mainly spent posting about the number of cases that were being reported on a given day and were therefore not relevant to this study. Although four of the hashtags are highly negative in tone, when compared to the results from the one neutral hashtag (#vaccinemandate), the tweets collected produced similar results.

The advanced search engine tool was used in order to include tweets posted between June 2021 until October 2021 and included tweets that contained links and replies. Tweets were collected that were posted within these specified dates, discussed a COVID-19 public health measure in Canada, and made a reference to either of specific right or rights in general. If the user of the tweet did not specifically state Canada or a Canadian location, their tweet was only collected if their account stated they were Canadian or if they had a Canadian flag or a maple leaf emoji within their biography/username. Tweets were collected from individuals, except those with verified Twitter accounts or those with bios that identified them as a health official, journalist, politician, or lawyer. A public health measure included the mandatory wearing of masks, social distancing, quarantining, travel restrictions, lockdowns, and vaccine passports/proof of vaccination. All tweets that fit into this category were collected, which created a dataset of 300 tweets.

It should be acknowledged that the advanced search engine tool did not take into account spelling errors, which could have prevented the collection of relevant tweets that contained such errors. In addition, the search tool did not allow for users to filter for location, which meant that tweets were only collected if the author specified the location they were tweeting about, which could have prevented applicable tweets form being collected. It could have also resulted in the collection of tweets which discussed Canada but where the author was not actually from Canada.

Analysis and Results of Twitter

Similar to the analysis of newspapers, the analysis of the discussion of rights on Twitter was divided into three categories: the nature of how rights were discussed, the tone surrounding the discussion of rights, and the types of limitations discussed within the tweets. Each category had the same codes as were used within the newspaper analysis.

The results from Twitter reveal that only two tweets (0.6 per cent) referenced a specific section of the Charter. This suggests that a high percentage of Canadians using Twitter did not discuss specific rights or what they entailed (including limits on those rights), and how these specific rights related to public health restrictions.

There was a slight increase in the number of tweets containing a close reference to a right, with 17 tweets (5.7 per cent) fitting into this category. The rights that were stated in order to fit into this category included freedom of choice, Indigenous rights, privacy right, and hate speech. The vast majority of tweets analyzed contained a broad discussion of rights, with it occurring in 281 tweets (93.7 per cent). The following is an example that would be considered a broad discussion (emphasis added):

> My irony meter is going off the charts! The Canadian Museum for Human Rights is *discriminating* against the unvaccinated & *violating rights*, but then proceeds to lecture attendees on global human rights #NoVaccinePassportsAnywhere. (@iJacap99)[20]

Tweets that discussed the public health mandates as being a form of discrimination or segregation were also included in this category as it insinuated a form of rights violation, without making reference to a specific constitutional right. Additionally, tweets containing the phrase "my body my choice" were included as users were applying the rights-based phrase for abortion rights to the discussion of vaccine mandates. The high percentage of tweets containing such a broad discussion supports the idea that the majority of Canadian users on Twitter did not discuss specific rights or what they entailed. This trend confirms the arguments of both Glendon and Macfarlane, which found that American and Canadian users were more likely to frame important issues in a simplistic manner and to discuss them in terms of rights, a trend that appears to be replicated in the discussion of public health measures on Twitter.

A significant majority of tweets, 255 out of 300 (85 per cent), discussed the rights implications in a negative tone, whereas, there were very few tweets that discussed the rights implications positively or in a neutral manner. The highly negative tone of the tweets are not surprising given the nature of the hashtags used, however, as stated previously, the one neutral hashtag (#vaccinemandate) produced very similar results. The following is an example that would be considered a negative discussion of rights:

> My grandfather fought for FREEDOM and I will also whether it's foreign or Domestic!! STAND UP for your RIGHTS #CANADIANS, WE will not let a HITLER take CANADA! #NoVaccinePassportsAnywhere Vote for @ppc_stpauls. (@jjh04)[21]

Less than one-sixth of the tweets (14 per cent or $n = 42$ tweets) discussed rights in a neutral manner. A number of tweets that were coded as neutral would simply hashtag the words "freedom" or "liberty" but would not expand further. For example:

> With the #election being called tomorrow. We need to blow up social with #PPC from now to election day. Let's get trending! #VotePPC #Peoples-PartyofCanada #MaximeBernier @MaximeBernier #Canada #Freedom #NoMoreLockdowns #NoVaccinePassport. (@theJasonWatts)[22]

Only two tweets (0.6 per cent) discussed rights positively, with an example of this discussion being:

> Let's be clear on one thing: this mandate does not violate the Canadian Charter of Rights and Freedoms. You're mistaking your argument with American politics. We line in Canada. There are actual differences between the 2 countries. #vaccinemandate. (@fromtheheartont)[23]

It should be noted that the two tweets that discussed rights positively contained the neutral hashtag (#vaccinemandate). There was one tweet that was coded as "unclear."[24]

Out of the tweets collected, the limitations that can be placed on rights received no mentions. The results from Twitter demonstrate that the discussion of rights, at least those discussions by opponents of pandemic measures, is much more absolutist and simplistic than compared to newspapers, containing no mention of limitations. This is quite noteworthy as it has been previously discussed by both Glendon and Macfarlane who have stressed that an absolutist view of rights could hinder democratic political discourse and make it difficult for politicians to implement policies.[25] In particular, policies that set boundaries on citizens' rights and freedoms and would likely invoke right-based responses from the public. This poses an issue in Canada's current political environment with regards to the policies related to public health measures, as these measures do limit the rights and freedoms of Canadians in order to ensure the safety of others. It is also worth noting that from a constitutional law perspective, courts will exhibit deference to reasonable COVID-19 mitigation policies because they have been implemented in response to an emergency and policy objectives aimed at protecting the safety and health of citizens will be considered pressing and substantial.[26] Therefore, it is likely that if such measures were to be challenged in a court of law, they would be upheld in a section 1 analysis.

There have been examples of these challenges being upheld since the pandemic began. For example, in September 2020, Kimberly Taylor sued the Newfoundland and Labrador government after she was denied entry into the province following the death of her mother due to the province's travel ban.[27] Taylor argued that the province misused its authority and violated her rights; however, a Supreme Court judge determined that the infringement was justified.[28]

Legislative Debate

We conducted a qualitative analysis of legislative debates in the Ontario Legislative Assembly with a focus on two pandemic measures: mask mandates and vaccine mandates. These protections were implemented during the pandemic in certain contexts (mask mandates in most indoor settings, including schools, and vaccine mandates in hospitals and long-term care facilities, and by many universities and colleges). Both mandates were mostly lifted at the provincial level in the spring of 2022. We also examine members' statements concerning the so-called "Freedom Convoy," a protest against pandemic measures that emerged that same spring during which several border crossings were blockaded (including the Ambassador Bridge linking Windsor, Ontario, to Michigan) and downtown Ottawa was occupied, resulting in the shutting of businesses and major disruption to the lives of nearby residents for a three-week period. We limit our scrutiny to debate from the floor of the legislature as recorded in *Hansard*, but we cover the entire period of the pandemic until the summer recess in May 2022.

The search term "mask mandate(s)" appeared on twelve sitting days from 28 September 2020 to 12 April 2022. The term "vaccine mandate(s)" appeared on twenty-three sitting days from 5 October 2021 to 13 April 2022. Discussion of the "Freedom Convoy"[29] appeared on seventeen sitting days from 22 February 2022 to 13 April 2022. Within these sitting days we then searched for "rights/right to," "freedom," or "Charter" to identify whether any members invoked or discussed rights in relation to these policies or events. We then turned to an analysis of how rights were employed by elected representatives in these contexts.

Findings and Analysis – Legislative Debate

Perhaps the most surprising finding is that rights were only very briefly mentioned in passing, just once, when mask mandates were discussed in the legislature. The NDP Member of Provincial Parliament (MPP) Gilles Bisson made quick reference to the idea that mask mandates were a restriction on civil liberties.[30] In general, debate from the floor focused on criticism by opposition members that the provincial government was slow to implement mask mandates near the beginning of the pandemic and, in the spring of 2022, failed to adhere to evidence and science when it lifted them.[31] Government members defended against both of these critiques, noting that their actions, including mask mandates, helped to curb transmission,[32] and arguing that Ontario was one of the last provinces to lift mask mandates while suggesting lifting mask mandates in schools was "vital to the mental health of children."[33] The government also justified the lifting of the mandate in the spring largely on people's desire to "return to normal."[34]

It is this context that helps to explain why rights were not central to the debate. For the period in which mandates were in place, each of the three major parties generally supported them. It would make little sense for the government to subsequently suggest that mask mandates infringed rights as a reason to lift them in spring of 2022 (as that would suggest they had violated rights). Perhaps more puzzling is why proponents of mask mandates did not cite the rights of people to public health protections in their arguments.

Debate and members' statements in relation to vaccine mandates were more likely to be accompanied by rights talk, with references to rights appearing on eight of the twenty-three days in which vaccine mandates were discussed on the floor of the assembly. As with debates over mask mandates, however, no members from any of the major parties engaged in absolutist rights talk. Two MPPs, Roman Baber and Belinda Karahalios, engaged in absolutist rights talk, but both members had at that point been removed from the governing Progressive Conservative caucus over their opposition to emergency pandemic measures.

As vaccine mandates were implemented in certain sectors like health care, Baber raised the spectre of the "termination of potentially hundreds of thousands of workers" and that this violation of "workers' rights" was forcing them to "decide between their health care and their ability to feed their family" (implying, wrongly, that vaccines were dangerous for their health).[35] By the spring of 2022, Baber referred to vaccine mandates as "one of the greatest injustices in 21st-century Ontario" and "one of the greatest assaults on Canadian democracy and human rights."[36] Here, Baber explicitly invoked the Charter of Rights, even while acknowledging that the Charter allowed rights to be subject to reasonable limits in a free and democratic society.[37] He stated that justifications for vaccine mandates had "proven to be false," citing a study that suggested similar infection rates between the vaccinated and unvaccinated, arguing that mandates "don't do anything except ruin lives and pit Canadians against one another."[38] NDP MPP Peggy Sattler responded that vaccine mandates had consistently been upheld in arbitration and had the backing of the Ontario Human Rights Commission as "generally permissible under the Human Rights Code … as long as protections are put in place to make sure people who are unable to be vaccinated for code-related reasons are reasonably accommodated."[39]

In the same debate, Karahalios argued that "no employer should have the right to fire an employee over the employee's choice not to reveal their vaccine status."[40] On 7 March 2022, Karahalios also introduced a petition decrying vaccine mandates as a violation of the International Covenant on Civil and Political Rights (medical experimentation) and stating that the Charter of Rights exists to protect against "assault, abuse, and intimidation."[41] Karahalios's conclusions, however, are contrary to the general constitutional and statutory rights jurisprudence in Canada.[42]

On one occasion, a particularly extreme form of rights talk was also cited by an MPP as an example of escalating societal anti-Semitism. Jill Andrew noted that a teacher compared "COVID-19 vaccine mandates to the yellow Star of David that Jewish people were forced to wear during the Holocaust."[43]

Overall, vaccine mandates were generally defended, by members of all major parties, as in the interest of public health and the protection of vulnerable people. The government was criticized for not extending vaccine mandates to public schools, something the government defended on the basis that while vaccines would be "voluntary," a testing regime was in place for school employees as added protection. Rich Nicholls, a third MPP removed from the Progressive Conservative Party for his anti-vaccine stance, also criticized mandates but did not invoke rights in doing so.[44]

That the absolutist forms of rights talk emerged only from MPPs on the extreme end of the spectrum and were generally criticized by other members suggests, overall, a healthy appreciation for mask and vaccine mandates as justified and reasonable pandemic measures. Yet, as with mask mandates, other members of the governing caucus who may have opposed vaccine mandates could not publicly suggest they constituted rights violations without fear of potential removal, as Baber, Karahalios, and Nicholls had been for their own opposition to pandemic measures. It is likely, although impossible to know for sure, that the government's willingness to remove dissenters had a chilling effect on the overall debate.

Debate over the "Freedom Convoy" resulted in a more substantive discourse around rights in the assembly. Much of the debate about the convoy saw members condemn the illegal border blockages and occupation of downtown Ottawa, and focused on the economic and trade disruptions that resulted. Some MPPs, like Nicholls, evinced sympathy for the convoy protesters, noting that while the blocking of bridges "was problematic," the protesters were simply "defending individual rights and freedoms."[45]

On 21 March 2022, and in the aftermath of the blockades, the provincial government introduced Bill 100, the *Keeping Ontario Open for Business Act*. The bill established provisions and enforcement mechanisms to protect transportation infrastructure against tactics and impediments like those witnessed during the convoy protests. Much of the discussion of rights surrounding the convoy protests occurred in relation to debate over Bill 100. With respect to the right to protest, the government defended its legislation as "very narrow in scope," noting it will "bear no impact on the right to peaceful, lawful and temporary protest in this province."[46] Attorney General Doug Downey stated, "While we support the right to peaceful and lawful protest, we will never hesitate to protect people's right to work and live freely and safely … The right to make a political statement does not outweigh the rights of citizens in our nation's capital to live peacefully in their own homes."[47] Other governing members reiterated this point,[48] as did members of the opposition,[49] although some raised concerns that the bill needed to be carefully scrutinized "to ensure that that law isn't weaponized in the future."[50]

Premier Doug Ford was criticized for initially supporting the "democratic rights" of the convoy protesters. NDP MPP Catherine Fife noted that many of the protesters were citing their "amendment rights" (i.e., mistakenly citing the US Bill of Rights, and in absolutist terms, instead of the Canadian Charter).[51] Liberal MPP Lucille Collard raised in depth rights concerns about the bill:

> The extraordinary measures that are meant to become permanent raise legitimate apprehensions about civil rights and the necessity to have proper oversight on the exercise of these new powers. Is the government being guided by a clear human rights framework? Did the Solicitor General and the Attorney General get supportive expert legal advice that the limitations being introduced in the bill under freedoms of expression, association and assembly are justified in the interests of national security or public safety?[52]

Despite these concerns, Collard also recognized the pressing problem at stake:

> What happened in Ottawa was opposing two fundamental rights, the right of expression against the right to live peacefully, based on the principle that one person's right ends where the right of another person begins. Not being able to open your business, not being able to go to work, not being able to sleep because of the noise, not being able to go to your local merchant, not being able to leave or stay in your apartment because of the

> intensity of the occupation activities are what drove people to question the ability of our government institutions to protect their rights, to protect them. There seemed to be no leverage, legal or political, to make it stop.[53]

This reflects a nuanced and non-absolutist understanding of the rights issues at stake.

By contrast, and in far more absolutist and simplistic terms, Karahalios described the bill as intended "to silence the Ontario public, to discourage individuals from engaging in the right to protest" and reflecting "the PC Party's disdain for freedom of speech and their love of unnecessary government overreach and draconian powers."[54] Similarly, Nicholls described the bill as "the worst, most tyrannical and draconian piece of legislation to be ever tabled in Canadian history," and a response to a largely peaceful protest that was merely opposing "loss of the freedom and rights of every Canadian and the overreach of governments with their mandates."[55] Bill 100 passed without amendment and received royal assent on 14 April 2022.

Members of the major parties generally invoked rights in a reasonable and balanced manner in relation to the convoy protests and Bill 100. Absolutist rights talk was also evident, but emerged from the more extreme members who had been removed from the PC caucus for their opposition to pandemic measures.

Conclusion

The analysis presented here suggests that rights discourse during the COVID-19 pandemic in Canada varied greatly, depending on the platform in which these discussions took place, as well as who the individual was discussing them. With regard to the legislative debates, members of the major parties generally demonstrated an informed and non-absolutist understanding of rights. The majority of MPs acknowledged the importance of pandemic health measures and the need for limits on such rights in order to guarantee public safety. In this sense, one could assume that Canada's rights talk differed greatly from the American rights talk described by Glendon. However, when looking at other platforms, such as news media and social media, the discussion of rights and the pandemic became less informed, less nuanced, and dramatically more absolutist.

Our analysis shows that news media had a balanced discussion of the pandemic health measures and exposed their readers to a variety of opinions on whether such measures were a violation of their rights. However, a large proportion of the articles discussed rights in a broad and absolutist manner, with only a third of the articles acknowledging the limitations that could be placed on rights. The analysis on social media demonstrated an even more concerning discussion of rights and pandemic health measures, at least from those opposed to such measures. The vast majority of users discussed their rights in an uninformed and absolutist manner. Although the results from Twitter were comprised of a small but vocal portion of the population, this form of discourse may have had a damaging impact. For example, it is likely that such extremist opinions online instigated the "Freedom Convoy," which resulted in weeks of illegal and excessively disruptive behaviour.

Overall, the analysis suggests that through the pandemic, although most elective representatives invoked rights in a relatively thoughtful and non-absolutist manner, news media and social media platforms continued to reinforce the idea that rights were absolute. This corresponds with the conclusions made by past scholars in that Canada does not have an especially distinct rights talk from the United States. This creates numerous political challenges, such as encouraging in citizens an uncompromising understanding of the relationship between public policy and rights. That this dynamic was evident even with respect to measures designed to deal with a global public health emergency is particularly revealing of the dangers this form of rights talk can present.

NOTES

1 Peter H. Russell, "Canadian Constraints on Judicialization from Without," *International Political Science Review* 15, no. 2 (1994): 165–75; Alan C. Cairns, *Charter versus Federalism: The Dilemmas of Constitutional Reform* (Montreal: McGill-Queen's University Press, 1992), 4.

2 Mary Ann Glendon, *Rights Talk: The Impoverishment of Political Discourse.* (New York: The Free Press, 1991), 3–4.

3 Ibid., 16.

4 Ibid., 44–5.

5 Ibid., 167.

6 Emmett Macfarlane, "Terms of Entitlement: Is there a Distinctly Canadian 'Rights Talk'?" *Canadian Journal of Political Science* 41, no. 2 (2008): 303–28.

7 Ibid., 324.

8 Ibid., 325.

9 Janet Hiebert, "Rights and Public Debate: The Limitations of a 'Rights Must be Paramount' Perspective," *International Journal of Canadian Studies* 7–8 (1997): 118.

10 Anthony A. Peacock, "Strange Brew: Tocqueville, Rights, and the Technology of Equality," *Rethinking the Constitution: Perspectives on Canadian Constitutional Reform, Interpretation, and Theory*, ed. Anthony A. Peacock (Toronto: Oxford University Press, 1996); Jeffrey Simpson, "Rights Talk: The Effect of the Charter on Canadian Political Discourse," *Protecting Rights and Freedoms: Essays on the Charter's Place in Canada's Political, Legal, and Intellectual Life*, ed. Philip Bryden, Steven Davis, and Peter Russell (Toronto: University of Toronto Press, 1994); Rainer Knopff, "Populism and the Politics of Rights: The Dual Attack on Representative Democracy," *Canadian Journal of Political Science* 31, no. 4 (1998): 683–705.

11 Harold J. Jansen et al., "Democratic Citizenship: How Do Canadians Engage with Politics Online?," *Digital Politics in Canada: Promises and Realities*, ed. Tamara Small and Harold J. Jansen (Toronto: University of Toronto Press, 2020), 188.

12 Anuppiriya Sriskandarajah, "Race, Space, and Media: The Production of Urban Neighbourhood Space in East-End Toronto," *Canadian Ethnic Studies* 52, no. 1 (2020): 8.

13 Linda Trimble and Shannon Sampert, "Who's in the Game? The Framing of the Canadian Election 2000 by the *Globe and Mail* and the *National Post*," *Canadian Journal of Political Science* 37, no. 1 (2004): 51–71; Macfarlane, "Terms of Entitlement."

14 Samuel E. Trosow and Julie Lowe, "Canadian Colleges and Universities Can Mandate COVID-19 Vaccination without Violating Charter Rights," *National Post*, 26 August 2021, https://nationalpost.com/pmn/news-pmn/canadian-colleges-and-universities-can-mandate-covid-19-vaccination-without-violating-charter-rights.

15 Gary Mason, "An Angry Public Is Forcing Timid Governments to Get Tough with Vaccine Resisters," *Globe and Mail*, 26 August 2021, https://www.theglobeandmail.com/opinion/article-an-angry-public-is-forcing-timid-governments-to-get-tough-with-vaccine/.

16 Paula Larsson, "The Inherent Racism of Anti-Vaxx Movements," *National Post*, 16 July 2021, https://nationalpost.com/pmn/news-pmn/the-inherent-racism-of-anti-vaxx-movements. The main discussion throughout the article was regarding how anti-vaxxers claimed their rights were being violated, however, they ignored the fact that the same freedoms were absent within low-income and racialized communities. As the rights discussion was complex and went beyond the discussion of public health mandates, the researcher found it difficult to code the tone surrounding the discussion of rights.

17 Frank Addario, "If the COVID-19 Pandemic Isn't an Emergency Demanding Real Leadership, What Is?," *Globe and Mail*, 8 September 2021, https://www.theglobeandmail.com/opinion/article-if-the-covid-19-pandemic-isnt-an-emergency-demanding-real-leadership/.

18 Christine Van Geyn, "Vaccine Passports Are an Unnecessary Infringement on Civil Liberties," *National Post*, 19 July 2021, https://nationalpost.com/opinion/christine-van-geyn-vaccine-passports-are-an-unnecessary-infringement-on-civil-liberties.
19 Megan A. Moreno et al., "Evaluating College Students' Displayed Alcohol References on Facebook and Twitter," *Journal of Adolescent Health* 58, no. 5 (2016): 528.
20 Jack H. (@iJacap99), "My irony meter is going off the charts!," Twitter, 16 July 2021, 11:29 PM, https://twitter.com/iJacap99/status/1416238623138238470?s=20.
21 Jack Hibbs (@jjh04), "My grandfather fought for FREEDOM," Twitter, 22 Aug 2021, 9:45 PM, https://twitter.com/jjh04/status/1429620839624839175?s=20.
22 Jason Watts (@theJasonWatts), "With the #election being called tomorrow," Twitter, 15 Aug 2021, 10:29 AM, https://twitter.com/theJasonWatts/status/1426914018455851019?s=20.
23 Rachel Concannon (@fromtheheartont), "Let's be clear on one thing," Twitter, 5 Sep 2021, 12:10 PM, https://web.archive.org/web/20210905191227/https://twitter.com/fromtheheartont/status/1434594759436378118.
24 Cyrus G., (@KingCyrus530) "Because Ontario is a bastion of freedom..#NoMoreLockdowns," Twitter, 14 July 2021, 7:50 AM, https://twitter.com/KingCyrus530/status/1415277540130893825?s=20.
25 Glendon, *Rights Talk*, 14; Macfarlane, "Terms of Entitlement," 325.
26 Emmett Macfarlane, "Public Policy and Constitutional Rights in Times of Crisis," *Canadian Journal of Political Science* 53, no. 2 (2020): 299–303.
27 Nicole Bogart, "Do Vaccine Mandates Violate Canadians' Charter Rights?" *CTV News*, 1 Spetmeber 2021; last updated 2 February 2022, https://www.ctvnews.ca/health/coronavirus/do-vaccine-mandates-violate-canadians-%20charter-rights-1.5569971.
28 Ibid.
29 Using search terms "convoy" or "blockade."
30 Legislative Assembly of Ontario, *Hansard*, 42nd Parl., 2nd Sess., No. 21, 22 November 2021, 1430 (Gilles Bison), https://www.ola.org/en/legislative-business/house-documents/parliament-42/session-2/2021-11-22/hansard.
31 See, for example, Legislative Assembly of Ontario, *Hansard*, 42nd Parl., 1st Sess., No. 267B, 20 May 2021, 1725 (Jessica Bell), https://www.ola.org/en/legislative-business/house-documents/parliament-42/session-1/2021-05-20/hansard-1; Legislative Assembly of Ontario, *Hansard*, 42nd Parl., 2nd Sess., No. 42A, 9 March 2022, 1035 (Andrea Horwath), https://www.ola.org/en/legislative-business/house-documents/parliament-42/session-2/2022-03-09/hansard.

32 Legislative Assembly of Ontario, *Hansard*, 42nd Parl., 2nd Sess., No. 21, 22 November 2022, 1530 (Rudy Cuzzetto), https://www.ola.org/en/legislative-business/house-documents/parliament-42/session-2/2021-11-22/hansard.
33 Legislative Assembly of Ontario, *Hansard*, 42nd Parl., 2nd Sess., No. 43A, 10 March 2022, 1030 (Stephen Lecce), https://www.ola.org/en/legislative-business/house-documents/parliament-42/session-2/2022-03-10/hansard.
34 Legislative Assembly of Ontario, *Hansard*, 42nd Parl., 2nd Sess., No. 49B, 29 March 2022, 1750 (Robin Martin), https://www.ola.org/en/legislative-business/house-documents/parliament-42/session-2/2022-03-29/hansard-1.
35 Legislative Assembly of Ontario, *Hansard*, 42nd Parl., 2nd Sess., No. 2, 5 October 2021, 1110 (Roman Baber), https://www.ola.org/en/legislative-business/house-documents/parliament-42/session-2/2021-10-05/hansard.
36 Legislative Assembly of Ontario, *Hansard*, 42nd Parl., 2nd Sess., No. 39B, 3 March 2022, 1800 (Roman Baber), https://www.ola.org/en/legislative-business/house-documents/parliament-42/session-2/2022-03-03/hansard-1.
37 Ibid.
38 Ibid.
39 Ibid., 1820. The validity of vaccine mandates as reasonable limits on rights and respecting the Human Rights Code was also noted on another occasions by other members. See, for example, Legislative Assembly of Ontario, *Hansard*, 42nd Parl., 2nd Sess., No. 4A, 7 October 2021, 1130 (John Fraser), https://www.ola.org/en/legislative-business/house-documents/parliament-42/session-2/2021-10-07/hansard.
40 Ibid.
41 Legislative Assembly of Ontario, *Hansard*, 42nd Parl., 2nd Sess., No. 40, 7 March 2022 1310 (Belinda Karahalios), https://www.ola.org/en/legislative-business/house-documents/parliament-42/session-2/2022-03-07/hansard.
42 Macfarlane, "Public Policy and Constitutional Rights in Times of Crisis."
43 Legislative Assembly of Ontario, *Hansard*, 42nd Parl., 2nd Sess., No. 35A, 24 February 2022 1110 (Jill Andrew), https://www.ola.org/en/legislative-business/house-documents/parliament-42/session-2/2022-02-24/hansard.
44 See, for example, Legislative Assembly of Ontario, *Hansard*, 42nd Parl., 2nd Sess., No. 55A, 7 April 2022, 1100 (Rich Nicholls), https://www.ola.org/en/legislative-business/house-documents/parliament-42/session-2/2022-04-07/hansard.

45 Legislative Assembly of Ontario, *Hansard*, 42nd Parl., 2nd Sess., No. 35A, 24 February 2022 1020 (Rich Nicholls), https://www.ola.org/en/legislative-business/house-documents/parliament-42/session-2/2022-02-24/hansard.

46 Legislative Assembly of Ontario, *Hansard*, 42nd Parl., 2nd Sess., No. 47A, 24 March 2022 1350 (Doug Downey), https://www.ola.org/en/legislative-business/house-documents/parliament-42/session-2/2022-03-24/hansard.

47 Ibid.

48 Ibid., *Hansard,* 1340 (Sylvia Jones), 1410 (Vijay Thanigasalm).

49 Ibid., *Hansard,* 1440 (Lisa Gretzky).

50 Ibid., *Hansard,* 1730 (John Vanthof).

51 Legislative Assembly of Ontario, *Hansard*, 42nd Parl., 2nd Sess., No. 48, 28 March 2022, 1340 (Catherine Fife), https://www.ola.org/en/legislative-business/house-documents/parliament-42/session-2/2022-03-28/hansard.

52 Ibid., 1410 (Lucille Collard).

53 Ibid.

54 Ibid., 1610, 1620 (Belinda Karahalios).

55 Legislative Assembly of Ontario, *Hansard*, 42nd Parl., 2nd Sess., No. 58B, 13 April 2022, 1930 and 1940 (Rich Nicholls), https://www.ola.org/en/legislative-business/house-documents/parliament-42/session-2/2022-04-13/hansard-1.

8 The Political Changes and Challenges to Third Party Election Advertising in Canada

ANDREA LAWLOR AND ERIN CRANDALL

On 8 June 2021, the Ontario Superior Court of Justice ruled that provisions of the province's *Election Finances Act* were unconstitutional.[1] The challenged provisions had been introduced earlier that year by the Progressive Conservative Government of Premier Doug Ford who, just days after the court's decision, responded by using the notwithstanding clause to re-enact the same legislation. It was the first time in Ontario's history that the clause had been implemented, igniting political shockwaves throughout the province. Contained in section 33 of the Canadian Charter of Rights and Freedoms, the clause lets Canadian legislatures pass an act that expressly operates notwithstanding the rights provided under section 2 or sections 7 to 15 of the Charter for five years (renewable). Use of the notwithstanding clause is almost always controversial and thus unlikely to be used unless to meet an important political objective.[2] The issue at play for Premier Ford, the regulation of third party election advertising, fits this general rule. In fact, the title of the bill that invoked the notwithstanding clause seemingly illustrates its importance for the government, titled no less dramatically than "Protecting Elections and Defending Democracy Act" (Bill 307).

Why were third parties important enough that the Ford government was willing to accept the public criticism that goes along with using section 33? Third parties are any person or entity, other than a political candidate, registered political party, or constituency association, who participate in elections, which in practice captures a wide range of political actors (e.g., unions, corporations, interest groups, and individuals). For critics, Premier Ford's actions were a brazen move to muzzle the government's harshest critics, particularly teachers' unions, by limiting the amount of money these groups could spend on political advertising. By contrast, the Ford government insisted that it was seeking to uphold the integrity of Ontario's democracy by ensuring that special interests with deep pockets did not unduly influence voters. But were Ontario elections and democracy really at risk as Bill 307's title suggests? And if they were, who was the source of this risk – the Progressive Conservative government or the well-financed third parties that Bill 307 is said to target? The answer is not necessarily straightforward.

The Ontario government's use of the notwithstanding clause is the latest, but by no means the first, time that a Canadian government has faced political controversy around how third party advertising should be regulated. In fact, the fraught question of how to regulate money in elections has spurred numerous political debates, legislative reforms, court challenges, and even a royal commission (for an analysis of third party spending at the federal level, see Small, this volume).[3] We take this question up in this chapter by using the Ontario government's regulatory decision-making in 2021 as an example of how ideological public policy making can run contrary to expectations given the empirical realities of the policy environment. To do so, we analyze recent third party spending in Ontario and federal elections, as well as the Ford government's approach to third party regulations. This provides us with an opportunity to not only see how this debate has played out in its latest iteration but also consider the evolution of election spending regulations in Canada. We use this case study to reflect on another critical moment for the regulation of third parties that occurred over thirty years ago, the 1988 federal election and the ensuing Royal Commission on Electoral Reform and Party Financing (1991). The recommendations issued by the royal commission informed the third party regulations implemented federally, and later provincially, that carry on today. Returning to the royal commission's reports illustrates how the challenges and debates around third party election advertising have remained constant, though the partisan motivations that may trigger regulatory reform have changed over time.

The 1988 Federal Election, the Royal Commission on Electoral Reform and Party Financing, and the Egalitarian Model of Political Finance

The federal election of 1988 stands out for at least two reasons. First, it focused almost exclusively on one policy issue: free trade with the United States, with the Progressive Conservative Party supporting free trade, and the Liberal and New Democratic parties opposed. Second, the election saw significant participation by third parties who spent more than $4.7 million on advertising advocating for or against free trade.[4] Notably, this spending was not distributed evenly between the two sides of the debate, with free trade supporters spending roughly four times more than third parties opposing free trade.[5] To put this spending in context, third parties spent about 40 per cent of the amount that the three main political parties spent on advertising.[6] As the only political party supporting free trade, the Progressive Conservative Party was seen as the clear beneficiary of this third party advertising, a perception that was further solidified with the party's decisive election victory. This connection between money spent and electoral success, in turn, raised questions around whether high spending by third parties had undermined the principles of fairness and equity that were seen as fundamental to Canada's electoral system.

In the midst of this election controversy, the Royal Commission on Electoral Reform and Party Financing was formed to assess whether existing election regulations required reform. While the royal commission's 1991 report is now over thirty years old,[7] its recommendations remain influential both in terms of the federal and provincial electoral regulations that operate today, as well as informing ongoing debates, like those recently seen in Ontario.[8]

To understand the task laid before the royal commission or, for that matter, any actor asked to consider the regulation of election financing, it is helpful to acknowledge the fundamental trade-offs to political participation that are at play. At the heart of all election spending regulations is a tension between free expression and fair participation. On the one hand, there is no question that all citizens in a democracy must be able to freely express their political views, with election campaigns being an especially critical time for this right to be exercised and protected. On the other hand, there is the practical reality that many forms of political expression, particularly advertising, are not free in terms of their monetary cost and that those with more money have enhanced opportunities to play an influential role in election campaigns.[9] The question that every democracy must address is how to reasonably balance these two tenants of fair elections in electoral regulations. At the extremes, we are presented with two very different scenarios. In one, where free expression is prioritized, elections will have few, if any, spending limits placed on candidates, parties, and third parties. On the other end, where fair participation is prioritized by placing strict spending limits on all participants, such measures help to ensure that no single voice can overawe others. In Canada, these two approaches are generally termed the libertarian and egalitarian models of election finance.[10] While neither approach is necessarily designed to favour one political ideology over another, it is also fair to acknowledge that the libertarian approach endorses conservative free-market principles, while the egalitarian approach prioritizes social democratic views of equality.

The royal commission's recommendations came out clearly on the side of the egalitarian model, advocating for strict third party spending limits in order to promote electoral fairness.[11] For the 1988 federal election, spending limits were in place for political parties and candidates, but not third parties. A starting point for the financial regulatory regime proposed by the commission was that political parties are the chief participants in elections, and moreover that there should be relative equity among parties and candidates, hence the use of campaign spending limits.[12]

The commission's principal study on third party spending, written by Janet Hiebert,[13] provides additional insights into the conception of a fair election process that informed the commission's recommendations. According to Hiebert, "It is difficult to conceive how the integrity of spending limits for candidates and parties can be preserved if interest groups are permitted to incur significant expenses to promote or oppose registered participants."[14] Third party spending is especially challenging in this regard given that it cannot be assumed that third party advertising will have a similar effect for each political party. The 1988 election is illustrative of this. In her study, Hiebert considers the four basic approaches available for regulating (or not) third parties, including (1) implementing no spending limits, (2) placing limits comparable to those on parties and candidates, (3) placing limits on interest groups consistent with their role as secondary participants, and, finally, (4) a total ban on all expenses during elections.[15] While noting that the most effective way of ensuring the integrity of spending limits for candidates and parties would be a ban on third party spending, Hiebert's conclusions, like those of the royal commission's final report, come down in favour of modest spending limits for third parties that would preclude the ability to run significant advertising during elections and thus preserve political parties and candidates as the chief participants in elections.

In Canada, any law that limits freedom of expression and democratic participation by placing a cap on election advertising raises the question of whether it can withstand a challenge under the Charter of Rights and Freedoms. Indeed the $1,000 third party spending limit that was implemented by the federal government following the recommendations of the royal commission was successfully challenged by an interest group before the Alberta Court of Appeal.[16] Writing in 1991, it was unclear to Hiebert whether modest third party spending limits would be upheld by the courts. However, in anticipation of a Charter challenge, she noted a constitutional remedy to uphold the royal commission's recommendation of modest third party spending limits – the Charter's notwithstanding clause (section 33).[17] While not taken up by the federal government in 1996 when these limits were initially struck down, it is interesting to observe that this option was eventually followed by another government several decades later – the Ford government of Ontario in 2021.

At first blush, Ontario Premier Doug Ford would not appear to be the standard bearer for the egalitarian model of election finance. After all, the political right is generally associated with favouring limited regulations around election contributions and spending, which is consistent with the libertarian approach. Moreover, the federal election best known for the alleged influence of big money was the 1988 free trade election, which was seen to benefit the Progressive Conservative Party over its rivals. But as correctly observed by Hiebert, "[n]o political party is immune from the effects of interest groups trying to influence the election agenda,"[18] and while the Progressive Conservative Party benefited from third party advertising in the 1988 election, there is no reason to presume that such an advantage is innate. This highlights the fundamental challenge of partisanship and political self-interest at play with the regulation of election finance. Put simply, the elected officials in charge of passing these regulations are the same ones who stand to potentially gain political advantages from the regulations themselves.[19] Thus, considering the types of third parties that are active in an election campaign can help us to understand why a particular political party in government may prefer one set of election regulations over another.

Put a different way, two things can be true simultaneously: (1) the egalitarian model of election finance can promote fair participation in elections by making sure that well-financed groups and individuals do not overawe the voices of others, and (2) by making sure that well-financed groups and individuals cannot overawe the voices of others, a party in government may be able to dampen the voices of its critics. To better understand how this has played out in Canada, we now turn to an analysis of federal and provincial third party regulations, with a particular emphasis on the recent policy changes that took place in Ontario. As these changes were the impetus for the Ford government's use of the notwithstanding clause in 2021, we give particular attention to the context surrounding these policy changes in Ontario and their potential effects on the application of the egalitarian model.

The Changing Landscape of Third Party Advertising

The past twenty years of federal elections have illustrated that third parties are a heterogeneous group of political actors that include individuals acting independently or within small community groups to large-scale, highly professionalized interest groups and associations with considerable budgets and resources. While the goals of third parties are not always clearly stated, they can vary widely, including the direct support or challenge of candidates to increasing issue salience around a policy issue.[20] Some third parties are ideologically defined, others not. The level of effort and money raised and spent also varies widely, resulting in the conclusion that there is no "typical" third party. Still, third parties are generally characterized as one of four types of actors: (1) individuals (or small groups of individuals operating independent of a larger interest); (2) business or corporate entities; (3) trade unions; (4) interest groups (with long-standing institutional structures or those that are struck solely for the purpose of one election campaign).

Federal third parties operate under the egalitarian model broadly speaking; however, there are a clear set of regulations stemming from the *Canada Elections Act* (the CEA) and more recently the *Elections Modernization Act* of 2018. Since 2006,[21] corporations, unions, and interest groups have been banned from making contributions to political parties; therefore, participating as a third party remains the only way for these organizations to participate formally in election campaigns. The *Elections Modernization Act* further updated the CEA to break down the regulated period for third parties into two distinct sections: the campaign period (the traditional period from the writ-drop) and the newly legislated pre-writ period[22] constituting the four months prior to the writ being issued, which begins on 30 June of a year in which there is an election held on a fixed date.[23]

The specific rules to be followed by third parties are available in Elections Canada's *Political Financing Handbook for Third Parties*.[24] While the original version of the CEA (2000) limited third party spending to $150,000 nationally, with no more than $3,000 spent in any electoral riding to promote or oppose a candidate, the rates have been indexed for inflation, and as of writing, assuming a fixed-date election, the third party spending limit in the pre-writ period is set at $1,023,400 with a maximum of $10,234 allowed in a given constituency. In the federal election campaign of 2021, third parties were able spend a total of $525,700, with no more than $4,506 in a constituency. By contrast, the CEA imposes a limit on partisan advertising expenses of registered parties for the pre-election period of a fixed-date election of $2,046,800. During the 2019 campaign, parties who ran a full slate of candidates could spend a total of $29,060,308.97.

Following the passage of the 2018 *Elections Modernization Act*, third party reports require a breakdown of funds spent along three lines.

Advertising (referred to as "partisan advertising" in the pre-election period and "election advertising" in the election period) includes express promotion or opposition to a political entity in the pre-writ period but also includes implied promotion or opposition through taking a position on an election issue to which a party or candidate is associated in the election period. Partisan activities are also regulated and include those activities, other than advertising, that directly promote or oppose a political party or candidate. Finally, money spent on election surveys is also subject to regulation and required for reporting.

The introduction of the pre-writ period was not without contestation. It represented a way in which parties, who may act in a self-interested fashion,[25] could limit the influence of non-party actors in the lead up to the campaign, effectively neutralizing attempts to influence voters' attitudes in the moments before the official campaign began. It was, in part, a response to the movement towards a "permanent campaign,"[26] where the constant up-to-the-moment availability of polling and media to citizens can provide campaign-style information in the inter-election period. However, it was also a response to the recognition that third parties can (and did) view this window as a last-minute political opportunity to influence the campaign dialogue. The federal government was not the only government to see this potential advantage. In 2016, the Ontario government introduced Bill 201, which instituted a $600,000 limit on political advertising during the six-month period immediately before the issue of a writ for a general election. The limit was lower than the federal regulation, yet the time covered by the regulation was two months longer, further restricting third parties' participation, prompting some conversation about whether the law went too far in regulating political activity.[27]

The *Canada Elections Act* requires third parties to act independently of political parties and candidates. To do otherwise would count as collusion, which is prohibited by the CEA. The CEA also includes provisions to prohibit circumvention of the rules (section 349), and the use of foreign funds for election advertising and survey activities. These activities come with strict administrative monetary penalties. Embedded within these sections reflects the earlier-mentioned principle: third parties are not primary actors within elections, and thus, should operate in a more restricted fashion than political parties and candidates. Importantly, there are no restrictions on the number of third parties that can participate in an election campaign. To do so would dramatically stifle both free speech and democratic deliberation in the election context.

Table 8.1. Third Parties by Actor Classification in Federal Elections (2004–2021)

Third Party Classification	2004	2006	2008	2011	2015	2019	2021
Individuals	15	27	16	8	9	7	5
Corporations	3	5	1	0	2	6	1
Unions	8	10	16	12	26	21	12
Interest Groups	21	24	24	31	69	88	73
Professional Associations	7	4	5	5	11	20	19
Charities	0	0	2	1	2	2	1
Total TPAs*	**47**	**66**	**57**	**51**	**106**	**122**	**91**

*Number of third parties includes only those who registered and reported a non-zero amount of funds spent in the campaign period. The 2019 and 2021 data includes both those who spent in the campaign and pre-writ period. Note that "Interest Groups" contains "Professional Associatons," "Charities," and other interest groups. We break those numbers out in the table for clarity.

The number of third parties participating in elections has grown incrementally since 2004, though there was a slight decline in participation in 2021. The vast majority of third parties are interest groups (see Table 8.1). That said, there is tremendous variation in this category with some interest groups being struck only for the purpose of a single election cycle (e.g., Team Climate 2021) and others representing long-standing organizations with considerable financial and personnel resources (e.g., the National Citizens Coalition). Some are grass-roots organizations (e.g., Canada Proud), whereas some are highly professionalized (e.g., the Canadian Real Estate Association). It is also important to acknowledge the presence of professional associations in the category of interest groups since they tend to make up a considerable proportion of this category and because their spending tends to be, on average, higher than that of other interest groups. Unions are also typically prominent third parties, representing the second largest group of participants in most elections (particularly more recently), and even more so in terms of money spent (see Table 8.2). The spending of professional associations that intersect the categorization of interest groups and unions (many professional associations are collaborations of various unions – such as Working Families or the Canadian Nurses Association) is of increasing importance. For example, in 2019, professional associations spent approximately 25 per cent or $1,338,114.80 of the total $5,498,668.94 spent by interest groups.

Table 8.2. Third Party Spending in Federal Elections by Actor Classification (2004–2021)

Third Party Classification	2004	2006	2008	2011	2015	2019	2021
N TPAs registered*	**47**	**66**	**57**	**51**	**106**	**122**	**91**
Total Spent	$720,404	$1,068,011	$1,260,680	$1,255,369	$6,048,501	$8,815,473	$6,933,254
Average expenditure of TPAs	$12,210	$14,630	$21,011	$22,824	$53,057	$63,420	$72,221
Total Spent by Unions	$198,511	$305,759	**$675,024**	$574,598	**$3,328,446**	$2,646,398	$1,561,247
Total Spent by Interest Groups	**$465,968**	**$601,592**	$532,887	$657,023	$2,698,184	**$5,498,668**	**$5,087,767**
Proportion of money spent by third parties (total) in comparison to top 3 political parties by vote share	2.1%	2.5%	2.1%	5.3%	7.4%	13.5%	8.7%

*Number of third parties includes only those that registered and report a non-zero amount of funds spent in the campaign period.

The data in Table 8.2 illustrates the total funds spent by third parties, with specific reference to the total dollars spent by unions and interest groups. The period is marked by a precipitous increase in total spending. The total amount spent in 2004 ($720,404.35, indexed to $980,244.85 in 2021 dollars) is only 10 per cent of that spent in 2015 and 14 per cent of the amount spent in 2021. Of this amount, unions and interest groups vie for the position of top spenders. Unions outspent interest group in 2008 and 2015; however, interest groups are the dominant third party spenders in all other years. While the increasing amounts may cause Canadians to consider whether third parties are becoming a dominant voice in elections, Table 8.2 also provides contextualization in the form of proportion of third party spending compared with that of the top three political parties by amounts spent during the campaign. Compared with the sum total of moneys spent by the Liberal Party of Canada, the Conservative Party of Canada and the New Democratic Party, third parties collectively spent only in the range of 2 per cent to a high point of 13.5 per cent in 2019 (though this amount declined to less than 10 per cent in 2021).

While measuring participation by third parties is reasonably straightforward, measuring efficacy is, by contrast, very difficult. Part of the challenge around measuring efficacy is that the goals of third parties are often not clearly understood by the public, sometimes because they are ill-defined at the organizational level, but more often because the goals are poorly communicated to the public. Furthermore, measuring the impact of a dollar raised and spent is unclear.[28]

Consideration of the efficacy of third party spending may appear an important topic for the public and legislators alike who have concerns around the voices of third parties drowning out those of candidates and parties. However, the egalitarian model does not consider the efficacy of the dollar spent, only the ability to spend funds in a manner that preserves the hierarchy between candidates and parties and third parties. Yet this concern about the potential for disruption to this balance is precisely what motivated policy change around third parties in the context of the 2018 and 2022 Ontario elections.

Case Study: Ontario's Bill 254, Bill 307 and the Application of the Notwithstanding Clause

At present, the Province of Ontario generally follows the Canadian federal egalitarian model. Up until 2017, third parties in Ontario were not subject to spending limits (though registration requirements were in place). Through the introduction of the *Election Finances Statute*

Law Amendment Act, 2016, which took effect in 2017, the Liberal government introduced spending limits on issue-based political advertising in the campaign period (to a maximum of $100,000, with no more than $4,000 spent in any electoral district, indexed for inflation) as well as the six-months prior to the campaign (to a maximum of $600,000, with no more than $24,000 spent in any electoral district, indexed for inflation). Similar to the federal system, the Ontario government also legislated a prohibition on corporate, union, or interest contributions to political parties. The 2018 election, won by the Progressive Conservative Party of Ontario (PCPO) was contested under this regulatory regime.[29] By comparison, the campaign spending limit for a political party running candidates in every Ontario riding was $8,009,999. Similar to third parties, political parties operated in a regulated pre-campaign period, where parties were restricted to a maximum of $1,000,000 in the six months preceding the campaign (indexed to $1,018,000 in the 2018 pre-writ period).[30] It is worth noting that candidates, who are almost always tied to an established party, are also permitted to spend a considerable amount during the campaign to support their candidacy.[31]

This model was altered by the introduction of Bill 254, "An Act to amend various Acts with respect to elections and members of the Assembly." The act amended Ontario's *Election Finances Act* in a number of significant ways. First, the Progressive Conservative government increased the pre-writ regulated period from six to twelve months with no corresponding increase to the spending limit, effectively diluting the ability for third parties to spend money on issues related to government action in the inter-election period. Specifically, the revised legislation held: "No third party shall spend (a) more than $24,000 in in any electoral district for the purpose of third party political advertising in that district during the 12-month period immediately before the issue of a writ of election for a general election [… and] (b) more than $600,000 in total for the purposes of third party political advertising during the 12-month period immediately before the issue of a writ of election."[32] While some Canadian jurisdictions regulate third party advertising in the months leading up to an election period, the periods are relatively short (i.e., six months or less, as was previously in place in Ontario). The federal pre-campaign spending period is only four months. Second, the act changed the definition of what constitutes "political advertising," thereby potentially constraining what gets caught by the legislation. Third, the legislation added new interim reporting requirements in addition to existing registration and reporting requirements. Finally, the act introduced an increased range of activity captured in a new anti-collusion provision. The discourse around these changes were largely framed by Attorney General Doug Downey as a mechanism to fight "big money" or "American-style super PACs."[33] In his comments to the media, Downey framed the change as a valence issue, stating, "We've seen members of the Liberal and NDP speak strongly in support of limits to influence of big-money political action groups and third party special interests on our elections to protect the voice of the individual by ensuring that we're reasonable on big-spending from third parties and special interest groups."[34]

The changes were contested in a coordinated effort by several labour groups, including Working Families, a coalition of professional unions, and the Elementary Teachers' Federation of Ontario, among other education unions. The case, *Working Families Ontario v. Ontario* 2021 ONSC 4076, reflected a challenge of the extension of the pre-campaign period from six to twelve months as an infringement on section 2(b) of the Charter of Rights and Freedoms. Ontario Superior Court Justice Edward Morgan released his opinion on the case on 8 June 2021, declaring the amendments to the *Election Finances Act* to be unconstitutional. While Attorney General Downey had argued that any constitutional limitations were captured under the section 1 reasonable limits clause as they reflected the government's objective of preventing third parties from overwhelming the political advertising environment, Justice Morgan found that the change was not minimally impairing.

The Government of Ontario chose not to appeal the legislation – perhaps reflecting the proximity to the next provincial election to be held within one year of Justice Morgan's decision – and instead invoked section 33 of the Charter. Just over one week following the declaration of unconstitutionality, the government reintroduced the legislation in the form of Bill 307, "Protecting Elections and Defending Democracy Act," and embedded text to invoke the notwithstanding clause within the legislation. The bill received little debate moving from first reading to royal assent in four days. Criticism of the revised bill and the application of the notwithstanding clause from unions and civil society associations was levelled quickly. Former attorney general and then executive director of the Canadian Civil Liberties Association, Michael Bryant, called the passage of the act "[a] day of infamy for Canada's constitution. The election gag law in question aids the incumbent government's re-election bid in 2022 by limiting political voices for the imminent election cycle."[35]

One week later, the same coalition of actors set forth a second Charter challenge against Bill 307, now based on a section 3 (democratic rights) claim, which would not be subject to the notwithstanding clause. In December of 2021, Justice Morgan upheld the legislation, stating, "The

Table 8.3. Third Parties by Actor Classification in Ontario Elections (2011–2022)

Third Party Classification	2007	2011	2014	2018 (pre-campaign)	2018 (campaign)	2022 (pre-campaign)	2022 (campaign)
Individuals	0	1	1	2	4	1	0
Corporations	0	0	1	1	1	0	0
Unions	8	13	19	5	9	12	11
Interest Groups	8	5	10	28	34	37	43
Professional Associations	2	2	1	12	13	14	14
Charities	0	0	0	0	0	2	2
Total TPAs*	16	19	31	36	48	50	54

*Number of third parties includes only those who registered and reported a non-zero amount of funds spent. Note that "Interest Groups" contains "Professional Associatons," "Charities," and other interest groups. We break those numbers out in the table for clarity.

object of the exercise is to ensure that the tailoring of the legislation is carefully calibrated with the need for broad and egalitarian participation; it is not to ensure that the political advertisements can pack a strong punch."[36] His comments underscore a view of the egalitarian model that promotes democratic involvement, but decouples it from the impact of spending. However, this interpretation of third party spending regulations did not stand. A three-judge panel of the Ontario Court of Appeal (Justice Benotto, dissenting) released a decision invalidating the Ford government's legislation[37] on section 3 grounds of the Charter in March of 2023.[38] Justices Zarnett and Sossin concluded that the appeal should be allowed because "the challenged spending restrictions infringe the informational component of the voter's s. 3 right to meaningful participation in the electoral process."[39]

While this debate between Premier Doug Ford and civil society (including members of the legal community) erupted, many were left wondering whether there was enough evidence to support the core tenet of Ford's decision – namely, whether third parties were really drowning out the voices of political parties and candidates. Table 8.3 presents data from the 2011 Ontario election (contested without limits, as was 2014) to the recent 2022 provincial election that was contested under the new regulatory framework of Bill 307. Much like the federal data, there is an increase in the number of third party participants over the course of the ten years presented here. Also similar to the federal third party spending environment, unions and interest groups are the dominant participants in the pre-campaign and campaign periods. While unions are the modal participants in 2011 and 2014, this shifts to interest groups for 2018 and 2022; however, it is worth observing that approximately one-third of these interest groups can be classified as professional associations in each year, many of which – like Working Families – are associations of unions.

The data from Ontario illustrates that the country's most populous province has a very active third party spending culture. Prior to the institution of the regulatory model used federally, third parties were spending in amounts very similar to federal levels. Total spending by Ontario third parties progressed from $1.7 million in 2007 to $8.6 million by 2014 (see Table 8.4). Contrast this with $1.2 million spent in the 2008 federal election by third parties and $8.8 million spent in the 2019 federal election. However, after the introduction of spending limits for the 2018 Ontario election, total spending by third parties dropped precipitously to $1.2 million with an additional $4 million spent in the six months leading up to the campaign period, increasing slightly to $1.5 million in the 2022 campaign period, with $6.7 million spent in the contested pre-election period. As was the case federally, unions and interest groups make up the majority of the spending, with unions collectively spending in the greatest amounts in 2011 and 2014 and interest groups spending in the greatest amounts in 2007, as well as the pre-campaign and campaign period in 2018 and the campaign period in 2022. Notably, third party spending levels during the 2018 and 2022 election campaigns in Ontario are vastly outpaced by third party spending in the election eleven years prior. Indeed, after third party spending limits were brought in by the Liberal government of Ontario, third party spending was reduced to 14 per cent of what it had been in the previous election and represented only 5.2 per cent of the spending by the top three political parties in the province in 2018 and 4.6 per cent of those parties' total expenditures in 2022. Looking at expenses in the context of the spending by political parties raises an important observation: while overall spending by third parties has increased in Ontario from 2018 to 2022, it remains a very small proportion of what major political parties are able to accomplish financially.

As a consequence of this sharp decline in third party spending from 2014 to 2018 and 2022, critics of Bills 254 and 307 noted that the government's continued regulation of third parties in an environment of relative constraint, may have been motivated by goals other than a desire to conform to the egalitarian model. Given the prominence of unions and professional associations who spent $5.2 million and $4 million, respectively, in 2014 (though only $368,000 and $380,000, respectively, in 2018) in third party advertising, some pundits suspected that the motivation for further regulation was less focused on the egalitarian model and

Table 8.4. Third Party Spending in Ontario Elections by Actor Classification (2007–2022)

Third Party Classification	2007 (unregulated)	2011 (unregulated)	2014 (unregulated)	2018 (pre-campaign) (regulated)	2018 (campaign) (regulated)	2022 (pre-campaign) (regulated)	2022 (campaign) (regulated)
N TPAs registered*	16	19	31	36	48	50	54
Total Spent*	$1,709,620	$6,082,961	$8,675,306	$4,012,825	$1,217,092	$6,697,238	$1,567,620
Average expenditure of TPAs*	$106,851	$320,155	$279,848	$111,467	$25,356	$133,944	$29,030
Total Spent by Unions*	$228,115	**$4,909,098**	**$4,544, 437**	$772,381	$367,948	**$3,528,372**	$740,105
Total Spent by Interest Groups*	**$1,481,504**	$1,067,805	$4,089,789	**$3,221,211**	**$820,259**	$3,155,473	**$827,515**
Proportion of money spent by third parties (total) in comparison to top 3 political parties by vote share	N/A	N/A	39.2%	N/A	5.2%	N/A	4.6%

*Number of third parties includes only those who registered and reported a non-zero amount of funds.

more positioned to stem the flow of advertising campaigns criticizing the Progressive Conservative Party and their suggested model of fiscal restraint in areas such as health care, education, and public sector wages. Indeed, in response to the application of the notwithstanding clause to the legislation, the Ontario Federation of Labour president, Patty Coates, stated that the decision to forge ahead with greater restrictions on third parties – namely, unions, was "an attempt to silence the people who lost family members in disastrous long-term care conditions, families and education workers who called for safer classrooms, and workers who demanded paid sick days."[40]

The Ontario case highlights an important disruption to the traditional understanding of the egalitarian model. In the past, some critics of the model have used the egalitarian framework as a stand-in for a critique of the absence of free-market or free speech principles in the election framework.[41] This traditional understanding was founded on data points such as the 1988 federal election and the American model of political finance that notes how large and well-moneyed corporate interests that typically favour the political right may be the most stymied by regulatory limits on election spending. Indeed, there is ample evidence to support this claim. It is not, however, reflective of the case in Ontario in the period leading up to the Ford government's re-regulation of third party spending. In this context, public employee unions were consistently the largest third party spenders in the provincial campaign environment, which challenged the egalitarian model's traditional left-right orthodoxy, even if the model itself is not intended to advantage or disadvantage any particular political ideology. Consequently, though further regulation of election spending may appear contrary to the ideological tenets of a small-c conservative party, it may have reflected a partisan dissatisfaction with the application of the model to Ontario's particular political environment.

Conclusion

This chapter began by asking a rather provocative question: Who should be considered the real source of risk being referenced in Bill 307, "Protecting Elections and Defending Democracy Act," the Ford government or third parties? As already noted, the answer is not necessarily clear. An interrogation of the efficacy of the egalitarian model would presumably focus on (1) whether the hierarchy of parties/candidates and third parties was being maintained, and (2) whether the voices of some third parties can overawe those of other third parties. The data in Tables 2 and 4 that illustrates the small proportion of third party spending in comparison with political party spending does not lend strong support to the first of these claims. Furthermore, the large number of third parties compared with a smaller, more focused concentration of political parties (who remain the clear recipient of media coverage in the political environment) may "water down" third parties' messaging, especially considering the heterogeneity of their interests and political claims. As it relates to the second claim, the existing regulatory framework that imposes declaration, reporting, and spending limit requirements on third parties leaves limited scope for one third party to drown out the voices of others.

The pre-campaign spending limits at the heart of the conflict in Ontario are a recent development in Canada and a product of the "permanent campaign" that had led some third parties to strategically use the unregulated period prior to the writ drop to spend a significant amount of money on political advertising. Introducing a spending limit in this pre-campaign period to make sure that a few well-financed third parties do not dominate the political discourse in the lead up to the election campaign can thus be understood as a continuation of the egalitarian model. Pre-campaign spending limits were never considered by the royal commission and thus it is not possible to know exactly how these limits would have been treated. However, given that the royal commission recommended quite stringent spending limits for third parties with the justification that third parties should be secondary to political parties, it seems reasonable to assume that this regulatory development is consistent with the election model it put forward. It is also a good reminder that there is no "perfect" set of electoral regulations that can stand the test of time. As political parties, advertising, and election campaigns evolve, so too must the regulations that govern them. On the other hand, Ontario already had a pre-campaign spending limit in place as of the 2018 election, with a regulated pre-writ period that was two months longer than that of its federal counterpart. Underlying the decision to double the length of that period, with no corresponding increase to the spending limit, was clearly the intention to constrain the voices of third parties in the inter-election period. The government was clear about this motivation in its public framing of the legislation.[42] Yet, there was less clarity around how the extension of the six-month regulated pre-writ period would accomplish any goal other than limiting these voices. Indeed, as Justice Morgan noted in his decision, "Without meaning to stress the obvious, it is hard to see how 12 months is minimal if 6 months will do the trick. In certain forms of minimalist design, less may be more."[43] If the quantity of third party spending was not a compelling reason for policy change, then a look at the content of third party spending is needed. Given that most money spent in recent Ontario election campaigns has been by unions and professional associations that have typically been critical of conservative policies, making a connection between partisan self-interest and policy change is not a big leap in logic. It is impossible to understand the timing and design of Premier Ford's reforms without acknowledging that many of the third parties affected by them, particularly teachers' unions, were vocal critics of the government. Perhaps, partisan self-interest is never far from the surface when dealing with election law.

Does this mean that the notwithstanding clause should never be used when dealing with election laws? Or that Canada's courts should not take a deferential approach when assessing the constitutionality of a government's election laws? Not necessarily. There is no single, universal third party spending limit that objectively meets the goals of the egalitarian model, nor one that would be appropriate across time and jurisdictions. Within some reasonable parameters, this is a political choice. There is no question that constitutional rights are at play, and it is appropriate for the courts to have a role in determining whether regulations are achieving a reasonable balance between political expression and equity in democratic participation. However, the balance between courts' and governments' roles in the area of election law is necessarily complicated. As observed by Hiebert, "Judicial review may serve an important role in assessing the rules of election engagement to ensure that they are not manifestly unfair, privilege specific parties or candidates or obviously disadvantage specific groups or particular individuals. But this oversight role is not the same as actually determining the substantive content of the rules themselves, decisions that required choices between competing normative values, a task that arguably does not comfortably fit with the role of judicial review or the method associated with judicial interpretation."[44] Election law is a policy area where governments must have a strong role too.

Then what is a reasonable way forward, especially given the identified challenge of partisan self-interest, which appears well on display in the case of the Ontario government of Premier Ford? At their core, limits on third party spending, like all spending limits that make up Canada's election regime, are part of what Hiebert refers to as "the normative project of promoting equality in citizen participation in elections."[45] Citizen participation and voice are therefore critical. A robust public debate on election regulations can take different forms, but a key point is that major changes to election regulations should not occur without meaningful citizen participation. When it comes to how citizen participation is translated into the passage of legislation, broad-based party support or even all-party support can be part of this path that emphasizes the voices of citizens. Even here, though, the risk of cartel-style policymaking must be acknowledged, which means that all-party support should not on its own be treated as sufficient.[46] Given the importance of election law to the broader practice of democracy, careful consideration should be given to changing campaign finance laws in any jurisdiction. In the case of the Ontario government's use of the notwithstanding clause, which was heavily criticized by opposition parties, media, interest groups, and eventually the Ontario Court of Appeal,[47] it is difficult to see how it can be argued that this policy change upheld those core principles of democracy.

NOTES

1 *Working Families Ontario v. Ontario*, 2021 ONSC 4076.

2 Janet L. Hiebert, "Notwithstanding the Charter: Does Section 33 Accommodate Federalism?," in *Canada at 150. Federalism and Democratic Renewal*, ed. Elizabeth Goodyear-Grant and Kyle Hanniman (Montreal: McGill-Queen's University Press, 2019), 59–84.

3 Andrea Lawlor and Erin Crandall, "Understanding Third-Party Advertising: An Analysis of the 2004, 2006 and 2008 Canadian Elections," *Canadian Public Administration* 54, no. 4 (2011): 509–29.

4 Janet L. Hiebert, "Interest Groups and Canadian Federal Elections," in *Interest Groups and Elections in Canada*, vol. 2, ed. F. Leslie Seidle (Toronto: Dundurn Press, 1991), 21.

5 Ibid., 22.

6 Ibid., 21.

7 Royal Commission on Electoral Reform and Party Financing, *Reforming Electoral Democracy: Final Report* (Ottawa: Government of Canada, 1991).

8 *Harper v. Canada (Attorney General)*, [2004] 1 S.C.R. 827, 2004 SCC 33; *Working Families Ontario v. Ontario*, 2021 ONSC 4076.

9 Janet L. Hiebert, "Money and Elections: Can Citizens Participate on Fair Terms Amidst Unrestricted Spending?," *Canadian Journal of Political Science* 31, no. 1 (1998): 91–111.

10 Yasmin Dawood, "Democracy, Power, and the Supreme Court: Campaign Finance Reform in Comparative Context," *International Journal of Constitutional Law* 4, no. 2 (2006): 269–93; Colin Feasby, "Libman v. Quebec (A.G.) and the Administration of the Process of Democracy under the Charter: The Emerging Egalitarian Model," *McGill Law Journal* 44 (1999): 5–38; Christopher Manfredi and Mark Rush, "Electoral Jurisprudence in the Canadian and US Supreme Courts: Evolution and Convergence,"

McGill Law Journal 52, no. 3 (2007): 457–94; Michael Pal, "Is the Permanent Campaign the End of the Egalitarian Model of Elections?," in *The Canadian Constitution in Transition*, ed. Richard Albert, Paul Daly, and Vanessa MacDonnell (Toronto: University of Toronto Press, 2019), 338–64.

11 Royal Commission on Electoral Reform and Party Financing, *Reforming Electoral Democracy: Final Report*.

12 Hiebert, "Interest Groups and Canadian Federal Elections," 6, 49.

13 Ibid.

14 Ibid., 51.

15 Ibid., 48–60.

16 *Somerville v. Canada (Attorney General)*, [1996] 184 A.R. 241.

17 Hiebert, "Interest Groups and Canadian Federal Elections," 59.

18 Ibid., 53–4.

19 Susan E Scarrow, "Explaining Political Finance Reforms Competition and Context," *Party Politics* 10, no. 6 (2004): 653–75, https://doi.org/10.1177/1354068804046912.

20 Andrea Lawlor and Erin Crandall, "Policy Versus Practice: Third Party Behaviour in Canadian Elections," *Canadian Public Administration* 61, no. 2 (2018): 246–65.

21 Bill C-2, "An Act providing for conflict-of-interest rules, restrictions on election financing and measures respecting administrative transparency, oversight and accountability," 39th Parl., 1st Sess., 2006, https://www.parl.ca/LegisInfo/en/bill/39-1/c-2.

22 *Elections Modernization Act*, S.C. 2018, c. 31 (Bill C-76).

23 Only fixed-date general elections have a pre-election period.

24 Elections Canada, "Political Financing Handbook for Third Parties, Financial Agents and Auditors – June 2021," https://www.elections.ca/content.aspx?section=pol&dir=thi/ec20227&document=index&lang=e.

25 Lisa Young, "Shaping the Battlefield," in *Deregulatory Moment? A Comparative Perspective on Changing Campaign Finance Laws*, ed. Robert G. Boatright (Ann Arbor: University of Michigan Press, 2015), 107–25.

26 Pal, Michael, "Is the Permanent Campaign the End of the Egalitarian Model of Elections?," in *Canada at 150: Constitutional Frontiers*, ed. Richard Albert, Paul Daly, and Venessa MacDonnell (Toronto: University of Toronto Press, 2017), 338–64.

27 Andrea Lawlor and Erin Crandall, "When More Isn't Better: Regulation of Third Parties in Ontario Elections," *Policy Options*, 29 July 2016, https://policyoptions.irpp.org/magazines/july-2016/when-more-isnt-better-regulation-of-third-parties-in-ontario-elections/.

28 Edward Fieldhouse and David Cutts, "The Effectiveness of Local Party Campaigns in 2005: Combining Evidence from Campaign Spending and Agent Survey Data," *British Journal of Political Science* 39, no. 2 (2009): 367–88, https://doi.org/10.1017/S0007123409000726.

29 The limit on third party advertising for the campaign was $101,800, while the limit for pre-campaign spending was $610,800.
30 As of 2021, this number increased to $1,062,000.
31 According to section 38(2) in the *Election Finances Act*, R.S.O. 1990, c. E.7, the total campaign expenses incurred by a registered political party and anyone acting on behalf of the registered political party during a campaign period must not exceed the amount determined by multiplying an indexed amount, currently set at 85 cents per elector. According to section 38(3.1) of the same, the "total campaign expenses incurred by a registered candidate's campaign, its registered constituency association, and anyone acting on behalf of the candidate's campaign or constituency association during a campaign period must not exceed the amount of $1.28 [in 2016 dollars; $1.36 in the 2018 election], multiplied by the number of electors in the candidate's electoral district."
32 *Election Finances Act*, R.S.O. 1990, c. E.7, s37.10.1 (2).
33 Legislative Assembly of Ontario, *Hansard*, No. 273A, 12 June 2021, 42nd Parl., 1st Sess., 14100 (Doug Downey), https://www.ola.org/en/legislative-business/house-documents/parliament-42/session-1/2021-06-12/hansard.
34 David Hains et al., "Notwithstanding Clause Legislation Poised to Pass Monday Following Contentious Weekend Sitting," QP Briefing, 13 June 2021, https://www.qpbriefing.com/2021/06/13/notwithstanding-clause-legislation-poised-to-pass-monday-following-contentious-weekend-sitting/.
35 Holly McKenzie-Sutter, "Ontario Government Passes Election Spending Bill with Notwithstanding Clause," *Global News*, 14 June 2021, https://globalnews.ca/news/7948024/ontario-election-spending-notwithstanding-clause-vote/.
36 Paola Loriggio, "Judge Upholds Ontario Rules Limiting Third-Party Election Advertising Spending," *Global News*, 8 December 2021, https://globalnews.ca/news/8433937/ontario-rules-limiting-third-party-election-ad-spending/.
37 Though the effect of the declaration was suspended for twelve months.
38 *Working Families Coalition (Canada) Inc. v. Ontario (Attorney General)*, 2023 ONCA 139.
39 Ibid., para. 14.
40 Ontario Federation of Labour, "Ford's Use of Notwithstanding Clause Threatens Democracy," Press release, n.d., accessed 11 October 2024, https://ofl.ca/ofl-fords-use-of-notwithstanding-clause-threatens-democracy/.
41 Léonid Sirota, ""Third Parties' and Democracy 2.0," *McGill Law Journal* 60, no. 2 (2015): 253–93.

42 Government House Leader Paul Calandra said the legislation would "protect the individual rights of Ontario voters and protect our elections from American-style super PACs (political action committees) and their big-money political influence."

43 *Working Families Ontario v. Ontario*, 2021 ONSC 4076, para. 66.

44 Janet Hiebert, "Elections, Democracy and Free Speech: More at Stake than an Unfettered Right To Advertise," in *Party Funding and Campaign Financing in International Perspective*, ed. Keith D. Ewing and Samuel Issacharoff (New York: Bloomsbury Publishing, 2006), 288.

45 Ibid., 280.

46 Lisa Young and Harold J. Jansen, "Cartels, Syndicates, and Coalitions: Canada's Political Parties after the 2004 Reforms," in *Money, Politics, and Democracy: Canada's Party Finance Reforms*, ed. Lisa Young and Harold J. Jansen (Vancouver: UBC Press, 2011), 82–103.

47 The Canadian Press, "Ford Government Pushes through Controversial Election Spending Bill with Notwithstanding Clause," *CBC News*, 14 June 2021, https://www.cbc.ca/news/canada/toronto/notwithstanding-clause-vote-ontario-1.6064952.

9 Understanding the Pre-Election: An Analysis of Third Party Spending in the 2019 Federal Election

TAMARA A. SMALL

Often when we think of the Liberal government of Justin Trudeau and electoral reform, we think of the failure of voting system reform. While in third place in the polls, the Liberal Party of Canada pledged in their platform that the 2015 election would be the last federal election to use the first-past-the-post voting system.[1] Less than eighteen months after their election, Trudeau was accused of abandoning voting system reform and breaking a key campaign promise.[2] However, as I argue elsewhere, focusing solely on voting system reform obfuscates that fact that the Liberal Party put a major stamp on the functioning of Canadian elections during their first term in office.[3] Indeed, the Liberal platform contained nine election related promises. Many of which were addressed in the *Election Modernization Act*, which amended the *Canada Elections Act* (CEA) in 2018. Despite the broken promise of voting system reform, the 2019 federal election was governed differently than 2015 on many fronts. One of those fronts was third parties.

A third party is a person or group other than a candidate, registered political party, or an electoral district association that participates in elections. This would include individuals, businesses, unions, and interest groups. Compared to other electoral actors, such as political parties and candidates, third parties are relevant to the discussion of the relationship between rights and institutions due to their long history of regulation and litigation. This is especially the case at the federal level but also more recently in the Province of Ontario (see Lawlor and Crandall, this volume). This chapter seeks to explore recent changes to third party regulation in the *Election Modernization Act*. Of particular attention is the establishment of a pre-election period which, as will be discussed, regulates the activities of political parties, candidates, and third parties in the approximately two and a half months before a fixed-date election. The 2019 federal election was the first (and only) election with a regulated pre-election period. The contribution of this chapter is to provide a first opportunity to consider the effects of this change. There are two objectives of this chapter. First, it traces the legislative changes to the regulation of third parties in Canadian elections with special attention paid to the pre-election period. Second, it conducts a systematic analysis of third party behaviour in the 2019 pre-election by considering the amount of money spent and the types of expenditures made. This is accomplished by analyzing the expenditure reports submitted by any third parties that incurred an expense in the 2019 federal election. This analysis will show that this pre-election was, in most parts, a lacklustre affair. This is because most federal third parties opted out of the pre-election by not incurring any expenses. That said, one class of third parties, labour unions, was heavily invested in the pre-election. When it comes to political advertising, Canadians were exposed to a lot of union messaging in the 2019 pre-election even compared to messaging by the political parties.

A More Comprehensive Third Party Regime

Before outlining the current state of third party regulations in Canada, including the pre-election period, it is worth beginning by putting these regulations in a broader context. Campaign finance are the legal rules governing who can contribute to political actors and how much they can spend during an election.[4] For nearly a century after Confederation, there was no comprehensive campaign financing regime in Canada. Things began to shift in the 1970s; now federal law imposes heavy restrictions on contributions and expenditures for political parties (both central and local) and candidates along with third parties.[5] Even though all three actors face regulation, it is only the regulation of third parties that has been and continues to be a significant rights issue. We have not seen political parties or candidates contest campaign finance rules within the courts. This is likely because while parties and candidates face more wide-reaching regulations, they also receive numerous benefits such as rebates from the government and tax breaks for supporters.[6]

Regarding third parties, the initial focus of regulation was on advertising spending. Advertising has been defined as "the transmission to the public by any means during an election period of an advertising message that promotes or opposes a registered party or the election of a candidate, including one that takes a position on an issue with which a registered party or candidate is associated."[7] Third party expenditures on advertising during the writ period have been regulated since the 2004 federal election after amendments were made to the *Canada*

Elections Act in 2000. Those rules required third parties to register with Elections Canada if they spent more than $500 on advertising. The law capped spending nationally and within a given electoral district.[8] Finally, third parties were required to identify themselves as sponsors in all advertising.

As is described elsewhere, the 2000 rules were not the first time the federal government had attempted to regulate spending on advertising by third parties.[9] Each time, however, these laws were struck down by lower courts in Alberta.[10] Opponents of third party regulation took these laws to court arguing the restrictions were gag laws.[11] That is, the limit on third party advertising was a limit of the ability of third parties to speak, thereby contravening the constitutional guarantee to freedom of expression in section 2(b) of the Charter of Rights and Freedom. This perspective is known as the free speech or libertarian approach to campaign finance, where political actors should be able to raise and spend unlimited amounts of funds from any source.[12] The Supreme Court of Canada ruled on the constitutionality of the CEA's third party regulations in *Harper v. Canada*. In 2004, the Court upheld the provisions suggesting the limits on third party spending was justifiable under the Charter because they were a means of promoting equality of participation. This decision is important in its articulation of a key principle of Canadian elections known as the *egalitarian model*, which states that the model is

> premised on the notion that individuals should have an equal opportunity to participate in the electoral process. Under this model, wealth is the main obstacle to equal participation. Thus, the egalitarian model promotes an electoral process that requires the wealthy to be prevented from controlling the electoral process to the detriment of others with less economic power.[13]

As articulated in the Final Report of the Royal Commission on Election Reform and Party Financing (the Lortie Commission), the egalitarian principle underlying third party regulation aims to ensure fairness *between* third parties and other electoral actors who are subject to spending restrictions (e.g., parties and candidates), and *among* different third parties.[14] The first objective is to recognize that political parties and candidates, and not third parties, are the primary actors in elections.[15] The primacy of political parties and candidates is related to the fact that they are elected and, subsequently, held accountable for actions or inactions, in a future election. Third parties are not subject to this democratic accountability. As such, the limits imposed on third parties are lower than political parties to ensure these primary actors remain at the centre of the political stage as pointed out by the Supreme Court in *Libman*.[16] The second objective stresses equity amongst the same type of political actors, in this case third parties, by recognizing that inequities exist when it comes to financial resources.[17] The category of third parties is broad, including corporations, partnerships, unincorporated businesses and associations, other groups, and individuals. Accordingly, it cannot be expected that each third party has a similar financial capacity to participate in elections: the resources available to a corporation or a trade union (which enjoy a permanent staff and significant budget) will outstrip more modest, grass-roots organizations or individuals. Therefore, these regulations seek to create a level playing field among third parties. Overall, as a rights issue, third party regulations limit free speech in favour of equity.

There are two main takeaways from this extremely brief overview of more than four decades of electoral history; first, the regulation of third parties in Canada was focused on only one aspect of their activities – advertising. Political parties and candidates faced significantly more regulation of their expenses, compared to third parties, given they are the primary actors in elections. Second, until it was settled in *Harper*, the regulation of third party advertising had been "distinguished for being one of the most legally contested election policies in Canada."[18]

As mentioned, the Liberals made major changes to the CEA with the *Election Modernization Act* (EMA) in 2018. One key aspect of the EMA was reversing some of the more problematic features of the *Fair Elections Act*, introduced by the previous Conservative government of Stephen Harper.[19] According to the 2015 Liberal platform, there was a need to restore the integrity and improve fairness in the electoral process.[20] While the platform did not mention third parties specifically, there was a pledge relating to campaign finance. The platform promised that the Liberals would "close political financing loopholes":

> When fixed election date legislation was introduced, it left a loophole that allows unlimited spending in the period before an election is called. That creates an uneven playing field. We will review the limits on how much political parties can spend during elections, and ensure that spending between elections is subject to limits as well.[21]

As part of this review, Elections Canada partnered with the Public Policy Forum to examine a wide variety of campaign financing activities in 2017. With regards to fixed dates, Elections Canada recommended the approach initially taken by the Ontario government: "that the regulation of spending of all political entities kick in six months before the fixed election date."[22] As will be discussed, fixed-date laws have significant implications for campaign finances. Beyond fixed dates, section 4 of the Public Policy Forum report focused on the lack of transparency of third parties. One main concern was related to the notion that post-election reporting by third parties was lax compared to political parties, where the former only reported on political advertising spending while parties reported on a wide variety of electoral activities, including salaries and surveys. While it is impossible to know the full extent to which the Public Policy Forum report impacted the policy process, the EMA made several similar changes to the regulation of third parties.[23]

First, the EMA establishes a pre-election period, which starts on 30 June and ends on the day before the general election is called for a fixed date election. During this period, third parties (and political parties and candidates) are subject to spending limits and reporting obligations for certain regulated activities. During the pre-election period, third party activities are limited to $700,000 of which no more than $7,000 can be spent in a given electoral district (subject to inflation). Second, third party spending rules were extended beyond advertising to include partisan activities and election surveys during both periods.[24] Elections Canada uses the umbrella term "regulated activities" to describe this broader category of expenditures.[25] Partisan activities are those carried out by a third party that "promote or oppose a political party, nomination contestant, potential candidate, candidate or party leader, other than by taking a position on an issue with which the political party or person is associated."[26] This would include robocalling, digital technologies (e.g., text messages, websites, free social media), door-to-door canvassing, rallies, and get-out-the-vote activities. Third party surveys are regulated when they are "about voting intentions or choices, or about an issue with which a registered party or candidate is associated" and/or the results are used by a third party in carrying out other regulated activities.[27] Third, the law requires third parties to report on all contributions related to election activities. Finally, there were some changes regarding foreign influence in Canadian elections. Specifically, regarding third parties, the EMA completely bans foreign third parties from incurring any expense while election advertising space cannot be sold to foreign actors.

These changes are directly related to the egalitarian principles discussed earlier. In her remarks introducing of EMA in Parliament, then minister of democratic reform, Karina Gould stated that the "changes will enhance transparency and ensure this fair and level playing field by defining a pre-election period with reporting requirements and spending limits."[28] She went on to note that the changes meant "more publicly available information for Canadians – and the media – about spending [by third parties] before and during an election." These were some of the most significant changes to the regulation of third parties federally since *Harper v. Canada* in 2004. Indeed, the Chief Electoral Officer described it as a "more comprehensive third party regime."[29]

Why the Pre-Election Matters

While the notion of a regulated pre-election period is relatively new in Canada, the idea that political actors were engaging in campaign-like activities outside the official campaign period, or permanent campaigning, is not. Permanent campaigning refers to the employing of strategies and tactics that are normally used in electioneering in between elections, especially for governing.[30] Despite its origins in American politics, the concept is regularly used to describe Canada. Government advertising in Canada is nothing new, nor has it ever been entirely without partisanship.[31] However, there have been growing concerns about the use of public money for partisan communication by governments.[32] However, there is evidence that a wide variety of political actors engage in permanent campaigning, including opposition parties and third parties. For instance, Mario Levesque's analysis of disability-related interest groups in Canada suggests that third parties engage in permanent campaigning. Based on interviews, he notes that disability organizations have come to adopt an electoral-preparedness mindset similar to that of political parties.[33] Alex Marland, Thiery Giasson, and Anna Esselment note that permanent campaigning has become "more prevalent with fixed-date election legislation."[34]

Fixed date laws are only around twenty years old, with British Columbia being the first province to introduce them in 2001. With Nova Scotia's passage of a fixed date law in 2021, every province now has one. In 2006, the Conservative government under Stephen Harper passed the federal law. As per the CEA, once an election was held, the following election would be set for the third Monday in October, four calendar years in the future. Only two of the five federal elections held since the law has been enacted have been on fixed dates: 2015 and 2019. This is likely related to the number of minority governments during this time. Minority governments are electorally precarious with most such governments lasting less than two years. For instance, in the five elections since the introduction of fixed dates in British Columbia, four have occurred on schedule. The only election that did not occur on the fixed date in 2020 was a minority situation.

One advantage of fixed-date elections is that it allows election officials, political parties, individual candidates, and third parties the opportunity to plan better for elections. However, fixed-date laws have implications for campaign finance. Because political actors know when the election will be called, it creates an unregulated period before the official election period, which as we know is highly regulated. According to Michael Pal, without regulation, voters would have little to no information about third party contributions and "in whose interests they were operating" during the pre-election.[35] He contends that this lack of transparency undermines the egalitarian model. The 2015 federal election highlighted two issues regarding an unregulated pre-election. The first issue was illustrated by the case of the Harper PAC.[36] Prior to the election, supporters of the Conservative Party, including several former political staffers, formed a group to run radio and television attack ads and use social media against the Liberal Party.[37] The Harper PAC shut down prior to the election call. The concern here was that third parties would shift their spending to the unregulated pre-election period in order to skirt the election period limits.[38] Moreover, unregulated pre-election spending arguably favoured political actors with the greatest financial resources, thereby threatening the egalitarian model.

The second issue has to do with one of the alleged reasons for the early election call in 2015. Normally, the federal election periods are thirty-six days; the 2015 election period was seventy-eight days. Several scholars have intimated that one reason that Prime Minister Stephen Harper called the campaign early was a ploy to disadvantage opponents. Faron Ellis suggests that the Conservatives were concerned about the large number of "Anybody but Harper" third parties.[39] For instance, in July 2015, Engage Canada, a group comprised of Liberal and NDP strategists with union financiers, launched a slick advertising campaign to persuade Canadians that it was time for a change in government.[40] Ellis estimates that pre-election period spending against Harper would have topped more than $20 million. Despite fixed election dates, the first minister retains the ability to request a dissolution of the legislature at any time as the governor general's or lieutenant governor's prerogative to grant an election remains intact.[41] Third party pre-election expenditure limits would ensure that starting the formal election period early could not be used as a weapon by political parties. Overall, the 2015 election demonstrated that third parties, on all sides of the political spectrum, were increasingly engaging political advertising prior to the election call. As electoral laws must keep up with changes in the campaigning environment, we see pre-election spending has been one of those changes that needed to be addressed in order to ensure the egalitarian principals continued in Canadian elections.[42]

Returning to the previous discussion, pre-election spending remains a rights issue in Canada. As shown in chapter 8 of this volume, Ontario's rules were contested by the Working Families Coalition. It is worth speculating why we did not see the same level of consternation by federal third parties around the pre-election as in Ontario, especially given that the EMA created more regulation for a longer period of time. Four reasons present themselves. First, even though pre-election regulations were new to third parties federally and in Ontario, the former have a long history of regulation during the writ period dating back to 2004 as was discussed. Ontario third parties were facing massive regulatory changes for the very first time.

Second, the federal pre-election period is comparatively short. As it starts on 30 June, it is approximately two and a half months' long, depending on the election date. In Manitoba, it is ninety days long. Alberta's pre-election is around five months as it starts on 1 January, with Election Day being on the last Monday in May. The Ontario pre-election period is very long, beginning twelve months prior to the election period. This longer period was at the heart of the two Charter challenges in Ontario.[43] In striking down the Ontario law in *Working Families I,* Justice Morgan noted, "Without meaning to stress the obvious, it is hard to see how 12 months is minimal if 6 months will do the trick."[44] As such, it would be reasonable for federal third parties to assume that the very short pre-election in the federal law was not worth contesting.

Third, federal pre-election regulations apply to third parties and political parties equally. That is, the regulation of Ontario third parties begins six months prior to the regulation of political parties. There is one pre-election period for both sets of actors in the federal rules, where parties, candidates and third parties face some level of regulation.

Finally, while not related to the pre-election, it is worth noting that the new federal expenditure limits seem to fairly take into account the new regulated activities. In 2015, the election limit for third parties was $150,000 (subject to inflation). The 2018 rules increased the limit to $350,000 (subject to inflation), which means there was $200,000 allotted to surveys and partisan activities. Overall, despite significantly more regulation of third parties in the 2018 law, it is certainly interesting we did not see the same sort of third party pushback in the courts as we did previously.

Understanding the 2019 Pre-Election

This section takes an empirical look at the 2018 legislative changes to third parties focusing on the pre-election. As there is little to no literature on the pre-election and campaign finance in Canada, this chapter along with chapter 8 are important contributions. I explore the 2019 pre-election by considering the amount of money spent, by whom, and the types of expenditures made in the new categories of regulated activities. As mentioned, the 2019 election is the first and only regulated pre-election in federal electoral history. As such, this chapter provides an empirical baseline for future analysis. The 2019 federal election was held on Monday, 21 October, with the writ being dropped on Wednesday, 11 September; the pre-election period was seventy-three days, starting on Sunday, 30 June. In this election, the total limit during the pre-election period was $1,023,400 with a limit of $10,234 in a given electoral district; in the election period, the limit was $511,700 with a limit of $4,386 in a given electoral district.

The data for this chapter comes from an analysis of the 2019 "Third Party Electoral Campaign Report" forms that third parties are required to submit at the completion of the election; these reports are found on the Election Canada website. In the analysis that follows, only third parties that incurred an expense on a regulated activity, in either the pre-election or the election period, are included.[45] Twenty-three third parties submitted an expenditure report, despite not spending any money on a regulated activity; they have been removed from the analysis as their inclusion skews the data downward and does not allow us to fully see trends in spending. The data shows that the 2019 pre-election was a relatively lacklustre affair. That is, most federal third parties were inactive during this period. That said, this finding is challenged by the participation of one class of third parties: unions. Labour unions were very active in the pre-election period in 2019. And when it comes to political advertising, Canadians were exposed to a lot of union messaging in the pre-election. These results are consistent with other research that shows that Canadian unions are important electoral actors and tend to outspend other classes of third parties during elections.[46]

Table 9.1 considers the importance of the two election periods by class of third party: 117 of 140 third parties incurred an expense on a regulated activity in either the pre-election or the election periods, or both. Table 9.1 divides the data into class of third party. By a wide margin, advocacy groups are the most common type of third parties. Advocacy groups are a broad category of organizations that seek to influence government but not govern.[47] This includes very established groups

Table 9.1. Participation of Third Parties in the 2019 Pre-Election and Election Period by Class

Class of Third Party	Pre-Election	Both	Election	TOTAL
Interest group	3	30	62	**95**
Union	2	8	6	**16**
Individual	2	0	4	**6**
TOTAL	**7**	**38**	**72**	**117**

such as the Friends of Canadian Broadcasting or Fair Vote Canada. It also includes industry and business groups such as the Egg Farmers of Canada. A new type of group of third parties we see in 2019 are a number of populist, anti-Trudeau groups using the "proud" or "strong" moniker including Canada Proud, Alberta Proud, and Quebec Fier. The breadth of this class of third parties explains the large number of them. Unions, both public and private, continue to be key third party actors in Canada. We also continue to see a small number of individual Canadians act as third parties.

Perhaps because the pre-election was new and unusual, only one in four third parties incurred an expense on a regulated activity during the pre-election. Indeed, only 32 per cent of third parties spent money on a regulated activity in both periods with a majority of them spending only in the election period (61 per cent). This finding suggest that third parties are interested in spending their money closer to election day. This appears to be a wise strategic decision for a couple of reasons. First, as per the data below, most third parties do not have the fiscal capacity to function in both periods. Second and relatedly, there is some evidence from the last few elections that suggests that many Canadians make up their minds about who to vote for during the official campaign.[48] Therefore, if one does not have a lot of money, it does not make sense to spend it in August when many Canadians are simply not paying attention to the election. However, we would be remiss not to acknowledge the possibility that pre-election regulations have been so chilling that third parties shunned spending during that period. However, it is impossible to empirically test this notion. Our findings also suggest that the pre-election is the purview of large, established third parties that have significant fiscal capacity. Indeed, we find that unions were more likely than other classes of third parties to spend in the pre-election. Of the sixteen unions that participated in the 2019 election, ten of the sixteen (62.5 per cent) incurred an expense in the pre-election. This is the first bit of evidence regarding the importance of unions in the pre-election period.

Table 9.2. Summary of Third Party Expenditures in the 2019 Pre-Election and Election Periods

Summary	Pre-Election	Election
Number of third parties spending	45	110
Total spent, all parties	$3,199,790.75	$8,438,067.95
Average spending	$71,106.46	$76,709.71
Average percentage of limit	6.95%	14.99%
Largest expenditure made by	Unifor	Unifor
Largest overall expenditure	$900,040.03	$505,358.62

Following the work of Erin Crandall and Andrea Lawlor, Table 9.2 provides summary data about the pre-election and election periods in 2019.[49] The data presented is consistent with the two claims of this chapter. Both the Total spent, Average spending and Average percentage of limit data all speak to the same point about the relative inactivity of third parties during the pre-election. Recall that in 2019 the pre-election limit for third parties in the pre-election was double that of the election period, at $1,023,400 and $511,700, respectively. This implies that if all third parties were spending comparable amounts of money in both periods, more money would be spent in the pre-election. But, in fact, we see the opposite. Row 2 reports the total amount of money spent in both periods and shows that $5 million more was spent in the election period than in the pre-election period. This is, of course, related to the small number of third parties active in the pre-election. Row 3, which shows the calculated average of all third parties that incurred a regulated expense in either period, makes a similar point. The average spending of regulated activities is slightly lower in the pre-election compared to the election period. Finally, turning to the average percentage of spending. For each third party, their total pending was divided by the period limit. For instance, Unifor, Canada's largest private sector union, spent $900,040.03 in the pre-election, therefore, the percentage of spending of the $1,023,400 limit is 87.95 per cent. Row 4 presents the average for all third parties in each period. It shows in a different way the importance of the election period compared to the pre-election. Moreover, it is worth noting that this finding is consistent with previous work by Crandall and Lawlor, which shows that the majority of third parties do not or cannot maximize the spending limit. Indeed, most third parties spend below the average amount.[50] In the pre-election, 73 per cent of third parties spent below the average while 75 per cent did in the election period. This is connected to an earlier point that most third parties simply do not have the fiscal capacity to participate in the pre-election,

Table 9.3. Summary of Third Party Expenditures on Regulated Activity in the 2019 Pre-Election and Election Periods

Election Period	Regulated Activity	Number of Third Parties	Total Amount Spent	Percentage
Pre-Election	Advertising	25	$2,419,821.82	75.62%
N = 45	Partisan Activities	35	$567,668.36	17.74%
	Surveys	7	$212,300.57	6.63%
	TOTAL		$3,199,790.75	
Election	Advertising	94	$6,477,630.70	76.77%
N = 110	Partisan Activities	51	$1,513,282.08	17.93%
	Surveys	18	$447,155.17	5.30%
	TOTAL		$8,438,067.95	

mainly because they barely have the fiscal capacity to participate in the election period. Rows 5 and 6 of the table highlight the importance of Unifor in the pre-election and election periods. Even though third party activity is dominated by interest groups (Table 9.1), the top spender is a labour union.

Recall, one of the key components of this new, more comprehensive third party financing regime is the expansion of the activities now regulated beyond the traditional category of political advertising. Table 9.3 provides a summary of third party expenditures in the three regulated activities in the two periods. Overall, the data shows little difference between the two campaign periods in terms of area of spending. Three-quarters of all spending was focused on political advertising. This speaks to the importance of advertising in election campaigns more broadly. While political parties also spend heavily on advertising, it is not the same extent as third parties. Jonathan Rose shows that advertising assumed more than 50 per cent of total election expenses for the three largest parties in the four federal elections between 2004 and 2015.[51] As we recognize that advertising, especially the production and placement of television advertising, is expensive compared to other types of activities that are captured under partisan activities, we do not want to overstate this number. Indeed, in the pre-election more third parties engaged in partisan activities than advertising. In both periods, spending on election surveys was very uncommon.

Thus far, the discussion has marshalled evidence towards the first claim about the lacklustre nature of the pre-election for third parties. Another way of making this point is to compare third parties against political parties. While comparing parties and third parties is useful, it is done with some caution. It is recognized that political parties are very

Table 9.4. Compared Spending on Advertising in the 2019 Pre-Election by Political Parties and Third Parties

Actor	Total	% of Limit
Major parties	$3,967,928.83	32.07%
Third parties	$2,419,821.82	5.25%
Minor parties	$54,069.49	0.53%

different actors than third parties. As mentioned, third parties are considered secondary actors compared to parties and candidates under the egalitarian model. During an election, political parties need to engage in more and different types of activities than third parties and, therefore, have a higher expenditure limit in the pre-election and election periods. In 2019, political parties were able to spend double what third parties could in the pre-election. Janet Hiebert made similar a comparison of political parties and third parties spending in her analysis of the 1988 federal election for the Lortie Commission.[52]

Table 9.4 compares the total amount and average percentage of the limit (discussed above) spent on political advertising in the pre-election across three groups: major political parties, minor political parties, and third parties.[53] The reason the focus is on advertising only is because whereas third parties must report an expense in any of the three regulated activities discussed above, political parties only need to report on political advertising in the pre-election period. Major parties include the five parties that had seats in the House of Commons in 2019 plus the People's Party of Canada, which was treated like a major party in that campaign.[54] Minor parties include the five parties that spent money in the 2019 pre-election that did not have seats in the House of Commons. The parties were the Animal Protection Party, Canada's Fourth Front, Canadian Nationalist Party, Christian Heritage Party, and Parti pour l'indépendance du Québec.

This comparison between parties and third parties is consistent with the main claims of this chapter. The pre-election period is one of minimal political activity regardless of actor. It is not just third parties that were not spending in the 2019 pre-election. While this varied by party, overall only 30 per cent of the limit on advertising was spent by the major political parties in the pre-election. Minor parties were all but absent in this period. Can we learn anything about unions by comparing advertising expenditures to parties? Table 9.5 takes the comparison further by rank ordering political actor by total amount spent on advertising. The results provide significant insight to the importance of unions during the pre-election. While the biggest spenders were the two parties vying

Table 9.5. Rank Order of Advertising Spending in the 2019 Pre-Election

Conservative Party	$1,763,952.58
Liberal Party	$1,669,811.96
Unifor	$836,765.00
United Steelworkers	$687,094.44
Bloc Québécois	$443,236.06
Fairness Works (Canadian Labour Congress)	$183,290.48
Public Service Alliance of Canada	$155,883.95
United Brotherhood of Carpenters and Joiners of America	$131,970.69
Canada Proud	$96,241.41
Canada Growth Council Inc.	$82,600.76
Friends of Canadian Broadcasting	$80,043.92
New Democratic Party	$66,264.02
True North Strong & Free Advertising Corp.	$59,890.00
Amalgamated Transit Union Canada	$26,544.19
Canadian Union of Postal Workers	$26,355.47
People's Party	$22,865.13
Union of Canadian Correctional Officers	$16,855.64
Green Party	$1,799.08

Note: Bold are union or labour organizations.

for government in the 2019 election (the Conservatives and Liberals), the next two biggest spenders were labour unions. Indeed, of the eighteen actors listed in Table 9.5, eight are unions. The NDP, Canada's third largest political party, was outspent by five unions in the pre-election period while every union in Table 9.5 spent more on advertising than the Green Party, which had three seats in the House of Commons at dissolution. In the pre-election, unions were major actors, as they participated more so than political parties in terms of spending. Given that the focus is on advertising, the implication is that Canadians during the 2019 pre-election received a significant amount of labour-related political messages on television, radio, and social media. That influence would have been drowned out during the election campaign when political parties and other third parties increased their participation.

Conclusion

The purpose of this chapter was to understand the federal pre-election period vis-à-vis third parties. Other than voters, no other electoral entity has had a more fraught relationship with political rights in Canada. While the introduction of the pre-election in Ontario was consistent with that history, the federal pre-election was not. Overall, the empirical portion of this chapter has demonstrated a remarkable inactivity on the part of most third parties, other than unions, in the 2019 pre-election period. As this chapter presents a first opportunity to consider the pre-election period, it is still too early to know the extent to which these findings are unique to 2019 or represent larger trends. The 2022 Supply and Confidence Agreement between the Liberal government and the NDP ended in Fall 2024, eventually resulting in an early election in Spring 2025.[55] That said, there may be opportunities for researchers to consider these trends provincially by exploring the pre-election period in Ontario in 2022 and the provincial elections in Alberta and Manitoba in May and October 2023, respectively.

The participation of unions in the pre-election period is interesting considering the two objectives of the egalitarian model discussed earlier: fairness between party and third parties, and among different third parties. In the case of the 2019 pre-election, not only were some unions not representative of the majority of third parties but also several unions outspent political parties. This could suggest that pre-election regulations are, in fact, effective. The fiscal capacity of most public and private sector unions in Canada is extensive. This is, in part, a result of union dues. In some Canadian jurisdictions, union dues are mandatory by law.[56] In the cases where it is not, collective agreements specify mandatory dues. Canadian federal parties and other third parties, on the other hand, are mainly funded by individual contributions. While it is clearly recognized that unions perform and spend money on a variety of internal services and external activities outside of elections, it is still fair to suggest that unions, especially the larger, pan-national ones, have a great ability to participate in elections.[57] It seems inevitable that the pre-election would be an important battleground for those groups with significant fiscal capacity. Indeed, there are reports that third parties, including unions, were spending big in the *pre*-pre-election in 2019 by advertising during the NBA Finals in June, which the Toronto Raptors won.[58] It appears that groups that have the fiscal capacity will take advantage of the unregulated period, regardless of when it begins. It is reasonable to conclude that the egalitarian principles, so central to Canada's electoral system, would have been upended in the 2019 federal election without the 2018 rules.

NOTES

1 Liberal Party of Canada, *Real Change: A New Plan for a Strong Middle Class* (Ottawa: Liberal Party of Canada, 2015), https://liberal.ca/wp-content/uploads/sites/292/2020/09/New-plan-for-a-strong-middle-class.pdf.

2 Laura Stone, "Trudeau Abandons Electoral Reform, Breaking Key Campaign Promise," *Globe and Mail*, 1 February 2017, https://www.theglobeandmail.com/news/politics/trudeau-abandons-electoral-reform/article33855925/.

3 Tamara A. Small, "Promises, Promises: Assessing the Liberal's Electoral Reform Agenda," *Études Canadiennes/Canadian Studies* 89 (2020): 41–64.

4 Lisa Young, "Money, Politics and the Canadian Party System," in *Canadian Parties in Transition: Recent Trends and New Paths for Research, Fourth Edition*, ed. A. Brian Tanguay and Alain-G. Gagnon (Toronto: University of Toronto Press, 2016), 28–43.

5 Yasmin Dawood, "Democracy, Power, and the Supreme Court: Campaign Finance Reform in Comparative Context." *International Journal of Constitutional Law* 4, no. 2 (2006): 269–93, https://doi.org/10.1093/icon/mol005.

6 William T. Stanbury, "Financing Federal Politics in Canada in an Era of Reform," in *Campaign and Party Finance in North America and Western Europe*, ed. Arthur B. Gunlicks (New York: Routledge, 2019) 68–120.

7 While this definition has not changed in the more recent version of the CEA, this particular definition is found in section 319 of the version in place between 1 January 2015 and 1 August 2015. For version of the CEA, see Justice Laws Website at https://laws-lois.justice.gc.ca/eng/acts/E-2.01/20150101/P1TT3xt3.html.

8 The limit in the CEA (2000) was a max of $150,000 during an election period and not more than $3,000 to promote or oppose one or more candidates in a given electoral district (subject to inflation).

9 See Janet Hiebert, "Elections, Democracy and Free Speech: More at Stake than an Unfettered Right to Advertise," in *Party Funding and Campaign Financing in International Perspective*, ed. Keith Ewing and Samuel Issacharoff (Portland, OR: Bloomsbury Publishing, 2006), 269–90.

10 *National Citizens' Coalition Inc. v. Attorney General of Canada* (1984), 32 Alta. L.R. (2d); *Somerville v. Canada (Attorney General)*, (1996) 184 A.R. 241 (CA).

11 Herman Bakvis and Jennifer Smith, "Third-Party Advertising and Electoral Democracy: The Political Theory of the Alberta Court of Appeal in *Somerville v. Canada (Attorney General)* [1996]," *Canadian Public Policy* 23, no. 2 (1997): 164–78, https://doi.org/10.2307/3551483.

12 Christopher P. Manfredi and Mark Rush, *Judging Democracy* (Peterborough, ON: Broadview Press, 2008).

13 *Harper v. Canada (Attorney General)*, [2000] 2 S.C.R. 764, para. 62

14 Royal Commission on Electoral Reform and Party Financing, *Reforming Electoral Democracy: Final Report*, vol. 1 (Ottawa: Royal Commission on Electoral Reform and Party Financing, 1991).

15 Pierre Lortie, "Principles of Electoral Reform: The Royal Commission on Electoral Reform and Party Financing," *Canadian Parliamentary Review* 16, no. 1 (1993): 2–6.

16 *Libman v. Quebec (Attorney General),* [1997] 3 S.C.R. 569. *Libman* is a case involving provisions in Quebec's *Referendum Act,* which limited third party spending in the 1995 referendum. The Supreme Court upheld the act suggesting that the limits on third party spending was justifiable under the Charter because they are a means of promoting equality of participation.
17 Manfredi and Rush, *Judging Democracy.*
18 Erin Crandall and Andrea Lawlor, "Third Party Policy and Electoral Participation after Harper v. Canada: A Triumph of Egalitarianism," in *Policy Change, Courts, and the Canadian Constitution,* ed. Emmett Macfarlane (Toronto: University of Toronto Press, 2018), 214.
19 Small, "Promises, Promises."
20 Liberal Party of Canada, *"Real Change: A New Plan for a Strong Middle Class."*
21 Ibid., 26.
22 Public Policy Forum, *Transparent and Level: Modernizing Political Financing in Canada* (Ottawa: Public Policy Forum, 2018), 12, https://www.ppforum.ca/publications/transparent-and-level-modernizing-political-financing-in-canada/.
23 The EMA is a significant revision of the CEA. It includes several other provisions, not mentioned in the platform, including provisions to combat misinformation on social media, to provide accessibility for disabled voters and voters in the Canadian Forces, and to ban foreign influence.
24 Karina Gould, "Remarks on the Introduction of Bill C-76: The Elections Modernization Act," Democratic Institutions, 13 June 2018, https://www.canada.ca/en/democratic-institutions/news/2018/05/national-press-theatre---remarks-on-the-introduction-of-bill-c-76-the-elections-modernization-act.html.
25 Elections Canada, *Political Financing Handbook for Third Parties, Financial Agents and Auditors – June 2021,* https://www.elections.ca/content.aspx?section=pol&dir=thi/ec20227&document=index&lang=e.
26 Ibid.
27 Ibid.
28 Gould, "Remarks on the Introduction of Bill C-76."
29 Election Canada, *Report on the 43rd General Election of October 21, 2019* (Ottawa: Elections Canada, 2020), 8, https://www.elections.ca/content.aspx?section=res&dir=rep/off/sta_ge43&document=index&lang=e.
30 Thomas Flanagan, foreword to *Permanent Campaigning in Canada,* ed. Alex Marland, Thierry Giasson, and Anna Lennox Esselment (Vancouver: UBC Press, 2017), xi–xvii; Anna Lennox Esselment, Alex Marland, and Thierry Giasson, "Permanent Campaigning: Changing the Nature of Canadian Democracy," in *Permanent Campaigning in Canada,* ed. Alex Marland, Thierry Giasson, and Anna Lennox Esselment (Vancouver: UBC Press, 2017), 298–321.

31 Jonathan Rose, "Government Advertising and the Creation of National Myths: The Canadian Case," *International Journal of Nonprofit and Voluntary Sector Marketing* 8, no. 2 (2003): 153–65.
32 Esselment, Marland, and Giasson, "Permanent Campaigning."
33 Mario Levesque, "Vulnerable Populations and the Permanent Campaign: Disability Organizations as Policy Entrepreneurs," in *Permanent Campaigning in Canada*, ed. Alex Marland, Thierry Giasson, and Anna Lennox Esselment (Vancouver: UBC Press, 2017), 288.
34 Alex Marland, Thierry Giasson, and Anna Lennox Esselment, "Welcome to Non-Stop Campaigning," in *Permanent Campaigning in Canada*, ed. Alex Marland, Thierry Giasson, and Anna Lennox Esselment (Vancouver: UBC Press, 2017), 3.
35 Michael Pal, "Three Narratives about Canadian Election Law," *Election Law Journal: Rules, Politics, and Policy* 16, no. 2 (2017): 255–62.
36 The choice of the name is interesting. In American politics, a Political Action Committee (PAC) is a popular term for an organization whose main purpose is to raise and spend money in order to elect and defeat candidates. Moreover, the name made it difficult to distinguish it from Conservatives, raising concerns regarding the independence.
37 Steven Chase, "Tory Supporters Form HarperPAC Advertising Unit to Target Election Rivals," *Globe and Mail*, 23 June 2015, http://www.theglobeandmail.com/news/politics/harper-supporters-form-political-advertising-group-to-target-election-rivals/article25064778/; Thomas Collombat, "Les syndicats en campagne contre Harper," in *Canadian Election Analysis 2015: Communication, Strategy, and Democracy*, ed. Alex Marland and Thierry Giasson (Vancouver: UBC Press/Samara, 2015), 56–7, https://www.ubcpress.ca/asset/1712/election-analysis2015-final-v3-web-copy.pdf.
38 Public Policy Forum, *Transparent and Level.*
39 Faron Ellis, "Stephen Harper and the 2015 Conservative Campaign: Defeated but Not Devastated," in *The Canadian Federal Election of 2015*, ed. Jon H. Pammett and Christopher Dornan (Toronto: Dundurn, 2016), 23–56.
40 Esselment, Marland, and Giasson, "Permanent Campaigning."
41 See section 52 of the CEA; Don Desserud, "Fixed-Date Elections: Improvement or New Problems?," *Electoral Insight (2004 General Election)* 7, no. 1 (2005): 48–53.
42 Public Policy Forum, *Transparent and Level.*
43 *Working Families Ontario v. Ontario, 2021 ONSC 4076 (Working Families I)* and *Working Families Coalition (Canada) Inc. v. Ontario, 2021 ONSC 7697 (Working Families II).*
44 *Working Families I,* paras. 65–6.
45 My thanks to Wesley Nicol for their research assistance on this project.

46 Andrea Lawlor and Erin Crandall, "Understanding Third Party Advertising: An Analysis of the 2004, 2006 and 2008 Canadian Elections," *Canadian Public Administration* 54, no. 4 (2011): 509–29; Collombat, "Les syndicats en campagne contre Harper."
47 Lisa Young and Joanna Everitt, *Advocacy Groups* (Vancouver: UBC Press, 2004).
48 Forum Research, "Post-Election Poll: Voters Wanted Change," Forum Research, 23 October 2015, http://poll.forumresearch.com/post/2417/big-vote-movers-niqab-balanced-budget-infrastructure-investment/.
49 Crandall and Lawlor, "Third Party Policy and Electoral Participation after Harper v. Canada."
50 Ibid.
51 Jonathan Rose, "The Pre-Eminence of Advertising in Canadian Elections," *Jonathan Rose* (blog), 8 July 2016, https://jonathanrose.ca/canadian-politics/electionads/.
52 Janet Hiebert, *Interest Groups and Canadian Federal Elections*, vol. 2 of the *Research Studies, Royal Commission on Electoral Reform and Party Financing* (Ottawa: Royal Commission on Electoral Reform and Party Financing, 1991).
53 For another research project, similar spending data for political parties in the 2019 federal election was collected and analyzed; see Tamara A. Small, "Did Digital Kill the Television Star? Political Advertising in Canadian Elections," Canadian Political Science Association, Remote Conference, 31 May–3 June 2022.
54 Brian Budd and Tamara A. Small, "'Many Thanks for Your Support': Email Populism and the People's Party of Canada," in *Election Campaigns, Media and the New World*, ed. Taras David and Richard Davis (Ann Arbor: University of Michigan Press, 2022).
55 Prime Minister of Canada, "Delivering for Canadians Now," 22 March 2022, https://pm.gc.ca/en/news/news-releases/2022/03/22/delivering-canadians-now.
56 David Doorey, "Are Ontario Laws on Union Dues and Membership 'Undemocratic'?" *The Law of Work* (blog), 3 April 2013, https://lawofwork.ca/canadian-laws-on-union-dues-and-membership/.
57 Collombat, "Les syndicats en campagne contre Harper."
58 Christian Paas-Lang, "Third-Party Advertisers Start Disclosing Ad Spending as Election Nears," *Toronto Star*, 29 June 2019, https://www.thestar.com/news/canada/third-party-advertisers-start-disclosing-ad-spending-as-election-nears/article_b2e114af-293d-575e-8517-b1c681787401.html.

10 Courts and Parliament: Defining Police Powers

TROY RIDDELL*

Writing in the early 1990s, Martin Friedland lamented that a codified set of police powers had not been introduced despite being championed by the Law Reform Commission in the 1970s.[1] Friedland made a number of arguments about democratic legitimacy and institutional capacity for favouring a leadership role by Parliament in defining police powers. Twenty years after he wrote, however, there is still no legislated code of police powers – in his 2022 book, Kent Roach stated that police powers in Canada were primarily defined by the Supreme Court of Canada under the Charter of Rights and Freedoms and that Parliament had largely "abdicated its potential role in defining police conduct."[2]

This chapter reviews the relationship between Parliament and the courts in defining police powers. Although it acknowledges the dominant role of the courts, it does highlight some nuances in the relationship. This includes examples of Parliament not simply following judicial decisions about police powers or acting on its own initiative with the courts being relatively deferential to these legislative efforts. The chapter renews calls for a code of police powers to be introduced in Canada, using the *Police and Criminal Evidence Act* (PACE) in England as an example.[3] Ideally, the relationship would be a coordinated one whereby Parliament leads through developing the code, the Supreme Court reviews under the Charter, and Parliament carefully considers any declaration of unconstitutionality – with a possible invocation of section 33, particularly in response to divided decisions. The chapter concludes by noting some prospects and challenges for introducing such a comprehensive reform.

Defining Police Powers in Canada

The *Constitution Act, 1867* gave the federal government the power over criminal law and procedure under section 91(27), while the provinces were responsible for the administration of justice under section 92(14). Although provincial policing statutes will often set out the general duties of the police (such as to preserve the peace, prevent crime, and protect life and property); outline police powers in relation to enforcing quasi-criminal legislation (such as traffic laws); and, more recently in some provinces, set guidelines for police "street checks," statutory police powers in relation to criminal law are provided primarily in federal statutes such as the Criminal Code and the *Controlled Drugs and Substances Act*.[4] For example, the Criminal Code sets out the powers of arrest in section 495. The Code also authorizes designated officers to engage in otherwise illegal behaviour so long as it is reasonable and proportionate (section 25.125.4). The bulk of police powers outlined in the Code, however, revolve around searches and seizures. These provisions are found in different parts of the Code. In Part VI of the Code (Invasion of Privacy), for instance, there are provisions that allow for the interception of private communications based on reasonable grounds to believe that a criminal offence has or will be committed. Section 186 allows for judicial authorization of intercepts where it would be in the best interests of the administration to do so and other investigative techniques are unlikely to succeed or there is urgency – the latter requirements are waived in investigations of terrorism or organized crime.

A number of other provisions are found in Part XV of the Code – Special Procedures and Powers. This includes the general warrant in section 487.01, which allows a judge to issue a warrant authorizing the use of "any device or investigative technique or procedure or do anything described in the warrant" if the judge is satisfied that on "reasonable grounds to believe" that an offence has or will be committed and that evidence will be found; it is in the "best interests of the administration of justice"; and no other act of Parliament could be used to authorize the device or procedure.

One of the more recent examples of a modification to police powers in the Code came from the Liberal government's introduction of Bill C-46 in 2017, which, among other things, provided enhanced powers to police to address driving while under the influence of alcohol or drugs. Part VIII.1 of the Criminal Code was modified to authorize police officers to demand a breath or bodily substance sample if the officer had reasonable grounds to suspect that an individual had alcohol or drugs in their body and had operated a conveyance within the previous three

Table 10.1. Expansion and Creation of Common Law Police Powers in the Charter Era[5]

Case	Common Law Powers Created
Dedman (1985)[6]	Spot-check program
Cloutier v. Langois (1990)[7]	Frisk incident to arrest
R. v. Caslake (1998)[8]	Vehicle search incident to arrest
R. v. Godoy (1999)[9]	Warrantless home entry after dropped 911 call
R. v. Golden (2001)[10]	Strip searches incident to arrest
R. v. Mann (2004)[11]	Investigative detention
R. v. Orbanski and Elias (2005)[12]	Roadside impairment stops but no right to counsel provided
R. v. Clayton (2007)[13]	Warrantless roadblock
R. v. Kang-Brown (2008), *R. v. A.M.* (2008)[14]	Warrantless dog-sniffer searches
R. v. Fearon (2014)[15]	Cell phone searches incident to arrest
R. v. MacDonald (2014)[16]	Protective searches at front door of home when responding to a noise complaint
R. v. Saeed (2016)[17]	Penile swabs incident to arrest
R. v. Stairs (2022)[18]	Search home incident to arrest

hours. Statements made by the accused could be used as a basis to form reasonable grounds for the demand.

Courts interpret and apply these powers in the Code and related statutes. For instance, should the general warrant provisions in section 487.01 be allowed to authorize searches other than for electronic surveillance?[19] Courts also define police powers under the common law. Indirectly, common law decisions about whether evidence will be admissible place parameters around police powers. For example, in *R. v. Hart* (2014),[20] the Supreme Court of Canada argued that statements made during "Mr. Big" undercover operations were presumptively inadmissible unless the presumption was rebutted by the Crown. Trial judges were to assess the reliability of statements made during a Mr. Big operation based in part on how frequently the suspect was contacted, what kinds of inducements were offered, and the presence and nature of threats.

Common law decisions also authorize and place limits around police powers directly. Some common law rules about police powers have long historical antecedents, such as the ability of the police to enter a home to arrest an individual in only limited circumstances or the ability of the police to search an individual incident to arrest.[21] Over the last few decades, the Supreme Court of Canada has been expanding certain common law powers – particularly the ambit of search incident to arrest – while also creating new common law powers using the "ancillary powers" doctrine. These powers are set out in Table 10.1.

Table 10.2. Supreme Court of Canada Declining Common Law Police Powers in the Charter Era[22]

Case	Common Law Powers Denied
R. v. Wong (1990)[23]	Warrantless electronic surveillance
R. v. Borden (1994)[24]	Warrantless DNA samples from individuals
R. v. Stillman (1997)[25]	Warrantless body impressions
R. v. Feeney (1997)[26]	Warrantless power to arrest at home (except in cases of hot pursuit)
Fleming v. Ontario (2019)[27]	Arrest for preventative breach of the peace

In some instances, however, the Court has declined to expand or create new common law powers or has indicated that older common law rules were no longer valid under the Charter. These instances are set out in Table 10.2.

There have been some other instances in which the Court has declined to recognize a police investigative technique, but such cases did not fit into the criteria to be counted in Table 10.2. For example, in *Silveira*,[28] the Court found that legislation did not authorize a search in exigent circumstances of a known drug house and, in *Campbell* and *Shirose*,[29] the Court indicated that a public interest exception to allow police to commit criminal acts during the course of an investigation should only be authorized by Parliament. Parliament responded to *Silveira*, *Campbell*, and *Shirose* and all of the cases in Table 10.2 (except the recent *Fleming v. Ontario*) with legislation authorizing police powers under certain conditions.

Under the common law, prior to the entrenchment of the Charter, regardless of how the police collected evidence, generally that evidence was not excluded from trial unless it was deemed to be unreliable (*R. v. Wray*).[30]

The entrenchment of the Charter, however, introduced a remedial clause that allowed for the exclusion of evidence if it was obtained in a manner that infringed or denied Charter rights and if its admission would "tend to bring the administration of justice into disrepute" (section 24(2)). Beyond providing the courts with an exclusionary rule, the Charter also included a number of legal rights that intersected with police powers, including rights against unreasonable search and seizure (section 8) and arbitrary detention (section 9) and the right to retain and instruct counsel without delay and to be informed of that right (section 10(b)).

The Court has significantly changed the rules around police investigative powers in the Charter era. Many of these decisions have constrained police powers compared to the pre-Charter era. For example, since detention in the Charter includes a psychological dimension, contrary to pre-Charter jurisprudence, a request to accompany a police officer to the station to provide a breath sample in a suspected drinking and driving case is now considered a "detention" and officers need to provide the right to counsel caution (*Therens*).[31] When providing cautions under section10(b), officers need to not only provide information about contacting counsel but also be proactive in helping individuals to contact counsel (*Manninen*).[32] The right against unreasonable search and seizure has been conceptualized around the "reasonable expectation of privacy," which, among other things, has limited police use of electronic and telecommunication surveillance techniques without prior judicial authorization (*Duarte*,[33] *Wong*[34]).

As noted above in Table 10.1, however, the Court has also authorized some uses of police powers, including investigative detentions, searches incidental to arrest, and roadblocks within certain parameters under the Charter. The Court has also indicated that accused individuals do not have a right to have a lawyer present during interrogation and can only recontact counsel under a few conditions. Police can also continue to question a suspect after they have spoken with counsel even if the person repeatedly states they do not wish to talk (*Sinclair*).[35] In other instances, the Court has ruled that in certain contexts individuals have diminished expectations of privacy; police, for example, can look through trash placed in a laneway without judicial authorization (*Patrick*).[36]

The Court's decisions about police powers under the Charter may ebb and flow in terms of whether their outcomes are more "due process" or "crime control" oriented,[37] but either way they play an important role in shaping police powers. If police are found to have violated constitutional rules while obtaining evidence, the Court has also created a series of tests to help trial judges determine whether that evidence should be excluded under section 24(2) of the Charter. The Court excludes evidence around 50 per cent of the time.[38] The percentages are higher at the trial level and somewhat lower at the court of appeal level.[39]

Empirical and Normative Analysis

The above overview indeed suggests that courts have been the dominant actor in defining police powers in the Charter era. However, analyses that argue that the Court creates the "vast majority" of rules[40] or that legislation tends to be passed as a result of "knee jerk" reactions to Court decisions[41] misses some nuances in the relationship between courts and Parliament. First, though in some instances Parliament has responded to Supreme Court decisions by mostly following the decision (e.g., requiring judicial authorization for recording suspect conversations with undercover police wearing body packs after *Duarte*;[42] passing a notification scheme and accountability measures for unauthorized emergency intercepts following *Tse*[43]) or in a way that showed considerable risk aversion to Charter challenges (e.g., the creation of the DNA databank),[44] in some instances Parliament has shown more independent decision-making. Parliament opted to follow the dissenting decision in *Feeney* by authorizing warrantless arrests in the case of "exigent circumstances" as opposed to only in cases of "hot pursuit" (as the majority concluded).[45] In response to *Wong*, rather than create a narrowly tailored warrant for electronic surveillance, Parliament created the general warrant described above which provides potentially wide latitude for police powers.[46]

Second, there have been important instances of Parliament taking initiative in the area of police powers. The recent overhaul of police authority to obtain breath and bodily samples to combat driving under the influence of alcohol or drugs is an example (Bill C-46). Another prominent example comes from police powers that were added to legislation that created an offence of cyberbullying (Bill C-13). The legislation provided a basis for the police to seek judicial authorization for the preservation of data and production orders from telecommunications companies, and for warrants for tracking individuals, transactions, and transmission data to combat online crime.[47]

Despite concerns about the constitutionality of the legislation, government officials defended the bills as an appropriate constitutional balance of addressing important societal needs while respecting rights in a way that was not unduly deferential to potential court challenges. For example, when introducing Bill C-46, Justice Minister Jody Wilson-Raybould explained the importance of mandatory screening without reasonable suspicion for enhanced deterrence and effectiveness, while noting that other countries have found success with this approach. In response to questions about whether such a power would lead to racial profiling, Minister Wilson-Raybould argued that "all investigative powers, including mandatory alcohol screening, must be exercised in a manner that is consistent with the Canadian Charter of Rights and Freedoms."[48]

Before the Standing Committee on Justice and Human Rights, Justice Minister Peter MacKay argued that Bill C-13 introduced much needed updates to police powers to investigate online crimes while trying to "minimizing the privacy impact on Canadians." He noted that the legislation raised the threshold for tracking individuals to one of "belief" (from "suspicion") and the legislation did not contain the controversial warrantless access provisions from the previous Bill C-30.[49] (Bill C-30 provided for warrantless access to internet subscriber information but the Bill was withdrawn after public outcry and opposition from organized groups).[50]

Interestingly, when courts have reviewed these pieces of legislation, even ones that do not simply implement a Supreme Court decision, the laws have largely been upheld. This is the final nuance that deserves mention. Lower courts have upheld sections 25.1–25.4 of the Criminal Code, which allows for designated police officers to engage in illegal acts during an investigation in a reasonable and proportionate way.[51] The Supreme Court found the DNA warrant scheme constitutional[52] and lower courts have tended to do the same for various warrant requirements, including those dealing with electronic surveillance and online investigations. The Ontario Court of Appeal, for example, upheld the general warrant provision and leave to appeal to the Supreme Court was denied (*R. v. Lucas*).[53] In *R. v. Otto* (2019), a judge of the Ontario Superior Court of Justice quoted Justice Minister MacKay's rationale for C-13 in upholding the ability for police to obtain a warrant for prospective transmission based on a reasonable suspicion standard.[54]

As of this writing, litigation concerning the government's new drinking and driving investigative powers is still in the initial phases. Although one trial court judge has declared that the legislation violates section 7 and cannot be saved by section 1,[55] other trial court judges have found no violations of sections 7, 8, or 9.[56] In *R. v. O'Connor*, the trial judge quoted from Minister Wilson-Raybould's "Charter statement" to buttress his conclusion that the legislation was constitutional. (See Dell and Harding, this volume, on Charter statements.)

Normative and Institutional Capacity Analysis

Despite these nuances, the Court is still the dominant actor in defining police powers. For some, this is the preferred institutional relationship, while others argue that Parliament should lead and the courts review (with the Court setting constitutional floors). After reviewing these models, I argue for a different approach, based on the English *Police and Criminal Evidence Act* (PACE), which provides a more robust role for Parliament compared to the dialogic model.

Don Stuart favours the courts developing police powers. According to Stuart, politicians see "few votes in being soft on crime" and Parliament's record shows that it "almost always" favours "law and order expediency" in the development of police powers.[57] In commenting on the Court's creation of police powers through the ancillary powers doctrine, he argues that "our independent judges in applying the ancillary powers doctrine do a better job than Parliament in their role as 'guardians of the constitution' in balancing minority rights of accused against the interests of law enforcement and public safety."[58] As an example, Stuart points to the Supreme Court's decision in *R. v. Golden* wherein the majority authorized that a strip search incident to arrest be subject to a detailed set of guidelines and conditions. Against the dissent's view that policy details should be left to Parliament, Stuart argues that perspective downplays the role of the courts as guardians of the Constitution and, moreover, Parliament had been aware of this issue since at least 1985 but did not act.[59]

Prior to his appointment to the bench, James Stribopoulos was sceptical about the role of courts in crafting policy around police investigations.[60] He argued that courts cannot look at the field in a comprehensive way, which creates unanswered questions that can only be answered as cases come before courts. Practical questions about investigative detentions or what kind of emergencies may also justify warrantless police entry into a home beyond 911 are cited as examples.[61] The possibility of more prospective law-making by courts also raises a host of issues as outlined by Stribopoulos and other commentators. These include the lack of specialized expertise in criminal investigations within the judiciary, limits on the ability of courts to collect and interpret social fact data, the desirability of debate in Parliament weighing the competing interests at stake in police investigations, the relative difficulty for groups to access courts to make their arguments compared to the parliamentary process, the lack of ability for courts to monitor the effects of their decisions, and the relative ease of changing rules that are shown to be undesirable through legislative means rather than judicial decisions.[62]

Borrowing from the dialogue model of Hogg and Bushell,[63] including the possibility that Parliament would respond in cases where no legislation was struck down but there was a successful challenge to police powers, Stribopoulos proposes that a dialogic process be used to guide the development of police powers. In this model, Parliament should create police power and not the courts – a relationship that would be facilitated by the courts refusing to create new police powers. Stribopoulos cites Parliament's responses to cases like *Duarte*, *Borden*, *Stillman*, and *Wong* as fruitful examples of dialogue at work in the 1990s.[64] He makes it clear, however, that courts would still play a key role in this dialogic model. In addition to interpreting the Criminal Code according to the principle of "strict construction," courts would also assess the constitutionality of police powers legislation. In doing so, they would "further elucidate the minimum constitutional standards governing the criminal investigative process." Finally, courts would also continue to adjudicate cases where the police are alleged to have violated Charter rights.[65]

A Parliamentary Code Model

As distinct from either the court-centric or dialogic model, Parliament should create a comprehensive code of police powers and the courts review for constitutionality; however, courts would not have the exclusive role of defining "minimal constitutional standards." England's PACE provides a model for this approach.

PACE was introduced in 1984 based on recommendations from the Royal Commission on Criminal Procedure following high-profile miscarriages of justice and general concerns about policing.[66] The legislation contains ten parts, including powers to stop and search; powers of entry, search, and seizure; arrest; detention; and questioning and treatment of persons by police. The legislation calls for codes of practice to further elucidate police powers.

For example, Code A begins by outlining the principles governing stop and search, including the need to stop and search without unlawful discrimination and that the intrusion upon liberty must be brief.[67] Utilizing the powers fairly, according to the principles in Code A, makes them more effective. In terms of stops based on reasonable grounds of suspicion, personal factors can never support a stop, and stops should be based on accurate and current intelligence to be more effective. In the absence of specific information, stops may be contextual based on behaviour, time, and location. Code A gives as an example of "someone on the street at night who is obviously trying to hide something."[68]

As for police questioning, compared to the pre-PACE regime, the legislation and code of practice provides for the right to legal representation, a requirement that interviews with suspects be recorded, and that limits be placed on detention before charges.[69] Code of Practice C for the detention, treatment, and questioning of persons by police officers is ninety-six pages long and contains details about a range of topics from interviewing youth and vulnerable individuals to rules around strip searches to the provision of menstrual products.[70]

Courts play a role in applying these rules in particular cases and make determinations if evidence should be excluded under section 78 of PACE. According to section 78, courts may exclude evidence if "having regard to all the circumstances, including the circumstances in which the evidence was obtained, the admission of the evidence would have such an adverse effect on the fairness of the proceedings that the court ought not to admit it."[71]

Michael Zander, who helped developed PACE, notes that section 78 has generated a considerable number of cases. Although he does not provide statistics, Zander argues that often trial courts will admit evidence and these decisions tend to be upheld upon appeal, but he indicates that "many" decisions have also excluded evidence. Often these are directed at concerns over reliability, though some reflect concerns over "procedural correctness" and "moral integrity."[72]

The courts play a limited role, however, in more directly influencing police powers either through review of legislation or the actions of police under the UK *Human Rights Act*. Laws outlining police powers have been largely untouched and challenges to police action have mostly not been successful. For example, Article 5 of the *European Convention on Human Rights*, which provides the right to "liberty and security of the person" save for certain situations, including "lawful arrest or detention," has had a "surprisingly limited" effect on policing according to Richard Edwards.[73] In many cases the courts have argued that police stops do not engage the Article 5 rights. Edwards would prefer that the courts expand the ambit of Article 5 by incorporating the concept of "psychological detention" from Canadian jurisprudence.

As it currently stands, though, defining police powers is driven by the British Parliament. There have been multiple reviews of PACE by the Home Office, consultations with stakeholders mandated by statutes on proposed revisions to its Codes of Conduct, and (sometimes controversial) legislative activity supplementing (and amending) PACE concerning matters such as online surveillance and intercepts and police powers over public demonstrations.[74]

The introduction of a series of detailed rules around police powers in Canada would have a number of benefits. First, such a code would help to leverage the institutional advantages that Parliament has in creating and monitoring policy. Police powers would be subject to democratic debate. The code would also contain provisions for periodic reviews and consultation with stakeholders prior to any revisions.

The code would also have more specific advantages related to policing. A code would help to make rules clearer, more accessible, and more coherent. Michal Fairburn, for instance, points out that Parliament's piecemeal approach to search and seizure law has "introduced unnecessary complexity into the Criminal Code. Officers are forced to debate which section of the Code governs their proposed investigative technique and which legislative demands, including jurisdictional concerns, apply."[75] The many other rules in case law can exacerbate difficulties with police knowing the rules. This is particularly important given the variability among police forces in providing quality information to officers about judicial decisions.[76] Sometimes the case law needs greater clarity and coherence. Penney and Stribopoulos, for example, argue the combined effect of *R. v. Grant* (2009)[77] – establishing contextual factors for what constitutes a "detention" and *R. v. Suberu* (2009)[78] – stating that the right to contact counsel applies immediately upon an investigative detention – can have negative consequences for both policing and civil liberties.[79] If the rules about detention are strictly applied, police may lose the opportunity to obtain valuable initial information; however, if courts try to avoid findings of detention so as to not have section 10(b) engaged (as the majority seemingly did in *Suberu* when it concluded that the police did not detain Suberu when they followed him and said, "Wait a minute. I need to talk to you before you go anywhere"), this could unduly infringe on liberties. Penney and Stribopoulos call for legislation that sets out clearer rules for detention and defers the section 10(b) caution until the individual is being asked targeted questions. They argue this deviation from the jurisprudence would have to be defended under the section 1 reasonable limits clause. Below I argue that it would also be legitimate for Parliament to use the section 33 notwithstanding clause in response to judicial decisions in certain situations.

A comprehensive code could also help to further professionalize policing and make processes more uniform across Canada. The code would mandate standardized police record-keeping, particularly in relation to race and stops, and procedures (such as recording interrogations) while reminding police, as does PACE, that a more professional approach often results in better policing. Although there would be important debates about trade-offs between police powers and civil liberties, sometimes a more proportionate and professional style of policing is both more effective and more respectful of liberty. Indeed, the introduction of PACE and the willingness of courts to exclude evidence for reliability, process, or fairness reasons helped spur the overhaul of interrogation techniques in England.[80] Police have moved to an "information gathering" model from an "accusatorial model" common in Canada and the United States, the latter of which has shown to contribute to false confessions.[81] In making these rules applicable across Canada, there would be less variation in the rights of individuals vis-à-vis the police. For instance, rules around police "street checks" would not be dependent on whether a provincial government or local community has regulated such stops (and how).

As well, a comprehensive code could address several important issues in policing that need attention. These would include the need for clearer directives around sexual assault investigations; harvesting of electronic data (such as facial recognition software); race and policing; undercover police techniques; and public order policing.

Finally, this code would include a rule to guide judges about when evidence should be excluded. This clause would lean more towards tying exclusion to reliability of evidence than the current jurisprudence. Steven Penney and Moin Yahya argue that, based on pre-Charter decisions and the legislative history of section 24(2), many expected exclusion to be an "extraordinary" remedy but that has clearly not been the case.[82] Removing reliable evidence from a trial can undermine justice and perceptions of justice while having little influence on police conduct.[83] It would be preferable to allow more reliable evidence at trial while directly addressing police misconduct through enhanced data collection, training, and discipline and possibly exploring enhanced options for civil restitution for individuals whose Charter rights have been breached.

Under this model, courts would still play an important role in interpreting and applying the code, including its exclusion of evidence provision and reviewing the substantive rules under the Charter. The Canadian model of stronger judicial review may provide additional benefits compared to the British model. Although I am not as pessimistic about Parliament simply unwittingly expanding police powers as others – the above review suggests that Parliament has been relatively moderate in this regard and the judiciary has tended to find legislation to be constitutional (and recall that Bill C-30 was withdrawn after interest groups and public concern around warrantless police access to internet subscriber information) – having a more robust judicial review provides another forum for carefully scrutinizing the balance between policing needs and civil liberties. Given the limitations of rights review by parliamentary actors[84] (see also Dell and Puddister, this volume) having a more robust judicial review would have its advantages over the "weak form" model of judicial review.

Judicial review, though, would not necessarily be the final say on police powers. Different theoretical models have been proposed for giving Parliament a less subordinate role in the interpretation of constitutional rights than found in the dialogue model (see, for example, Grégoire Webber, this volume). Dennis Baker has proposed a "coordinate construction" role for Parliament.[85] Under this theory, an important indicator of when it is legitimate for Parliament to respond with legislation that does not reflect a Supreme Court decision is when the

Court is clearly divided on an issue. Parliament's response to the *Feeney* decision (5–4) in which the legislation followed the dissent's view as to when police could make a warrantless arrest in a dwelling place would be such an example.[86] Currently, there are a number of divisions on the Supreme Court around such questions as what constitutes a detention (*Omar*[2019],[87] *Le* [2019],[88] and *Lafrance* [2022]),[89] balancing the right to electronic privacy against effective policing (*Fearon* [2014][90] and *Marakah* [2017]),[91] and access to lawyers during interrogation (*Sinclair* [2010][924] and *Lafrance* [2022][935]). Although there would be grey areas in which it is unclear whether Parliament should invoke section 33 in response to a Supreme Court decision that strikes down part of the code, generally courts would play an important role in defining police powers but would not have the final say in setting minimal standards.

Prospects and Challenges for Implementation

Given that there has been only sporadic attention given to police powers by Parliament over the past several decades, the prospects for a comprehensive code being introduced may not be high. However, crisis events in policing in both England and New South Wales in Australia helped usher in comprehensive codes for policing.[94] In Canada, recent attention has been given to police and racial profiling;[95] wrongful convictions;[96] police investigations in sexual assault cases;[97] and a series of public order policing issues, including the 2022 "Freedom Convoy" occupation in Ottawa.[98]

Even if the political will were generated to develop a code, however, there are institutional considerations that complicate comprehensive police reform. One is federalism. Jonathan Bilton and Philip Stenning note that no precise definition of the federal power over "criminal procedure" has been provided by the courts, but the term does encompass "many aspects of criminal law enforcement, such as warrants, evidence, right to counsel, arrest, interim release – that is, the manner in which police powers are exercised."[99] Therefore, many of the police powers contemplated by a federal code would not offend the division of powers. Jurisdictional questions could arise, however, if the code included aspects of policing that may fall under provincial jurisdiction over the administration of justice and the enforcement of quasi-criminal regulation. The Supreme Court has noted that criminal procedure cannot be defined too broadly to drain provincial power over the administration of justice, leading Bilton and Stenning to conclude that the contours of "criminal procedure" represent a "delicate balance" between federal and provincial power over policing.[100] Would rules around public order policing by the federal government upset this delicate balance?[101] What if the federal government created rules around street checks in a code of policing (including record-keeping requirements) and they differed from provincial rules around street checks, such as those enacted in Ontario or Nova Scotia?[102] Given the paucity of current guidance, some issues around police practice would have to be worked out through negotiation, contestation, judicial decisions, and practice.

Other processes that would be helpful to professionalization in the broader context – particularly training, accountability, and disciplinary matters – are exercised by provinces under their authority for the "administration of justice," though complexities arise as the federal government largely has responsibility for these matters in the context of Indigenous police forces and RCMP officers who are contracted to perform policing duties in a number of provinces.[103] While a comprehensive code of police powers would be beneficial on its own, ideally it would be part of a broader effort at police reform. PACE is considered to have led to a number of improvements,[104] but ongoing concerns about matters such as racial discrimination in policing[105] and other issues around implementation, rights, and accountability,[106] underscore the need for a holistic approach to policing. In Canada, such an approach would require federal-provincial cooperation and coordination to be effective.

Another institutional wrinkle is that the Charter's exclusionary rule is not subject to the section 33 notwithstanding clause. Even if a piece of the code is struck down by a court and then allowed to operate notwithstanding the decision by an invocation of section 33, in individual cases courts could exclude evidence even if police followed the code but judges ruled that their conduct contravened the Charter. Judges would not be constitutionally bound to follow the exclusionary rule proposed in the code. What kind of norms would develop in the jurisprudence?

The question of norms also applies to Parliament's use of section 33. It should be used only after careful reflection in response to a judicial decision striking down part of a code – and usually only after a split Supreme Court decision; however, the pre-emptive use by section 33 in some provinces indicates that this practice is not a given. Improvements could also be made to how Parliament considers rights issues when creating policy.[107]

Although the challenges are considerable, there appears to be a window of opportunity for introducing a long-awaited code for policing in Canada. Commenting on revelations of dysfunctional policing by the Commission investigating the invocation of the *Emergencies Act* in response to the "Freedom Convoy," journalist Chris Selley tweeted that if "the current highway pile-up of policing disasters isn't enough to trigger serious reform, I shudder to think what would be."[108] Reforms that included a comprehensive code of police powers would help to reconstitute the relationship between Parliament and courts in this policy area and, compared to the current context, result in improved coherence, legitimacy, and consistency in the definition and application of police powers across Canada.

NOTES

* The author would like to thank Carter Bray and Marc Zanoni for their research assistance.

1 Martin L. Friedland, "Reforming Police Powers: Who's in Charge," in *Police Powers in Canada: The Evolution of Practice and Authority*, ed. R.C. Macleod and David Schneiderman (Toronto: University of Toronto Press, 1994), 100–19. Codified rules around police investigations were to be part of an overall reform to Canadian criminal law and procedure.

2 Kent Roach, *Canadian Policing: Why and How It Must Change* (Toronto: Irwin Law, 2022), 52.

3 Roach offers PACE as a potential example for Canada to follow, see *Canadian Policing*, 76–7.

4 See Roach, *Canadian Policing*, chap. 5, for an overview of policing governance.

5 Richard Jochelson et al., "Generation and Deployment of Common Law Police Powers by Canadian Courts and the Double-Edged Charter," *Critical Criminology* 28 (2020): 107–26.

6 *Dedman v. The Queen*, [1985] 2 SCR 2.

7 *Cloutier v. Langois*, [1990] 1 SCR 158.

8 *R. v. Caslake*, [1998] 1 SCR 51. The Supreme Court of Canada argued that both preventing the destruction of evidence and finding evidence related to the specific charge could justify a vehicle search incident to arrest. In this case, however, the Court ruled that the police searched the car only to inventory the contents, which was a violation of section 8 of the Charter. See Coughlan, *Criminal Procedure*, 122–3, 127, 141.

9 *R. v. Godoy*, [1999] 1 SCR 311.

10 *R. v. Golden*, 2001 SCC 83.

11 *R. v. Mann*, 2004 SCC 52.

12 *R. v. Orbanski, R. v. Elias* 2005 SCC 37.

13 *R. v. Clayton*, 2007 SCC 32.

14 *R. v. A.M*, 2008 SCC 19; *R. v. Kang-Brown*, 2008 SCC 18.

15 *R. v. Fearon*, 2014 SCC 77.

16 *R. v. MacDonald*, 2014 SCC 3.
17 *R. v. Saeed*, 2016 SCC 24.
18 *R. v. Stairs*, 2022 SCC 11.
19 Daniel W. Watt, "General Warrants Take the Wrong Path: Challenging the Constitutionality of Section 487.01 of the Code," *Canadian Criminal Law Review* 12, no. 3 (2008): 297–326; *R. v. Noseworthy* 1997 CanLII 1853 (ON CA).
20 *R. v. Hart*, 2014 SCC 52.
21 Steve Coughlan, *Criminal Procedure*, 4th ed. (Toronto: Irwin Law, 2020), chap. 4.
22 Jochelson et al., "Generation and Deployment of Common Law Police Powers."
23 *R. v. Wong*, [1990] 3 S.C.R. 36.
24 *R. v. Borden*, [1994] 3 S.C.R. 145.
25 *R. v. Stillman*, [1997] 1 S.C.R. 607.
26 *R. v. Feeney*, [1997] 2 S.C.R. 13.
27 *Fleming v. Ontario*, 2019 SCC 45.
28 *R. v. Silveira*, [1995] 2 S.C.R. 297.
29 *R. v. Campbell*, [1999] 1 S.C.R. 565.
30 *R. v. Wray*, [1971] S.C.R. 272.
31 *R. v. Therens*, [1985] 1 S.C.R. 613.
32 *R. v. Manninen*, [1987] 1 S.C.R. 1233.
33 *R. v. Duarte*, [1990] 1 SCR 30.
34 *R. v. Wong*, [1990] 3 S.C.R. 36.
35 *R. v. Sinclair*, 2010 SCC 35.
36 *R. v. Patrick*, 2009 SCC 17.
37 Roach, *Canadian Policing*, chap. 4.
38 See Troy Riddell, "Measuring Activism and Restraint: An Alternative Perspective on the Supreme Court of Canada's Exclusion of Evidence Decisions under Section 24(2) of the Charter," *Canadian Journal of Criminology and Criminal Justice* 58 (2016): 87–111.
39 Steven Penney and Moin Yahya, "Section 24(2) in the Trial Courts: An Empirical Analysis of the Legal and Non-legal Determinants of Excluding Unconstitutionally Obtained Evidence in Canada," *Osgoode Hall Law Journal* 58 (2021): 509–66; Lori Hausegger, Danielle McNabb, and Troy Riddell, "Provincial Courts of Appeal and s.24(2) of the Charter," in *Constitutional Crossroads: Reflections on Charter Rights, Reconciliation and Constitutional Change*, ed. Kate Puddister and Emmett Macfarlane (Vancouver: UBC Press, 2022), 311–30. They found variability among the rate of exclusion in British Columbia, Saskatchewan, Ontario, and Nova Scotia but the average among the four courts was 33 per cent pre-*Grant* and 31 per cent post-*Grant*.

40 Roach, *Canadian Policing*, 52.
41 Michal Fairburn, "Twenty-Five Years in Search of a Reasonable Approach," *The Supreme Court Law Review: Osgoode's Annual Constitutional Cases Conference* 40 (2008), https://doi.org/10.60082/2563-8505.1110.
42 *R. v. Duarte*, [1990] 1 SCR 30.
43 *R. v. Tse*, 2012 SCC 16.
44 Janet L. Hiebert, *Charter Conflicts: What Is Parliament's Role?* (Montreal: McGill-Queen's University Press, 2002), chap. 6.
45 Ibid., chap. 7.
46 Watt, "General Warrants Take the Wrong Path."
47 For a good summary of the legislative changes, see the submission of the Privacy Commissioner of Canada, "Bill C-13, the Protecting Canadians from Online Crime Act," 19 November 2014, https://www.priv.gc.ca/en/opc-actions-and-decisions/advice-to-parliament/2014/parl_sub_141119/.
48 Jody Wilson-Raybould, "Bill C-46 (Historical)," Open Parliament, accessed 11 October 2024, https://openparliament.ca/bills/42-1/C-46/.
49 Hon. Peter McKay, "Standing Committee on Justice and Human Rights, Evidence, 1 May 2014," https://www.ourcommons.ca/DocumentViewer/en/41-2/JUST/meeting-21/evidence
50 Canadian Press, "Conservatives Kill Controversial 'Child Pornographers' Internet Surveillance Bill," *National Post*, 11 February 2013.
51 *R. v. Lising*, 2010 BCCA 390.
52 *R. v. S.A.B.* 2003 SCC 60.
53 *R. v. Lucas* 2014 ONCA 561 (CanLii).
54 *R. v. Otto* 2019 ONSC 2473, para. 21.
55 *R. v. Korduner*, 2022 ABPC 139.
56 *R. v. O'Connor*, 2022 QCCQ 3773; *R. v. Pratt*, 2022 ABQB 407.
57 Don Stuart, "Charter Standards for Investigative Powers: Have the Courts Got the Balance Right?," *The Supreme Court Law Review: Osgoode's Annual Constitutional Cases Conference* 40 (2008), 3, 13, http://digitalcommons.osgoode.yorku.ca/sclr/vol40/iss1/2.
58 Ibid., 13.
59 Ibid., 13–16.
60 James Stribopoulos, "In Search of Dialogue: The Supreme Court, Police Powers and the Charter," *Queen's Law Journal* 31, no. 1 (2005): 1–74.
61 Ibid., 24–9.
62 See Coughlan, *Criminal Procedure*, 21; Friedland, "Reforming Police Powers"; and Stribopoulos, "In Search of Dialogue."
63 Peter W. Hogg and Allison A. Bushell, "The Charter Dialogue between Courts and Legislatures (Or Perhaps the Charter of Rights Isn't Such a Bad Thing after All)," *Osgoode Hall Law Journal* 35 (1997): 75–124. Hogg

and Bushell argued that legislation struck down under the Charter is normally replaced by legislation that fulfills the goal of the original legislation; therefore, a Charter review by the courts should not be seen as undemocratic but as a "dialogue" between institutions.

64 Stribopoulos, "In Search of Dialogue," 66. Interestingly, Stribopoulos in a footnote also includes the legislation passed by Parliament in response to *Feeney* but does not comment on the fact that the law followed the dissent in *Feeney* rather than the majority.

65 Ibid., 71.

66 David Cowan, "Pace Odyssey," *The Law Society Gazette,* 16 March 2020; Michael Zander. *The Police and Criminal Evidence Act 1984*, 8th ed. (London: Thomson Reuters, 2018), ix–xi.

67 Home Office, Gov. UK, "PACE Code A 2015, Policy Paper," 19 March 2015, https://www.gov.uk/government/publications/pace-code-a-2015#:~:text=This%20revised%20PACE%20Code%20A,of%20a%20stop%20or%20encounter..

68 Home Office, Gov. UK, "PACE Code A 2015," 8.

69 Cowan, "Pace Odyssey."

70 Home Office, Gov. UK, "PACE Code C 2019, Statutory Guidance," 20 August 2019, https://www.gov.uk/government/publications/pace-code-c-2019.

71 *Police and Criminal Evidence Act*, 1984, s. 78, https://www.legislation.gov.uk/ukpga/1984/60/section/78.

72 Zander, *The Police and Criminal Evidence Act 1984,* 489. For an overview of some of the principles developed in the jurisprudence, see Richard Stone, "Exclusion of Evidence under Section 78 of the Police and Criminal Evidence Act: Practice and Principles," *Web Journal of Current Legal Issues* 3 (1995), http://www.bailii.org/uk/other/journals/WebJCLI/1995/issue3/stone3.html.

73 Richard A. Edwards, "Police Powers and Article 5 ECHR: Time for a New Approach to the Interpretation of the Right to Liberty," *Liverpool Law Review* 41 (2020): 331–56.

74 Zander, *The Police and Criminal Evidence Act 1984,* xi–xvi; Home Office, Gov. UK, "Public Order Bill: Factsheet," 20 August 2023, https://www.gov.uk/government/publications/public-order-bill-overarching-documents/public-order-bill-factsheet#:~:text=The%20Public%20Order%20Bill%20builds,intentionally%20or%20recklessly%20causing%20public; Legislation.Gov.UK, *Investigatory Powers Act 2016*, https://www.legislation.gov.uk/ukpga/2016/25/contents.
For an overview of the controversy over the most recent public order policing provisions, see BBC News, "What Is the Police and Crime Bill and How Will It Change Protests?," BBC News,

28 April 2022, https://www.bbc.com/news/uk-56400751. For a brief review of previous public order legislation in the UK (as well as New South Wales, Australia), see Wesley Pue and Robert Diab, "The Gap in Canadian Police Powers: Canada Needs 'Public Order Policing' Legislation," *Windsor Review of Legal and Social Issues* 28 (2010): 88. In noting that police powers legislation in the UK has sometimes been controversial, Roach argues that "controversial" legislation is better than the "inertia" of Parliament not acting in defining police powers. See Roach, *Canadian Policing*, 76–7.

75 Fairburn, "Twenty-Five Years in Search of a Reasonable Approach," 80.

76 Kathryn Moore, Kathryn, "Police Implementation of Supreme Court of Canada Charter Decisions: An Empirical Study," *Osgood Hall Law Journal* 30, no. 3 (1992): 547–77; Troy Riddell and Dennis Baker, "The Charter Beat: The Impact of Rights Decisions on Canadian Policing," in *Policy Change, Courts and the Canadian Constitution*, ed. Emmett Macfarlane. (Toronto: University of Toronto Press, 2018), 169–88.

77 *R. v. Grant*, 2009 SCC 32.

78 *R. v. Suberu*, 2009 SCC 33.

79 Steven Penney and James Stribopoulos, "'Detention' under the Charter after *R. v. Grant* and *R. v. Suberu*," *Supreme Court Law Review* 51, 2nd ser. (2010): 439–77.

80 Cowan, "Pace Odyssey."

81 Cowan, "Pace Odyssey"; Jeaneé C. Miller, Allison D. Redlich, and Christopher E. Kelly, "Accusatorial and Information-Gathering Interview and Interrogation Methods: A Multi-Country Comparison," *Psychology, Crime and Law* 24 (2018): 935–56; Jeffrey Manishem, "Reid Technique Is Problematic," *Law Times*, 11 December 2017, https://www.lawtimesnews.com/archive/reid-technique-is-problematic/262844.

82 Steven and Yahya, "Section 24(2) in the Trial Courts," 524n67.

83 Cristin Schmitz, "Moldaver Led SCC on Criminal Law for 11 Years but Spent First Three Looking for an Exit," *Lawyers Daily*, 26 September 2022; Julianne Parfett, "A Triumph of Liberalism: The Supreme Court of Canada and the Exclusion of Evidence," *Alberta Law Review* 40 (2002): 299–332; Alan Bryant et al., "Public Attitudes Toward the Exclusion of Evidence: Section 24(2) of the Canadian Charter of Rights and Freedoms," *Canadian Bar Review* 69 (1990): 1–45; Matthew Wolfson, "Public Opinion and Excluding Evidence under Section 24(2) of the Charter: A Recent Poll," *Windsor Review of Legal and Social Issues* 2 (2016): 40–79.

84 Janet L. Hiebert and James B. Kelly, *Parliamentary Bills of Rights: The Experiences of New Zealand and the United Kingdom* (Cambridge: Cambridge University Press, 2015).

85 Dennis Baker, *Not Quite Supreme: The Courts and Coordinate Constitutional Interpretation* (Montreal: McGill-Queen's University Press, 2010).
86 See Hiebert, *Charter Conflicts*, chap. 7.
87 *R. v. Omar*, 2019 SCC 32.
88 *R. v. Le*, 2019 SCC 34.
89 *R. v. Lafrance*, 2022 SCC 32.
90 *R. v. Fearon*, 2014 SCC 77.
91 *R. v. Marakah*, 2017 SCC 59.
92 *R. v. Sinclair*, 2010 SCC 35.
93 *R. v. Lafrance*, 2022 SCC 32.
94 Zander, *The Police and Criminal Evidence Act 1984*, ix–xi; David Brown et al., *Criminal Laws: Materials and Commentary on Criminal Law and Process of New South Wales*, 6th ed. (Annandale: The Federation Press, 2015).
95 See Roach, *Canadian Policing*, chap. 3, for an overview.
96 See Kathryn M. Campbell, *Miscarriages of Justice in Canada: Causes, Responses, Remedies* (Toronto: University of Toronto Press, 2018).
97 See Robyn Doolittle, "Unfounded: Why Police Dismiss 1 in 5 Sexual Assault Claims as Baseless," *Globe and Mail*, 3 February 2017.
98 CTV News, "Emergencies Act Inquiry: What Initial Police Testimony Says about 'Freedom Convoy' Preparation and Response," *CTV News*, 21 October 2022.
99 Jonathan H. Bilton and Philip C. Stenning, "Extra-Jurisdictional Authority of Provincially Appointed Police Officers in Canada: A Discussion Paper Prepared for the Uniform Law Conference of Canada," June 2001, 35, https://cacole.ca/resources/publications/ExJuAuPoliceLeg01-eng.pdf.
100 Ibid., 34. Note, though, that the Supreme Court has also protected the federal power over criminal procedure from provincial encroachment. For example, in *Scowby v. Glendinning* [1986] 2 S.C.R. 226, the Court invalidated a section of Saskatchewan's Human Rights Code that provided for freedom against arbitrary detention arguing that the provision ran contrary to the federal government's power over criminal law and procedure.
101 Pue and Riab call for legislation to govern public order policing but argue this should be passed by provincial legislatures. See Pue and Diab, "The Gap in Canadian Police Powers."
102 In a 2021 report, the Civilian Review and Complaints Commission for the Royal Canadian Mounted Police noted that the current policy was that RCMP officers designated as providing provincial or municipal police services had to abide by any provincial rules around street checks. The commission recommended creating clearer guidance around street checks for officers working under a federal mandate. See *Review of the RCMP's*

Policies and Procedures Regarding Street Checks, 26 February 2021, https://www.crcc-ccetp.gc.ca/pdf/SAR_street-check-Review-en.pdf.

103 Some complexities arise out of these arrangements. For instance, provinces have been allowed to establish commissions of inquiry over the actions of the RCMP acting under contract (such as the Braidwood inquiry) but public complaints about the RCMP cannot go through a provincial complaints commission. See Roach, *Canadian Policing*, 154–6; also, see *Bentley v. Braiwood*, 2009 BCCA 604 (CanLII). In a particularly memorable passage from a decision involving questions about whether the federal or provincial government should be responsible for the pension plan for members of a First Nation's police force, the trial judge of the Federal Court noted: "Constitutional jurisdiction over police forces is not an exercise in pure rhetoric. It cannot be based on some constitutional fallacy. It calls for pragmatism. And that is where the necessary cooperation between the federal and provincial authorities comes into play. It will help put in place these statutory glia that ensure the cohesion and support of all the neurons of the Canadian system of justice and enforcement of federal and provincial administrative, criminal and penal laws." *Picard v. Canada (Attorney General)*, 2018 FC 747 (CanLII), para. 50.

104 Cowan, "Pace Odyssey." For various perspectives, see Ed Cape and Richard Young, eds., *Regulating Policing: The Police and Criminal Evidence Act 1984: Past, Present and Future* (Oxford: Hart Publishing, 2008).

105 UK Parliament, "Urgent Action Needed to Tackle Deep Rooted and Persistent Racial Disparities in Policing," 30 July 2021, https://committees.parliament.uk/work/347/the-macpherson-report-twentytwo-years-on/news/157006/urgent-action-needed-to-tackle-deep-rooted-and-persistent-racial-disparities-in-policing#:~:text=New%20scrutiny%20and%20transparency%20is,in%20policing%20are%20not%20working.

106 Cape and Young, *Regulating Policing*; Geoff Pearson, Mike Rowe, and Liz Turner, "Policy, Practicalities, and PACE s.24: The Subsuming of Necessity Criteria in Arrest Decision-Making by Frontline Police Officers," *Journal of Law and Society* 45 (2018): 282–308; Information Commissioner's Office, *Mobile Phone Data Extraction by Police Forces in England and Wales: Investigation Report*, June 2020, https://ico.org.uk/about-the-ico/what-we-do/mobile-phone-data-extraction-by-police-forces-in-england-and-wales/.

107 See Emmett Macfarlane, Janet Hiebert, and Anna Drake, *Legislating under the Charter: Parliament, Executive Power and Rights* (Toronto: University of Toronto Press, 2023). The authors argue that significant improvements

need to be made to Parliament's consideration of rights when creating legislation – they offer suggestions for reform.

108 Chris Selley (@cselley), "If the current highway pile-up of policing disasters isn't enough to trigger serious reform, I shudder to think what would be." Twitter, 28 October 2022, 3:10 p.m. (tweet no longer posted).

11 Consequences of Weak Parliamentary Rights Review: A Study of Harper-Era Mandatory Minimum Sentencing

BRENDAN DELL AND KATE PUDDISTER

During the Harper government (2006–15), the number of offences in the Criminal Code and *Controlled Drugs and Substances Act* (CDSA) that carry mandatory minimum sentences (MMS) significantly increased. These sentencing provisions require judges to impose a minimum sentence on an offender upon conviction, limiting judicial discretion. Research demonstrates that MMS are an ineffective means of controlling crime, have extensive implications for the justice system, can disproportionately affect marginalized groups, and may be vulnerable to Charter challenges under section 12 of the Canadian Charter of Rights and Freedoms, which protects against cruel and unusual punishment.[1] As an area of public policy, sentencing is unique as both the legislature and the judiciary play distinct and significant roles – Parliament enacts criminal law with general sentencing principles, and the judiciary applies the law and sentences with discretion.[2] However, MMS alter this institutional dynamic as they represent a clear decision by policymakers to limit the discretion of judges in sentencing. The Harper government pursued a tough on crime policy agenda, including an overwhelming focus on sentencing policy, which led to the creation of upwards of fifty MMS. The government's approach to criminal justice policymaking has been characterized as one that disregards expertise and evidence.[3] Given all of this, little is known about the creation of such policies, including whether Charter rights were seriously considered in the policymaking process.

The wave of MMS enacted by the Harper government provides a unique case study to analyze legislative rights review in Canada under a government that prioritized a law-and-order approach to criminal justice policy. Because this case study focuses on a single policy area that spans the minority and majority Parliaments of one government, it also allows for a novel comparison of legislative rights review under different legislating scenarios while holding the policy area constant. Additionally, when criminal justice policy is framed by penal populism, the terms of debate can be narrowed as the opposition may be hesitant to raise Charter concerns at the risk being perceived as soft on crime, which creates unique conditions to analyze legislative rights review.

By analyzing the parliamentary debates and committee hearings for all bills passed by the Harper government that contained MMS, this chapter asks the following research questions: What role did the Charter play in the MMS policymaking process during the Harper government? How did the Harper government respond to Charter-based arguments while enacting MMS legislation? We find that the Charter was brought up frequently (and increasingly so after Bill C-10) by opposition parliamentarians in an attempt to hold the Conservative government and its legislative goals in check with Charter rights. However, Charter-based critiques were rarely met with a substantive response or justification from the Conservative government. We find that the MMS legislation passed without much consideration of the criticisms raised in debates and that, ultimately, the Charter did not play a significant role in the MMS policymaking process for the Harper government. We argue that this demonstrates Parliament's weak role in legislative rights review, a finding consistent with previous studies that highlight the strength of the centre of government under Canada's style of Westminster Parliament. Implications of this finding are further explored in this chapter.

How Governments Legislate with the Charter

Policymaking in Canada should be done in a manner that respects the Constitution and, in particular, the rights set out in the Charter of Rights and Freedoms. It follows that concerns regarding constitutionality and the potential for judicial invalidation of legislation on Charter grounds should shape the beginning stages of policy development for governments.[4] Understanding this process is particularly important because legislation often represents a final decision on balancing government objectives and constitutionally protected rights.[5] Indeed, Janet Hiebert reminds us that only a fraction of laws will be subject to Charter litigation in court; therefore, Parliament retains a predominant position to define the scope of the legislation it enacts, allowing the executive to generally achieve its legislative agenda.[6] Thus, the goal of legislative rights review is to ensure that the government advances policies that are in line with the Charter before the judiciary reviews legislation for its constitutionality.[7] Legislative rights review can occur in both Parliament and the bureaucracy, the former being when members of Parliament (MPs),

Senators, and parliamentary committees scrutinize proposed laws on Charter grounds, a process that is especially weak and ineffective in Canada.[8] In contrast, bureaucratic rights review, which is pre-legislative review of bills for consistency with rights, is particularly institutionalized in Canada due to the strength of Cabinet and the Department of Justice. However, this does not ensure robust rights review.

Bureaucratic rights review occurs in two separate streams: (1) an advisory stream for policy development, and (2) a statutory reporting obligation for Charter inconsistency.[9] The first stream is characterized as "legal risk management," where the Department of Justice, in partnership with other departments, thoroughly assesses the risk of rights infringement and future judicial nullification, and suggests amendments to limit the potential for judicial nullification on Charter grounds.[10] Interpretations of Charter inconsistency with proposed legislation is said to range from "very low to manifestly unconstitutional."[11] However, advice and risk-assessment from government lawyers at this stage is just that: advice.

While Charter vetting of legislation has been a significant step in bridging the government's legislative agenda with Charter values, Cabinet ultimately decides whether to proceed with a legislative proposal.[12] Therefore, as Hiebert notes, a policy of questionable constitutionality that is central to a government's agenda, or an electoral commitment, may be implemented despite the advice of the Department of Justice.[13] Hiebert's interviews with government lawyers indicate that decisions about whether departments and ministers accept Charter advice boils down to a government's tolerance for risk.[14] Hiebert likens significant elements of the Harper government's criminal justice policy – such as MMS – to high risk taking, where government is intent on pursuing legislation despite having been forewarned that it was constitutionally vulnerable.[15] Hiebert finds it difficult to imagine that government lawyers did not make it clear that these specific pieces of legislation were highly vulnerable to invalidation by the courts.[16] Macfarlane and colleagues explain that if a government's approach to a particular policy area is grounded in a strong ideological position (such as penal populism or a desire to be "tough on crime"), it may tolerate a greater level of risk for potential judicial invalidation.[17]

The second stream in the bureaucratic arena includes the minister of justice's statutory reporting requirement set out in section 4.1(1) of the *Department of Justice Act*, which requires the minister to certify that bills comply with the Charter and, when inconsistent, report this fact to Parliament.[18] In contrast to the first stream, this mechanism seems to tolerate much higher levels of Charter risk.[19] The minister of justice has never issued a report of inconsistency under section 4.1(1) to Parliament. It is argued that this reporting duty does not facilitate a "robust rights culture" in bureaucratic rights review.[20] Thus, Hiebert concludes that the Charter has encouraged "risk avoidance" by refusing to acknowledge instances where proposed legislation may be vulnerable to judicial invalidation.[21]

In the parliamentary arena, the Standing Committee on Justice and Human Rights (SCJHR) and the Standing Senate Committee on Legal and Constitutional Affairs (SSCLCA) are the primary committees responsible for assessing proposed bills for constitutionality. However, neither of these committees has a formal mandate to engage in legislative scrutiny of government bills for compatibility with the Charter and their effectiveness is undermined by the executive branch, which can generally pursue policy objectives regardless of criticism from committees.[22] Outside of scrutiny by parliamentary committees, backbench MPs and opposition parties have rarely amended proposed legislation or convinced the government to accept amendments regarding compatibility with rights.[23] The ineffectiveness of Parliament as a policy actor and rights protector can be partially explained by Canadian Westminster factors such as executive dominance of the legislative process, centralizing nature of strong majority governments, party discipline, and extreme partisanship within the House of Commons.[24] These factors "allow the executive to dominate legislative proceedings … and exert sufficient power over members of the governing party to support the government and overcome opposition attempts to defeat the government's agenda."[25] Thus, arguably Parliament has not been an adequate check on the legislative agenda of the executive branch.[26]

Although Parliament has not served as a robust check on the executive, it is not inconsequential.[27] There are significant effects from Parliament's adversarial role and from the public criticism of proposed government bills. For example, questioning the prime minister or minister of justice in the House of Commons could be reported in the media, which could stimulate public debate on the merits of a proposed bill.[28] While the government does not advise Parliament about the degree of Charter risk or compliance associated with proposed bills, Parliament can be viewed as a chamber for debate regarding controversial bills that could result in Charter challenges in court.[29]

Finally, it is important to note the obscurity or secretive nature of legislative rights review within the executive arena, due to the closed nature of the policy process and the principle of cabinet solidarity.[30] Those who hold the responsibility to identify potential Charter risks in the Department of Justice are reluctant to speak about specific policies and the nature of the advice given, due to concerns regarding legal privilege.[31] This means that the internal process of reviewing proposed legislation for Charter compliance is difficult to assess.

Emmett Macfarlane, Janet Hiebert, and Anna Drake suggest that governments are willing to pursue policy objectives that may be constitutionally suspect when the policies reinforce a government's ideological position, such as a desire to appear tough on crime.[32] We take up this notion through our analysis of the mandatory minimum sentence (MMS) policies enacted by the Harper government. MMS are a policy tool favoured by governments that wish to appear tough on crime because they capitalize on the public's fear of crime and perception that sentencing is too lenient,[33] thus making it an excellent case study for assessing the nature of legislative rights review in Canada. The Harper government was determined to position itself as tough on crime, which translated into significant reforms to sentencing policy.[34] By analyzing the parliamentary debates and committee meetings of bills that enacted MMS, the goal of this chapter is to understand the role that the Charter played in the Harper-era mandatory minimum sentencing policymaking process and how the Harper government responded to Charter-based arguments in Parliament.

The Harper Government's Mandatory Minimum Sentences: Legislative Rights Review and Parliamentary Process

Under the Harper government, 11 bills were passed that contained at least one new or increased MMS. From these 11 bills, 29 new MMS were added to the Criminal Code and the CDSA, and the minimum sanction for 22 pre-existing MMS were increased. In total, 51 MMS in the Criminal Code and the CDSA were created or increased by the Harper government. Of the 51 MMS enacted, 39 (76.5 per cent) were passed when the Harper government governed with a majority (2011 to 2015). Our analysis of parliamentary debates and committee hearings is based on all MMS enacted by the Harper government.

The constitutionality of MMS was discussed in the debates and committee meetings for seven of the eleven MMS bills enacted by the Harper government.[35] The nature of this discussion can be split into two periods, pre-Bill C-10[36] (the *Safe Streets and Communities Act*) and post–Bill C-10. Bill C-10, an omnibus bill that grouped together nine pieces of legislation, received an overwhelming amount of criticism from expert witnesses and opposition members of Parliament, which influenced legislative review of MMS policy going forward. Bill C-10 was also one of the first bills introduced by the Harper government after forming a majority government. Five MMS bills were enacted pre-Bill C-10 and only two featured a minimal discussion of constitutionality.

Bill C-10 saw an overwhelming increase in critiques of MMS constitutionality, which trickled into the debates for nearly every bill after it. As expected, most Charter concerns focused on section 12, which was mentioned by the opposition and experts for every bill post–Bill C-10. Policymaking discussions also considered the impact on sections 7 and 15 of the Charter. For example, in reviewing the mandatory victim surcharge in Bill C-37, NDP MP Craig Scott argued that the variance in fine option programs[37] between provinces could violate section 7 of the Charter.[38] This is notable because when the Supreme Court of Canada later heard a challenge of the mandatory victim surcharge in *R. v. Boudreault*,[39] it commented on this very issue regarding fine option programs. Section 15 was also mentioned by critics because MMS can disproportionately impact women, Indigenous peoples, and people with disabilities.

When questions or criticisms of MMS constitutionality arose in debates and committee meetings, a substantive response from the Conservative government was uncommon and members of the government often passed questions to the Department of Justice. In the infrequent occurrence that a Conservative parliamentarian responded to concerns regarding the constitutionality of the proposed MMS provisions, the responses were either political in nature or did not seem to adequately address the question or concern. For example, in a response to critics regarding the constitutionality of Bill C-10, Minister of Justice Rob Nicholson stated that MMS "send out the right message" and "this complies with the Charter" without providing much of a justification.[40] The Harper government defended its MMS policies by stating that they had already been vetted by the Department of Justice. For example, Minister of Justice Peter MacKay responded to a question on the constitutionality of a proposed MMS by saying: "It is an important question. The Department of Justice has lawyers with the necessary experience and training to study each bill and each article of the Criminal Code to ensure Charter compliance."[41]

"Has this bill been Charter tested?": The Policymaking Process and the Department of Justice

Before Bill C-10, the Department of Justice was infrequently discussed. However, after Bill C-10, apart from Bill C-36,[42] much of the debates focused on questioning the policymaking process and critiquing Charter scrutiny by the Department of Justice. For example, after questioning the constitutionality of MMS provisions in Bill C-10, Liberal MP Irwin Cotler criticized Minister of Justice Rob Nicholson for not responding to his request for "the Minister to table the constitutional opinion that the government received … to demonstrate to us that the government had put it through that constitutional filter in order to determine that Bill C-10 … adhered to the Canadian Charter of Rights and Freedoms."[43] Cotler continued to press the government on this point in later debates on Bill C-10 explaining to the House that the minister "would have had to refer this matter to the constitutional experts within the Department of Justice" and that he had his doubts as to whether that question was even put to the Department of Justice because if it were "he would have received the response that they were invalid."[44]

After Cotler's speeches regarding the policymaking process and Charter scrutiny from the Department of Justice, the question "Has this bill been Charter tested?" was routine from opposition members for the remainder of debates on the Harper government's MMS policies. When the government was asked whether a bill had been scrutinized under Charter standards, the question was typically deferred to Department of Justice counsel, which responded with a brief "yes" without further explanation. For example, after Liberal Senator George Baker asked if the MMS provision in Bill C-10 (2014) passed the constitutionality test for section 12 of the Charter, Department of Justice counsel offered up the following response: "In short, yes. In fact, the department always verifies the constitutionality of any of the provisions that we propose, especially when minimum penalties are involved."[45]

After Bill C-10, debates moved towards criticizing the Conservative government's approach to Charter scrutiny and policymaking. For example, Liberal Senator Serge Joyal pushed back on Department of Justice response regarding Charter implications of the mandatory victim surcharge in Bill C-37 by asking "How can we be assured that those studies are conducted seriously and that we can satisfy ourselves as legislators that when you come forward with such a proposal, it accords with the levels of scrutiny that the *Charter* will impose upon it?"[46] For Bill C-35, Liberal MP Wayne Easter gave a lengthy speech in the second reading which criticized the government and its use of the legal advice from the Department of Justice:

> I hope that the minister will be willing to provide that evidence … to show where the legal advice came from. Is it from the Department of Justice? It is outside advice? Is there Charter compliance, especially as it relates to consecutive and mandatory minimums jointly in this particular bill? …

> The concern we may have is whether the government is taking into serious consideration some of the advice that is given to it, probably by the minister's own department.[47]

Relatedly, for Bill C-10 (2014), NDP MP Françoise Boivin implied that the government was not concerned with advice regarding Charter compliance by stating that "I still have no guarantee that the bill complies with our Charters because the government does not seem to be too worried about that."[48]

To bolster their criticisms regarding the Conservative government's lack of concern with Charter compliance, parliamentarians referenced the case of Edgar Schmidt who took the Department of Justice to court for using a very low standard for determining Charter consistency for statutory reporting purposes.[49] This case was significant as it brought to light the systematic use of weak Charter standards that the Conservative government employed when drafting bills. According to Hiebert, Schmidt claimed that during the Harper era, the standard used for advising the minister of justice on a bill's consistency with the Charter was "so low as to be essentially meaningless."[50] Thus, the fact that opposition members picked up on the *Schmidt* case[51] and used this critique in the parliamentary debates further demonstrates the concerns regarding constitutionality of the Harper government's MMS policies held by opposition parliamentarians.

While criticism regarding the Harper government's approach to policymaking and Charter scrutiny did not emerge until Bill C-10, much of the debate during and after Bill C-10 (2012) focused on this aspect and the government was heavily criticized for not engaging in serious rights review of its proposed legislation. The lack of substantive response from the government or Department of Justice to these concerns demonstrates James Kelly's findings regarding the obscurity or secretive nature of legislative rights review within the executive arena and policymaking with the Charter.[52] As demonstrated by opposition members, the secretive nature of the internal process of reviewing proposed legislation for Charter compliance makes it difficult to assess.

"Quebec refuses to pick up the tab": Federalism Issues with MMS

In Canada, both the provincial and federal governments have roles to play in the criminal justice system and criminal justice policy.[53] Even though the federal government possesses exclusive authority over sentencing policy, the division of responsibility in the criminal justice system means that implementation often falls to provincial governments.[54]

As a result, Canada's justice system relies on cooperation between the two orders of government.[55] Federalism-based tensions arose in the parliamentary debates regarding issues such as increasing judicial administration costs for provinces and the disparities throughout the country regarding the mandatory victim surcharge and fine option programs. While the literature on legislative rights review has focused on the Charter, an examination of the concerns for provincial jurisdiction allows us to assess another form of legislative constitutional review – that is on federalism grounds.

Concerns regarding federalism were raised in roughly half of the debates (5 of 11). In Bill C-10 (2012), we see the principle of federalism raised as a broad concept that ought to be respected and in regard to specific concerns with the MMS provisions. An example of the former is when Liberal MP Irwin Cotler stated, "Another transformative impact is on the whole question of federal-provincial relations … the government always spoke about an open federalism, about a covenantal federalism, that we were going to cooperate with the provinces."[56] Federalism was also raised with specific concerns regarding the financial burden for provinces because many MMS provisions dealt with terms of imprisonment of two years or less (thus served in provincial correctional institutions). This issue was raised by opposition parliamentarians, legal experts, and provincial officials in four of the bills' debates and committee meetings (bills C-2, C-10, C-26, and C-35). For example, Minister of Justice and Attorney General of Quebec Jean-Marc Fournier testified at the Standing Committee on Justice and Human Rights (SCJHR) for Bill C-10 stating, "[T]his Bill fails to provide the financial support for its implementation and Quebec refuses to pick up the tab."[57] Fournier continued by citing the Constitution and stating that the two orders of government must work together on such matters. Further, in the debates for the same bill, NDP MP Ryan Cleary echoed a message from the Premier of Ontario who warned that Ontario "will not pick up the tab for any new costs associated with the omnibus crime bill."[58]

Responses from the Conservative government to these objections were rare and inadequately addressed the concerns being raised. For example, in response to criticism regarding off-loading expenses to provinces, Minister of Justice Rob Nicholson stated: "The provinces are very well aware of what we are doing … and they have underlined to me what a problem drug trafficking is within the provinces. So, they're well aware of the components of this bill."[59] Additionally, in response to a Liberal Senator's concerns regarding the provincial administration of justice budgets, Minister of Public Safety Vic Toews responded by saying: "… many of these changes were made at the request of the provinces. They recognize that there is an issue with respect to cost."[60] As illustrated, responses to federalism-based criticism by the Conservative government seemed to deflect the responsibility to the provincial governments.

Another area in which the issue of federalism was raised was with respect to the mandatory victim surcharge in Bill C-37. At the SCJHR, NDP MP Craig Scott argued that the mandatory victim surcharge could result in "a differential application of the criminal law" because multiple provinces lack fine option programs for offenders.[61] In response to this, Minister of Justice Rob Nicholson stated that "this will apply across the country ... but it is administered at the provincial or territorial level ... They're all dealing with the same penalty scheme ... The where and how of its administration is delegated, of course, to the provinces," ignoring the concerns regarding the lack of availability of these programs in some provinces.[62] This lack of access to fine option programs in some provinces was a key concern for the Supreme Court when it invalidated the mandatory victim fine surcharge in *Boudreault*.[63]

Along with criticisms regarding the compatibility of the Harper government's MMS policies with Charter rights, the government's policies were also subject to constitutional concerns regarding the federalism and the provincial jurisdiction over the administration of justice. As illustrated, responses from the Conservative government regarding these concerns were infrequent, deflected responsibility, and lacked guidance for provincial governments.

Opposition Parties' Patterns of Scrutiny

The opposition parties attempted to hold the Conservative government accountable for its duty to ensure constitutionality of its legislation by using expert evidence on the effectiveness and impacts of MMS and through assessments of compliance with the Charter. That said, the level of criticism by the opposition was not consistent in the debates of all eleven bills. In bills enacted during the first years of the Harper government, members of the Bloc Québécois were most vocal against MMS provisions. However, this vocal opposition dropped after the 2011 election where the party went from forty-seven seats in the House of Commons to just four, resulting in the loss of official party status.[64]

Parties that held the role as Official Opposition during the Harper-era – the Liberal Party from 2006–11 and the NDP from 2011–15 – did not always oppose MMS. For example, the NDP supported the MMS provisions in Bill C-2 (2008). In the debates for Bill C-2, an NDP MP stated that "the mandatory minimums that are in there (C-2) and some of the provisions around impaired driving are badly need in our society."[65] Additionally, in the debates for Bill S-9, a Liberal MP said, "[W]e feel that these mandatory minimums placed in this stand-alone section for auto theft are reasonable ... The mandatory minimum that attaches with it is proportionate."[66] However, as discussed above, Bill C-10 marked a significant shift towards the criticism of all MMS introduced by the Harper government. For example, in contrast with the above quotes, in the debates for Bill C-26 (which occurred after Bill C-10) a Liberal MP stated, "While we have supported mandatory minimums in this area in the past, we no longer support them as a matter of policy, given that they are ineffective in achieving their stated objectives and may violate the Charter."[67] This passage marks an explicit shift in philosophy regarding MMS from the Liberal Party. After Bill C-10, the NDP and Liberals consistently criticized and opposed MMS by relying on Charter compliance as a mechanism to hold the government accountable in this policy area.

Conclusion

The secretive nature of bureaucratic rights review makes it difficult to fully understand the decision-making process that occurred between the Department of Justice and the Harper government before a bill was officially introduced in the House of Commons. For example, other than the short excerpts provided by Department of Justice lawyers that testified in parliamentary committees we do not know the extent to which the Department of Justice scrutinized proposed bills, whether the Department of Justice determined if the legislation is in line with Charter values, and to what extent the Department of Justice believed the government could successfully defend these policies once enacted. Considering that 76 per cent of the Harper government-enacted MMS provisions have been found unconstitutional by Canadian appellate courts,[68] it is possible that the Department of Justice advised that the bills could be constitutionally vulnerable, but the government decided to pursue these policies anyway.[69] Additionally, as Hiebert demonstrates, the advice at this stage from the Department of Justice and the decision by the government to proceed with the legislation boils down to the government's tolerance for risk.[70] Given that the Harper government may have been engaging in penal populism and that its criminal justice policy has been likened to high-risk taking in this regard, it could be the case that the government was intent on pursuing this legislation despite possibly being forewarned by the Department of Justice.[71] In the time since, MMS has been one of the more active areas where the Supreme

Court has invalidated the Harper government's policies. However, it is possible that the advice from the Department of Justice at the time would have suggested that these policies were indeed constitutional. The Supreme Court's jurisprudence until that point was deferential to Parliament's creation of MMS.[72] Until the Court's 2015 decision in *R. v. Nur*, it upheld MMS created by Parliament having only invalidated one MMS in *R. v. Smith* (1987). Indeed, prior to *Nur*, the Court often noted, "It is not for the court to pass on the wisdom of Parliament … [that] the court should be reluctant to interfere with the considered views of Parliament."[73] That said, while the Harper government was still in office, many lower courts, including provincial courts of appeal, were striking down some of these policies. Ultimately, although we have no way of knowing, it is quite possible that the Department of Justice advised the government that MMS were likely constitutional, and certainly not manifestly unconstitutional.

The second stream of legislative rights review in the bureaucratic arena concerns the minister of justice's reporting duty under section 4.1(1) of the *Department of Justice Act* when proposed legislation is inconsistent with the Charter. Other intended purposes of section 4.1(1) were to facilitate intra-institutional scrutiny of proposed legislation as well as potentially acting as a restraint on the government's legislative agenda.[74] However, in the nearly four decades since the *Department of Justice Act* has been in effect, no such report has ever been made by a minister of justice under this provision, including in relation to the Harper government's MMS legislation. It is important to note, though, that the fact that there have been no reports under section 4.1(1) does not mean this is an indication of a "robust rights culture" within the bureaucratic arena of rights review.[75] Instead, the lack of section 4.1(1) reports casts doubt on the nature of bureaucratic assessments of Charter compliance.[76]

For the Harper government MMS provisions, the question then remains: What does it mean if the minister of justice is required to certify that bills have been assessed to comply with the Charter and no reports of inconsistency were made, but 76 per cent of the provisions challenged have been invalidated by courts? Additionally, what level of assessment took place to satisfy that these laws were consistent with the Charter? Due to the secrecy of this stage of legislative rights review, it is difficult to completely understand. This secrecy was demonstrated in the parliamentary debates when opposition parliamentarians asked the Conservative government to provide evidence that the Department of Justice advised that the MMS policies were consistent with the Charter and the government did not provide such evidence.

Instead, Department of Justice lawyers briefly testified that the provisions were constitutional. These brief comments regarding constitutionality by Department of Justice lawyers are unsurprising given that they are responsible to the government, not Parliament.[77] However, the claims from the opposition parliamentarians regarding the lack of consideration for the Charter calls into question the threshold for reporting inconsistencies with the Charter under section 4.1(1).

The existing literature on this reporting duty and the *Schmidt* case helps us understand this threshold in more depth.[78] James Kelly and Matthew Hennigar highlight how the lack of transparency regarding the minister of justice's statutory duty under section 4.1(1) obscures the "constitutional basis on which certification is determined."[79] Hiebert demonstrates that there is an existing presumption in the Department of Justice that such a report under section 4.1(1) will never be made.[80] While one explanation is that this is because the government ensures that the legislation is completely in line with the Charter, a more sceptical explanation suggests that this is because such a report would make it difficult or impossible to (a) pass the legislation into law and (b) defend such legislation in court, if challenged.[81] Additionally, *Schmidt* brought to light an allegedly weak systematic use of Charter standards by the Conservative government when creating bills.[82] While ultimately unsuccessful in court, the claim that the reporting obligation was only engaged when a bill was "more likely than not inconsistent" with the Charter, provides valuable insight into understanding how the Harper government legislated with Charter standards and why no such report under section 4.1(1) was made.[83] If this claim is accurate, it has serious implications for how rights are protected in Canada's legislative process. First, it may signal to Parliament that it does not need to engage in serious rights scrutiny because no report under section 4.1(1) was made. Second, if meaningful rights-based scrutiny of legislation does not occur in Parliament, then potentially unconstitutional legislation may be passed into law.

In contrast to the institutionalized state of legislative rights review in the bureaucratic arena, legislative rights review in the parliamentary arena is seen as particularly weak in Canada. Parliamentary rights review is effectively captured in the above analysis of parliamentary debates and committee hearings. While we did find some clear examples of opposition parliamentarians attempting to hold the government accountable for the constitutionality of its legislation, these efforts were essentially ignored as the government was able to pursue its legislative agenda regardless of criticisms from the opposition. Throughout our study, opposition parliamentarians and expert witnesses relentlessly criticized the proposed legislation on Charter grounds (especially post–Bill C-10 when the Harper government held a majority) and attempted to make amendments to the legislation in committee; however, no criticisms were seriously considered by the government, nor were any proposed amendments adopted. The fact that the legislation was enacted into law without much concern from the government in the face of substantial critical discussion regarding rights compatibility demonstrates the weak state of parliamentary rights review in Canada.[84]

This weak nature of parliamentary rights review is directly related to the institutionalized state of bureaucratic rights review in Canada.[85] First, once the Department of Justice confirms that the proposed legislation is constitutional, there is essentially no chance that the government's stance will change. Second, the secrecy of the bureaucratic rights review process also hinders the ability of the House of Commons to deliberate the constitutional merits of proposed bills to its fullest ability. Thus, there must be more transparency at this stage. If it is the job of the Department of Justice to vet proposed bills for consistency with the Charter and provide legal advice to the government, this advice should be transparent and reported to Parliament when the laws are being introduced and debated. In order for Parliament to have an effective and more legitimate role in legislative rights review, it must be privy to the legal advice and expertise regarding the constitutionality of proposed legislation, not just the executive.[86] It is no surprise that parliamentary rights review is weak in Canada if the legal advice given to the government regarding constitutionality is not shared with the House of Commons – the democratic institution in charge of debating the merits of the bill. Improving the function of parliamentary rights review would ultimately allow Parliament to engage in a meaningful discussion regarding the constitutionality of proposed provisions and provide a check on the power that the executive has over the legislative process in Canada. For example, one could look to Hiebert's suggestion of a hybrid-approach that implements aspects of Australia's establishment of scrutiny committees in Parliament, which if supplemented with Canada's model, could provide a stronger role for Parliament and a more robust model for protecting rights.[87]

Parliamentary rights review is also impacted by the Canadian style of the Westminster system of government. As James Kelly and Alex Marland both argue, the inability of parliamentary committees and opposition MPs to amend legislation can be attributed to executive dominance of the legislative process.[88] This is also shaped by other Westminster factors such as the centralizing nature of strong majority governments, party discipline, and extreme partisanship in the House of Commons.[89]

Viewed this way, when applied to the Harper government MMS legislation, Parliament is not an adequate check on the legislative agenda of the executive branch in Canada. Further, in this case, this weakness of Parliament has one significant consequence: constitutionally suspect legislation was easily passed through Parliament by the government despite being heavily criticized and forewarned by opposition MPs and expert witnesses on its potential lack of compliance with the Charter.

As for the future of MMS in Canada, it appears that as more of these provisions are challenged in Canadian courts, more will be invalidated under the Charter. The government has a number of options as to how to deal with these provisions: (1) stay the course and allow these constitutionally suspect provisions on the books to be challenged and – more than likely – struck down by courts, (2) remove certain MMS, but not all,[90] (3) remove all MMS except for the most serious offences (e.g., murder),[91] or (4) enact a safety valve that could act as a compromise for those that support MMS and those that are concerned about their inconsistencies with the Charter in certain circumstances.[92]

The findings from this study of the Harper government's MMS policies – specifically that no report regarding constitutional incapability was made, that the legislation was criticized by opposition MPs in the House of Commons, and that these provisions have been found unconstitutional 76 per cent of the time in appellate courts – demonstrates legislative rights review by Parliament is not an effective restraint. Due to the weak function of parliamentary rights review, Parliament is susceptible to passing unconstitutional legislation under governments that do not legislate in good faith within the parameters of the Charter.

NOTES

1 Debra Parkes, "From Smith to Smickle: The Charter's Minimal Impact on Mandatory Minimum Sentences," *Supreme Court Law Review* 57 (2012): 149–72; Kate Puddister, "Protecting against Cruel and Unusual Punishment: Section 12 of the Charter and Mandatory Minimum Sentences," in *Policy Change, Courts, and the Canadian Constitution*, ed. Emmett Macfarlane (Toronto: University of Toronto Press, 2018), 189–209.

2 Lauren Witten, "Proportionality as a Moral Process: Reconceiving Judicial Discretion and Mandatory Minimum Penalties," *Ottawa Law Review* 48, no. 1 (2016): 81–134.

3 James B. Kelly and Kate Puddister, "Criminal Justice Policy during the Harper Era: Private Member's Bills, Penal Populism, and the *Criminal Code of Canada*," *Canadian Journal of Law and Society* 32, no. 3 (2017): 391–416.

4 Janet Hiebert, *Charter Conflicts: What Is Parliament's Role?* (Montreal: McGill-Queen's University Press, 2002).
5 Ibid.
6 Ibid.; James B. Kelly, *Governing with the Charter: Legislative and Judicial Activism and Framers' Intent* (Vancouver: UBC Press, 2005).
7 Kelly, *Governing with the Charter*.
8 Ibid.; Emmett Macfarlane, Janet Hiebert, and Anna Drake, *Legislating Under the Charter: Parliament, Executive Power, and Rights* (Toronto: University of Toronto Press, 2023).
9 Janet Hiebert, "The Charter, Policy, and Political Judgment," in *Policy Change, Courts, and the Canadian Constitution*, ed. Emmett Macfarlane (Toronto: University of Toronto Press, 2018), 81–102.
10 Ibid., 88; Kelly, *Governing with the Charter*.
11 Hiebert, "The Charter, Policy, and Political Judgment," 88.
12 Kelly, *Governing with the Charter*.
13 Janet Hiebert, "The Charter's Influence on Legislation: Political Strategizing about Risk: Presidential Address to the Canadian Political Science Association, Regina, Saskatchewan, May 31, 2018," *Canadian Journal of Political Science* 51, no. 4 (2018): 727–47.
14 Ibid.
15 Ibid.
16 Ibid.
17 Macfarlane, Hiebert, and Drake, *Legislating Under the Charter*.
18 Hiebert, *Charter Conflicts*; Janet Hiebert and James B. Kelly, *Parliamentary Bills of Rights: The Experiences of New Zealand and the United Kingdom* (Cambridge: Cambridge University Press, 2015).
19 Hiebert, "The Charter, Policy, and Political Judgment."
20 Hiebert and Kelly, *Parliamentary Bills of Rights*, 60.
21 Hiebert, "The Charter, Policy, and Political Judgment."
22 Kelly, *Governing with the Charter*.
23 James B. Kelly, "Legislative Capacity and Human Rights in the Age of Populism – Two Challenges for Legislated Rights: Discussion of Legislated Rights – Securing Human Rights Through Legislation," *Jerusalem Review of Legal Studies* 21, no. 1 (2020): 94–111.
24 Christopher J. Kam, *Party Discipline and Parliamentary Politics* (Cambridge: Cambridge University Press, 2009); Donald J. Savoie, *Governing From the Centre: The Concentration of Power in Canadian Politics* (Toronto: University of Toronto Press, 1999).
25 Hiebert, "The Charter, Policy, and Political Judgment," 96.
26 Ibid.; Kelly, *Governing with the Charter*.
27 Hiebert, *Charter Conflicts*.
28 Ibid.

29 Ibid.
30 Kelly, *Governing with the Charter*.
31 Hiebert, *Charter Conflicts*.
32 Macfarlane, Hiebert, and Drake, *Legislating Under the Charter*.
33 Julian V. Roberts et al., *Penal Populism and Public Opinion: Lessons from Five Countries* (Oxford: Oxford University Press, 2002).
34 Kelly and Puddister, "Criminal Justice Policy during the Harper Era"; Kate Puddister, "How the Canadian Sentencing System Impacts Policy Reform: An Examination of the Harper Era," *Law & Policy* 43, no. 2 (2021): 149–69.
35 The debates and committee meetings for Bill C-13 (a bill that enacted two MMS for impaired driving), Bill S-9 (a bill that enacted an MMS for motor vehicle theft), Bill C-21 (a bill that enacted an MMS for fraud over $1 million), and C-36 (a bill that enacted seven MMS regarding prostitution and trafficking) did not discuss the proposed MMS provisions in regards to the Constitution or the Charter.
36 There are two Bill C-10s that relate to MMS in our study. Unless indicated otherwise, when discussing Bill C-10, we are referring to the *Safe Streets and Communities Act* (2012). Any discussions of Bill C-10 (2014), *An Act to Amend the Criminal Code (trafficking in contraband tobacco)* will be indicated as such.
37 Fine option programs allow individuals who have been ordered to pay a fine to satisfy the fine by performing work for volunteer or not-for-profit organizations approved by the Department of Justice.
38 Craig Scott, Standing Committee on Justice and Human Rights, Evidence, 23 October 2012, https://www.ourcommons.ca/documentviewer/en/41-1/JUST/meeting-46/evidence.
39 *R. v. Boudreault*, [2018] 3 S.C.R. 599.
40 House of Common Debates, *Hansard*, 41st Parl., 1st Sess., Vol. 146, No. 053, 18 October 2024, 3549 (Hon. Rob Nicholson), https://www.ourcommons.ca/DocumentViewer/en/41-1/house/sitting-53/hansard.
41 House of Common Debates, *Hansard*, 41st Parl., 2nd Sess., Vol. 147, No. 095, 3 June 2014, 6074 (Hon. Peter MacKay), https://www.ourcommons.ca/DocumentViewer/en/41-2/house/sitting-95/hansard.
42 The debates for Bill C-36 focused more on the criminalization of certain areas of sex-work, rather than on the MMS provisions.
43 House of Common Debates, *Hansard*, 41st Parl., 1st Sess., Vol. 146, No. 059, 2 December 2011, 3929 (Hon. Irwin Cotler), https://www.ourcommons.ca/DocumentViewer/en/41-1/house/sitting-59/hansard.
44 House of Common Debates, *Hansard*, 41st Parl., 1st Sess., Vol. 146, No. 093, 9 March 2012, 6040 (Hon. Irwin Cotler), https://www.ourcommons.ca/DocumentViewer/en/41-1/house/sitting-93/hansard.

45 Paul Saint-Denis, Proceedings of the Standing Senate Committee on Legal and Constitutional Affairs, 18 September 2014, https://sencanada.ca/en/Content/Sen/Committee/412/LCJC/16EV-51571-E.
46 Serge Joyal, Proceedings of the Standing Senate Committee on Legal and Constitutional Affairs, 7 March 2013, https://sencanada.ca/en/Content/Sen/Committee/411/LCJC/31EV-50016-E.
47 House of Common Debates, *Hansard*, 41st Parl., 2nd Sess., Vol. 147, No. 095, 3 June 2014, 6080 (Hon. Wayne Easter), https://www.ourcommons.ca/DocumentViewer/en/41-2/house/sitting-95/hansard.
48 House of Common Debates, *Hansard*, 41st Parl., 2nd Sess., Vol. 147, No. 093, 30 May 2014, 5928 (Hon. Francoise Boivin), https://www.ourcommons.ca/DocumentViewer/en/41-2/house/sitting-93/hansard.
49 Hiebert, "The Charter, Policy, and Political Judgment."
50 Ibid., 91–2.
51 *Schmidt v. Canada (Attorney General)*, [2016] FC 269.
52 Kelly, *Governing with the Charter*.
53 Dennis Baker, "Criminal Justice and Criminal Law," in *Canadian Federalism: Performance, Effectiveness, and Legitimacy*, ed. Herman Bakvis and Grace Skogstad (Toronto: University of Toronto Press, 2020), 114–37.
54 Puddister, "How the Canadian Sentencing System Impacts Policy Reform."
55 Ibid.
56 Irwin Cotler, Standing Committee on Justice and Human Rights, 17 November 2011, https://www.ourcommons.ca/documentviewer/en/41-1/JUST/meeting-12/evidence.
57 Jean-Marc Fournier, Standing Committee on Justice and Human Rights, 1 November 2011, https://www.ourcommons.ca/documentviewer/en/41-1/JUST/meeting-9/evidence.
58 House of Common Debates, *Hansard*, 41st Parl., 1st Sess., Vol. 146, No. 056, 29 November 2011, 3746 (Hon. Ryan Cleary), https://www.ourcommons.ca/DocumentViewer/en/41-1/house/sitting-56/hansard.
59 Rob Nicholson, Standing Committee on Justice and Human Rights, Evidence, 6 October 2011, https://www.ourcommons.ca/documentviewer/en/41-1/JUST/meeting-4/evidence.
60 Vic Toews, Proceedings of the Standing Senate Committee on Legal and Constitutional Affairs, 2 February 2012, https://sencanada.ca/en/Content/Sen/Committee/411/LCJC/09EV-49287-E.
61 Craig Scott, Standing Committee on Justice and Human Rights, Evidence, 23 October 2012, https://www.ourcommons.ca/documentviewer/en/41-1/JUST/meeting-46/evidence.
62 Rob Nicholson, Standing Committee on Justice and Human Rights, Evidence, 23 October 2012, https://www.ourcommons.ca/documentviewer/en/41-1/JUST/meeting-46/evidence.

63 *R. v. Boudreault*, para. 72.
64 Loss of official party status meant that the Bloc Québécois could ask fewer questions in the House and could not sit as voting members on parliamentary committees.
65 House of Common Debates, *Hansard*, 39th Parl., 2nd Sess., Vol. 142, No. 025, 27 November 2007, 1425 (Hon. Joe Comartin), https://www.ourcommons.ca/DocumentViewer/en/39-2/house/sitting-25/hansard.
66 House of Common Debates, *Hansard*, 40th Parl., 3rd Sess., Vol. 145, No. 095, 5 November 2010, 5872 (Hon. Brian Murphy), https://www.ourcommons.ca/DocumentViewer/en/40-3/house/sitting-95/hansard.
67 House of Common Debates, *Hansard*, 41st Parl., 2nd Sess., Vol. 147, No. 094, 2 June 2014, 6058 (Hon. Sean Casey), https://www.ourcommons.ca/DocumentViewer/en/41-2/house/sitting-94/hansard.
68 Brendan Dell, "Return to Smith? Harper-Era Mandatory Minimum Sentences in Canadian Courts (2008–2023)," *Ottawa Law Review* 55, no. 2 (2024): 327–62.
69 Brendan Dell, "Rights Review and the Institutional Roles in Sentencing: A Study of Harper-Era Mandatory Minimum Sentences" (MA thesis, University of Guelph, 2022).
70 Hiebert, "The Charter's Influence on Legislation."
71 Ibid.; Kelly and Puddister, "Criminal Justice Policy During the Harper Era"; Macfarlane, Hiebert, and Drake, *Legislating Under the Charter*.
72 See *R. v. Ferguson*, [2008] 1 S.C.R. 96; *R. v. Goltz*, [1991] 3 S.C.R. 485; *R. v. Latimer*, [2001] 1 S.C.R. 3; *R. v. Morrisey*, [2000] 2 S.C.R. 90.
73 *R. v. Goltz*, [1991] 3 S.C.R., 502.
74 Janet Hiebert, "Parliamentary Engagement with the Charter: Rethinking the Idea of Legislative Rights Review," *The Supreme Court Law Review: Osgoode's Annual Constitutional Cases Conference* 58, no. 1 (2012): 87–107.
75 Hiebert and Kelly, *Parliamentary Bills of Rights*, 60.
76 Macfarlane, Hiebert, and Drake, *Legislating Under the Charter*.
77 Stephen Gardbaum, *The New Commonwealth Model of Constitutionalism Theory and Practice* (Cambridge: Cambridge University Press, 2013).
78 *Schmidt v. Canada (Attorney General)*, [2016] FC 269.
79 James B. Kelly and Matthew A. Hennigar, "The Canadian Charter of Rights and the minister of justice: Weak-form review within a constitutional Charter of Rights," *International Journal of Constitutional Law* 10, no. 1 (2012): 35–68.
80 Hiebert, "The Charter's Influence on Legislation."
81 Hiebert, "The Charter, Policy, and Political Judgment."
82 Ibid.
83 Ibid., 92.
84 Kelly, *Governing with the Charter*.

85 Ibid.
86 Macfarlane, Hiebert, and Drake, *Legislating Under the Charter*, reach similar conclusions.
87 Janet Hiebert, "A Hybrid-Approach to Protect Rights? An Argument in Favour of Supplementing Canadian Judicial Review with Australia's Model of Parliamentary Scrutiny," *Federal Law Review* 26, no. 1 (1998): 115–38.
88 Kelly, "Legislative Capacity and Human Rights in the Age of Populism"; Alex Marland, *Whipped: Party Discipline in Canada* (Vancouver: UBC Press, 2020).
89 Hiebert, "A Hybrid-Approach to Protect Rights?"
90 At the time of writing, the Liberal government has a bill before Parliament (Bill C-5) that aims to remove certain MMS from the Criminal Code and CDSA.
91 In 2016, Green Party MP Elizabeth May introduced a PMB to eliminate MMS for most offences except murder and high treason.
92 At the time of writing, safety valve legislation has been proposed in Parliament on six separate occasions by individual MPs or Senators – none of which made significant progress.

12 Enhancing Legislative Review: A New Voice for the Legislature

CHRIS MCCORKINDALE AND JANET HIEBERT

Unlike acts of the United Kingdom Parliament, primary legislation made by the Scottish Parliament is not immune from judicial review.[1] An act of the Scottish Parliament "is not law" in so far as a court determines, inter alia, that it "relates to" a matter reserved to the UK Parliament (as defined in Schedule 5 to the *Scotland Act 1998*) or is incompatible with the European Convention on Human Rights.[2] For those engaged in the law-making process – from civil servants, to legislators, to ministers and their advisors, to courts and to those private citizens and public or private bodies who rely on the rights and duties conferred by legislation – the consequences where legislation does stray outside of legislative competence are therefore severe.

In order to protect against the prospect of judicial censure the *Scotland Act 1998* established a framework of pre-introduction checks and cross-checks for legislative competence. Consistent with systems of legislative rights review in Canada, New Zealand, Australia (in the Australian Capital Territory and in Victoria), and the UK,[3] the minister responsible, on or before its introduction, must report to Parliament their view that a bill as introduced would be within devolved competence. If the minister, acting on the basis of legal advice provided by the Scottish Government Legal Directorate (SGLD) and by the Scottish Government's Law Officers,[4] reaches a view that a bill would *not* be within legislative competence then (unlike, say, the section 19 reporting requirement in the *Human Rights Act 1998* [HRA]), it would be unlawful to proceed to introduction. However, and unique to the devolution statutes, a parallel and independent report on legislative competence must also be made upon a bill's introduction by the Presiding Officer of the Scottish Parliament. The Presiding Officer's view is reached on the basis of legal advice, provided by the Office of the Solicitor to the Scottish Parliament (OSSP). Passed concurrently with the HRA, the reporting requirements created by the *Scotland Act* share simultaneously inward and outward facing purposes. On the one hand, these statements of competence ensure that the executive "has properly considered the issues and made a proper judgement that the measure is within the power and competence of the Scottish Parliament."[5] On the other hand, they serve to enhance the scrutiny of legislation by the Scottish Parliament, allowing them to "ask questions about the statement[s], raise queries about whether [they] are entirely correct, and no doubt identify particular provisions in the Bill where there may or may not be some doubt" about legislative competence.[6]

While some have expressed doubt about whether the independent assessment by the Presiding Officer is anything more than needless duplication, in this chapter – which is based on a number of interviews with Scottish government lawyers, Scottish Parliament lawyers, and Scottish Parliament legislators – we argue that the statutory function of the Presiding Officer in relation to legislative competence is impactful on legislation that strays close to constitutional boundaries, provides an independent check on the executive that is missing in other jurisdictions with executive-only reporting requirements, and provides a source of independent scrutiny by lawyers that – unlike government legal advice – can support legislators in the exercise of their legislative and scrutiny functions. While this strengthening of pre-introduction reporting requirements may not (yet) have achieved the aim of better informing the Scottish Parliament to take legislative review seriously, and while the impact on legislation at the pre-introduction stage may (so far) come at the cost of transparency, we believe that the role of the Presiding Officer in the devolution statutes offers a promising alternative to those schemes that rely on the good will of the executive to mark its own homework and on the good faith of the executive accurately to inform legislators where there are doubts about the rights compatibility of proposed legislation.

The Presiding Officer's Statutory Function

The Presiding Officer's statutory function with regard to legislative competence is set out in section 31(2) of the 1998 act:

> The Presiding Officer shall, on or before the introduction of a Bill in the Parliament, decide whether or not in his view the provisions of the Bill would be within the legislative competence of the Parliament and state his decision.

As per section 31(3), "the form of any statement and the manner in which it is to be made" is set out in standing orders. Rule 9.3 of the Scottish Parliament's standing orders states:

1. A Bill shall on introduction be accompanied by a written statement signed by the Presiding Officer which shall-
   a. Indicate whether or not the Presiding Officer's view the provisions of the Bill would be within the legislative competence of the Parliament; and
   b. If in the Presiding Officer's view any of the provisions would not be within legislative competence, indicate which those provisions are and the reasons for that view.

This is to say that *every* bill that is introduced into the Scottish Parliament must be accompanied with a (positive or negative) statement of legislative competence by the Presiding Officer, and that every negative statement must be issued with reasons that explain the Presiding Officer's view that the bill, as introduced, would not be within the legislative competence of the Parliament. Unlike the parallel ministerial statement – Scottish ministers cannot make a statement of competence (in other words, cannot introduce legislation) unless they are satisfied, on the basis of legal advice and with clearance by the Scottish government's Law Officers,[7] that the bill as introduced *would be* within the legislative competence of the Parliament – the Presiding Officer's view is just that: a view. A negative statement of competence by the Presiding Officer is *not* a veto on the introduction of a bill. It is perfectly competent for the Scottish government to introduce – and for the Scottish Parliament to pass – legislation notwithstanding a negative statement by the Presiding Officer.

The question to which the Presiding Officer must set their mind – "would the provisions of a bill be within the legislative competence of the Parliament" – is legal in character: the duty to make a statement of competence is a creature of statute; the tests for legislative competence are set out in the 1998 act and in the subsequent jurisprudence of the House of Lords/Supreme Court; a bill that troubles the boundaries of legislative competence is susceptible to a pre-enactment reference to the Supreme Court by the Scottish or UK government Law Officers; and, an act of the Scottish Parliament that sits outside of legislative competence "is not law" and is vulnerable to judicial strike down. For this reason, the Presiding Officer is assisted in the exercise of their statutory function by OSSP – a team of Parliament lawyers (no longer, as they once were, formally part of the Government Legal Service of Scotland [GLSS] – now "associates" thereof) headed by the solicitor to the Scottish Parliament. OSSP's main function in relation to primary legislation is to advise the Presiding Officer on the question of legislative competence. However, while the character of the section 31(2) function is legal, the Supreme Court has said that neither the Presiding Officer's statement nor the parallel statement by the Scottish ministers (nor any decision made by the Scottish or UK government Law Officers *whether or not* to refer a bill to the Supreme Court for pre-enactment review of competence issues, under section 33 of the *Scotland Act*), have any bearing on the courts' judicial function. In *Anderson v. Scottish Ministers*, Lord Hope said:

> Important though these two safeguards [the parallel section 31 statements and the section 33 reference power] may be in practice to the work of the Scottish Parliament, they are no more than statements of opinion which do not bind the judiciary.[8]

Lord Hope returned to the theme a little more than a decade later in a leading case on legislative competence, *Imperial Tobacco v. Lord Advocate*. "If an issue as to legislative competence arises," he said – noting the positive statements of competence relating to the legislation at stake, as well as the decision by the Law Officers *not* to refer the relevant bill for a pre-enactment challenge – "it will entirely be a matter for the courts to determine."[9]

As these statements indicate, though legal in *character*, the Presiding Officer's statement serves political/parliamentary rather than legal/judicial *purposes*. These purposes were set out by Lord Sewel, the minister of state in the Scottish Office (as it then was) responsible for steering the Scotland bill safely through the House of Lords. On the one hand, he said, the Presiding Officer's statement provides parliamentarians with "important guidance about the competence of the Parliament" that might inform subsequent scrutiny of the bill. On the other hand, it provides the Presiding Officer with an opportunity "to express his concerns [to Parliament and to Government] if he has any."[10] Put differently, the Presiding Officer's statement serves both a scrutiny function, as each bill is made subject to OSSP's scrutiny and to the Presiding Officer's assessment, and a reporting function, as Parliament is informed – at introduction – not only of the Scottish government's view about legislative competence but also, separately and independently, about the Presiding Officer's assessment.

Vetting Bills for Legislative Competence

The Presiding Officer will come to a view on legislative competence during the three week "pre-introduction" period that precedes the formal introduction of a bill into the Scottish Parliament. During this period, the draft bill, and a note on legislative competence prepared by SGLD, will be shared with the Lord Advocate (who must clear the parallel ministerial statement) and with the OSSP. At this point, an iterative process takes place between SGLD and OSSP that will inform the advice given by the latter to the Presiding Officer about legislative competence. We were told that, while SGLD's note on legislative competence is a useful point of reference, Parliament lawyers will make their own assessment of legislative competence, both to avoid their view being "tainted" by assessments already made by SGLD and to maximize concerns about legislative competence that might have been missed or interpreted differently by SGLD. Where a positive statement of competence is made this (so far, and in identical terms to the statement made by the responsible minister) comprises a standard single line statement: that, in the Presiding Officer's view, "the provisions of [the bill] would be within the legislative competence of the Scottish Parliament."

When asked about the criteria applied by the Presiding Officer and by OSSP in the exercise of the section 31(2) function we were told that no formal test had been articulated, and that a percentage-based approach (for example, that a bill would be 50.01 per cent more likely than not to survive a challenge in the Supreme Court) would not necessarily be helpful. Rather, it was said that parliamentary officials must quickly develop an understanding of how each Presiding Officer likes to work, on the one hand ensuring that all advice offered to the Presiding Officer is based on "robust evidence" and the "proper application of relevant legal principles," and on the other hand respecting that the Presiding Officer is a politician, that it is the Presiding Officer's statement – *qua* political actor – to make and so it is for the Presiding Officer to decide which factors (including legal advice from OSSP) to consider – and what weight to give to those relevant factors – in reaching their view.

An important factor for the Presiding Officer is the government's democratic mandate to pass its legislation, with the consequence that – where there is a very close call – the Presiding Officer might be minded to give to the government the benefit of the doubt by making a positive statement of competence. This political presumption of competence chimes with a "strong" legal presumption that is hardwired into the *Scotland Act 1998* by section 101(2). That section places an obligation on the courts, where such a reading is possible, to read acts of the

Scottish Parliament "as narrowly as is required … to be within competence." Parliamentary officials told us that, when pushed on legislative competence concerns, the Scottish government will often – sometimes more persuasively than others – point to section 101(2) as something of a panacea: that no matter the concern it will be available to the court at a later date to "read down" legislative provisions so as to bring them within competence. This approach, it was said, might raise issues of transparency where Scottish ministers claim outwardly to be taking a power to be used in a particular – and expansive – way while inwardly conceding behind the veil of the pre-introduction period that the court is likely to construe the power in much more narrow terms. It is also an approach that might have been pushed to its limits. In its 2021 judgment in the *UNCRC Bill Reference*, the Supreme Court was unimpressed by attempts to draft provisions

> whose plain meaning does not accurately represent the law, and to rely on the courts, applying section 101(2) of the Scotland Act, subsequently to impose a variety of qualifications upon the provisions on a case by case basis, so as to give it a different effect which is lawful.[11]

For the Supreme Court, not only would such an approach be incompatible with accessibility and legal certainty as fundamental tenets of the rule of law,[12] but – pushed to its logical conclusion – it would render nugatory the section 31 safeguards. If the expansive approach to section 101(2) advocated for by the Scottish government was accepted, the Supreme Court said:

> … then the person in charge of the Bill, and the Presiding Officer, can be satisfied that the provisions of a Bill are within competence, even where they plainly exceed competence on their face, by relying on the future application of section 101(2) by the courts. On that basis, their statements of compatibility are liable to be reduced to a formality.[13]

At the time of writing, a little more than two decades after the opening of the Scottish Parliament and with the introduction of some 296 government bills during that time, only *one* government bill – the "UK Withdrawal from the European Union (Legal Continuity) (Scotland) Bill" – has been introduced with a negative statement of competence by the Presiding Officer.[14] However, that record – one negative statement in 296 – is a poor indicator of the occurrence, nature, and resolution of concerns about legislative competence between OSSP and SGLD during the three-week pre-introduction period. Rather, with approximately fourteen government bills introduced in a typical year, we were told (1) that it is rare for OSSP not to raise *some* concerns about a bill – most of which are easily smoothed over with further clarification from SGLD during the pre-introduction period – but also, (2) that one or two bills each year might raise serious concerns about legislative competence or be considered a "close call," and where more pressure is placed on that iterative process. The *sources* of more significant disagreement might include the absence of case law to guide SGLD/OSSP in their interpretation of reserved matters or of Convention rights, differences in the proportionality assessments made by SGLD and OSSP where Convention rights are engaged, disagreement about the necessity or adequacy of safeguards – and whether these should feature on the face of a bill or in extraneous guidance – where the government takes/creates a power via primary legislation or engages Convention rights, or where the government pushes knowingly at the boundary between reserved and devolved matters.

The Pre-introduction Period

A number of factors explain the gap between the solitary negative statement of competence (so far) and the more regular concerns raised by OSSP, or disagreements between OSSP and SGLD, about legislative competence.

One significant factor is *ministerial priorities*. We asked whether legislative competence concerns were high on the list of ministerial priorities. The answer was that, because legislative competence concerns normally relate to specific provisions within a bill, rather than to a statutory scheme as a whole, or to the way in which a policy objective might be achieved rather than the policy objective itself, concerns about legislative competence do not rank highly in the order of ministerial priorities. Rather, the more immediate and pragmatic concern for Scottish ministers, "impatient for results,"[15] is to navigate as safely as possible through "unnecessarily complex and time consuming process[es]"[16] that might risk their place in a legislative queue that might be as long as three years in the making. There are two important consequences of this. First, political and policy actors in government will rarely engage directly in the competence vetting process and will defer heavily to the legal assessments made by SGLD and by the Lord Advocate – the exception being those rare occasions when a fundamental problem puts the statute or policy objective itself at risk. Second, where serious concerns about competence are raised by OSSP, we were told that ministers and their advisers tend to be risk averse, conceding (in the view of some government officials too readily) to OSSP, so as to insulate policy and legislative objectives from additional changes that might alter the government's policy agenda or (recalling that packed and long legislative queue) delay a bill's introduction.

Despite the fact the Presiding Officer's statement is a view only, with no power of veto or other legal effects that would compel ministers to satisfy the Presiding Officer as to its view on legislative competence, government officials told us that it would be "less than ideal" and "politically awkward" for Scottish ministers to proceed to introduction with a negative statement. So, we were told that every effort will be made during the pre-introduction period to reach a mutually agreeable position and to obtain a positive statement of competence from the Presiding Officer. For ministers, this might mean making amendments to – or withdrawing altogether – offending provisions in order to save the overall policy and bill, or it might mean making a so-called *Pepper v. Hart* statement (a statement made to Parliament by the responsible minister to place on the official record, and for possible future reference by the courts in the event of a legal challenge, the overall purpose of legislation or the meaning of particular provisions) regarding the exercise of contested powers.

Government officials offered mixed views about this process. Indeed, although not representative of the government view, some went so as far as to say that the Presiding Officer's statement – and the process that underpins it – amounts to unnecessary duplication of work already done by government lawyers. Frustration was expressed with the frequency, the helpfulness and the "too legalistic" nature of OSSP's interventions and with the overly cautious approach that is often taken by ministers. As regards the latter, government officials told us that ministers and their political advisers have in the past been too quick to make concessions not because they were persuaded to the Presiding Officer's view but because of those pragmatic reasons discussed above – the introduction of legislation on time and in good health. It is the view of some government officials, aware that any aim to achieve a positive statement from the Presiding Officer is a self-imposed one, that a more assertive approach by ministers to concerns raised by OSSP might have allowed the government to be bolder in its legislative agenda without crossing the boundaries of competence. While it is too strong to say that there is a *presumption* against proceeding with a negative statement, we were told that ministers would have to "think very carefully" about doing so, taking into account the political importance of the policy at stake, the possibility of post-introduction scrutiny and pre- or post-enactment legal challenge, the knock-on effect on a packed legislative timetable and the political consequences of challenging openly the Presiding Officer's judgement.

On the one occasion that a government bill was introduced with a negative statement by the Presiding Officer some of these considerations came into clear view. Having refused legislative consent to a UK bill (what would become the *European Union (Withdrawal) Act* 2018) that dealt with the continuity of European Union (EU) law in (and as) domestic law post-Brexit, and also with the repatriation of powers to the UK from the EU post-Brexit, the Scottish government introduced a bill that would cater for the continuity of EU law in devolved areas and that would give powers to Scottish ministers to adjust the statute book to deal with any deficiencies arising as a result of Brexit. This was a high stakes political act – a response to the political decision to reject the terms of the UK legislation but also (and recognizing the difficulty of implementing a parallel regime) putting political pressure onto the UK government to amend its bill so as to meet concerns from the devolved authorities about the way in which it planned to repatriate powers in devolved areas. As such the conditions were satisfied for the Scottish government to proceed confident in its view of the bill's legality even in the face of the Presiding Officer's negative statement.

Having made a negative statement, the Presiding Officer produced reasons as required (indeed, reflecting the political stakes, detailed reasons were produced) to the effect that, in the Presiding Officer's view, provisions of the Bill that would allow Scottish Ministers – post-Brexit – to amend the Scottish statute book in ways that would be incompatible with EU law brought the bill outside of legislative competence. "[P]ostponing the exercise of powers until a future date [in this case, until after the Brexit process was complete and the UK stood outside of the EU]", the Presiding Officer said, "may change the legal effect of a Bill but does not resolve the question of its legal validity."[17] As it happened, the Supreme Court held that the bill was outside of devolved competence but it rejected the reasons put forward by the Presiding Officer – "absent such legal effects," the Supreme Court held, "there is no incompatibility with EU law."[18] While the authority of the Presiding Officer was called into question in some quarters for expressing a view with which the Supreme Court ultimately did not agree, this criticism was misplaced. He was, here, acting (a) in the exercise of a statutory function, (b) on the basis of legal advice, (c) on a point of law that surely was a "close call," that (d) was offered to him with only limited judicial guidance on the point, and (e) which focused minds during the legislative process on a range of possible *vires* concerns that otherwise might not have attracted scrutiny. It remains to be seen if the experience will have a chilling effect on the Presiding Officer, in light of judicial disagreement and political backlash, or an emboldening effect on the Scottish government, who introduced a bill with a negative statement by the Presiding Officer and who – at least on that specific ground – lived to tell the tale.

A second factor in play, albeit one that is linked to the issue of ministerial priorities, is the *pressure of time*. Government and Parliament lawyers alike described as "challenging" the constraints of a three-week pre-introduction period. Those three weeks are inclusive of weekends, holidays and the constituency days of the Presiding Officer and of the minister responsible for the relevant Bill. This creates a series of significant pressures – pressure on OSSP to make an assessment and to inform the Presiding Officer; pressure to do so in time for SGLD to receive comments, to inform the responsible minister, and to engage in discussions with OSSP; and, pressure to do so in time for settled positions to be fed back and for the Presiding Officer to reflect on advice, to seek further clarification as necessary and to reach a view. In exceptional cases – where it is clear from an early stage that serious or complex competence issues might arise – the three week period might be extended with the agreement of both parties and/or the SGLD might choose to engage OSSP in "without prejudice" discussions about specific problematic provisions ahead of the three week period. In most cases, however, officials on both sides will work within the confines of the three week period.

While OSSP works with a smaller team and with fewer resources than does SGLD, and while Parliament lawyers come to a bill fresh and from a standing start as opposed to the time that SGLD will have engaged with a bill from the policy formulation to the drafting stages, for some officials the pressure of the three-week period works in favour of OSSP. As the end of the three-week period nears, and with (self-imposed) anxiety on the part of ministers about the possibility of a negative statement of competence by the Presiding Officer, ministers will themselves feel pressure to err on the side of caution. With the clock ticking – where disagreement persists towards the point of introduction – the Scottish government – by virtue of *its* three-week pre-introduction timeframe and by virtue of *its* strong preference for a positive statement by the Presiding Officer – is presented with a stark choice: to face down the Presiding Officer's view in the hope that they will give way, or – and as we were told, more commonly – to stand down, by amending or withdrawing the relevant provision(s). To the extent that section 31(2) serves a *scrutiny* function, this is served by the separate and independent treatment given to every bill introduced into the Scottish Parliament in parallel to internal scrutiny by SGLD and by the Lord Advocate. A bill that is introduced into the Parliament should throw up no surprises even if it is later subject to pre- or post-enactment judicial review. However, to the extent that the Presiding Officer's view serves an executive-facing *reporting* function – that opportunity to make government aware of concerns about legislative competence – the record is much more mixed. Government *is* made aware of concerns and very often government *does* make pre-legislative changes as a result, but as we have seen this is not often attributable to persuasion or to a developing culture of constitutional (including rights) compliance between and across the devolved institutions. Rather, this is more often attributable to pure pragmatism – finding the path of least resistance to a bill's introduction.

Members of the Scottish Parliament

So much for the executive-facing aspect of the Presiding Officer's statutory function. What about its Parliament-facing function – offering guidance to the Scottish Parliament about legislative competence and informing members about particular concerns that might inform the subsequent scrutiny of bills?

The dynamics of the pre-introduction period have been criticized both for lacking transparency and for having a "chilling effect" on elected members themselves. As Bruce Adamson, a leading human rights lawyer in Scotland, has said, "there may be a risk that it offers a false sense of security to MSPs who may rely on the [Presiding Officer's] statement of competence, without having the benefit of seeing the legal advice which will have identified the potential risks."[19] In our interviews with officials and elected members we were told that Adamson's fear is well founded. Neither in plenary nor in committees would parliamentarians "second guess" the view reached by the Presiding Officer. A variety of reasons were offered that explain this position. First, it is rare that legislative competence will remain a live issue when a bill is introduced into the Parliament. As one parliamentary official put it, given that most bills are government bills that have been made subject to scrutiny by the Presiding Officer as well as by SGLD and the UK and Scottish government's Law Officers, there is a reasonable working assumption that, when introduced, bills will not manifest by ultra vires. It would be "re-inventing the wheel" and, as such, an inefficient use of the Scottish Parliament's resources, to revisit that pre-legislative scrutiny. Second, the legal nature of competence questions – that involve close analysis of the *Scotland Act 1998*, the ECHR and related case law both in domestic courts and in the European Court of Human Rights (and in some cases, the Court of Justice of the European Union), as well as vires limits in other pieces of

UK and Scottish legislation – is of a sort that is likely to be beyond the experience or expertise of many elected members. Third, a number of officials and elected members told us that to second-guess the Presiding Officer's statement would be to "[disrespect the]" judgement of the Presiding Officer. Finally, we were told that for backbench and opposition MSPs the policy implications of a bill are more salient than questions of legislative competence, with two possible implications. On the one hand, members might take the "easy" option of deferring to the Presiding Officer on the competence question. On the other hand, members might see strategic advantage in reframing questions about legislative competence into questions about policy objectives and effects.[20]

However, and as we have seen, in "close call" situations the Presiding Officer might be inclined give the benefit of the doubt to the government on democratic grounds and make a one-line positive statement even where there is a significant (but, in the Presiding Officer's view, tolerable) risk that provisions of a bill would not survive judicial scrutiny. On such occasions we were told that the binary nature of the Presiding Officer's statement, along with the absence of reasons that support the making of a positive statement, can be a source of frustration. This frustration might be mitigated or alleviated, it was suggested, if committees and their clerks could be shown more of the Presiding Officer's working (either by the publication of reasons or on a less formal and confidential basis) about possible risk factors and opportunities for challenge. This, it was said, would help committees to identify areas of risk, to identify relevant witnesses as alternative sources of advice that might affirm, challenge or qualify single-line s31 statements and would break down the "boss mentality" that sees elected members defer too readily to the view reached (or, with undisclosed risk, conceded) by the Presiding Officer. This is to say that, taking seriously the Parliament-facing reporting function of the Presiding Officer's statutory function means a two-way shift in behaviour. On the one hand, a greater willingness on the part of the Presiding Officer and OSSP to be transparent about the hitherto undisclosed risk that might underpin single-line statements of legislative competence. On the other hand, a greater willingness on the part of elected members and Parliament officials to look behind those single-line statements and where appropriate to test, rather than defer to, the view reached by the Presiding Officer. While we were told that the publication of reasons underpinning positive statements in some cases had been considered – and in some cases even drafted – these "have never seen the light of day."

Interestingly, in the Senedd (Welsh Parliament) there have been no negative statements made by the Llywydd (Presiding Officer) but – unlike in Scotland – a practice *has* emerged of providing reasons and setting out risks where the question of legislative competence is a "close call" but a positive statement of competence is made. There are mixed views about this practice. Whereas Welsh government officials have expressed frustration that the publication of reasons provides a "sign post" to potential pre- or post-enactment litigants, we were told not only that the practice was in the public interest on transparency grounds but was also protective of the Llywydd's own position by providing reassurance to elected members and to the wider public that risks had been recognized, fully considered and that there were credible arguments that support the view that ultimately was reached.[21]

Officials were keen to stress the value of informal channels of communication that – on a case by case basis – could see OSSP raise "risks" about legislative competence (a positive statement notwithstanding) with a committee/clerk as a means of making those risks known and inviting due consideration by the committee during the bill's legislative passage. Again, there was a mixed assessment of the value of such engagement. For some officials this informal engagement provides the basis for a more regular dialogue between OSSP and legislators/clerks where there are known risks that are worthy of robust scrutiny. On the other hand, however, some officials expressed doubt about the capacity or willingness of elected members – particularly where the political stakes are high – to put political differences aside and to engage with competence arguments on their own terms. As with its executive-facing reporting function, then, the Parliament-facing reporting function has not yet lived up to its aim to provide guidance about legislative competence that can inform the political scrutiny of bills after their introduction.

Conclusion

The absence of published (or privately shared) reasons on the part of the Presiding Officer, a culture of deference amongst members towards the Presiding Officer, a reluctance to second-guess the legal advice that underpins the Presiding Officer's view and a reluctance on members' parts to put political lines to the side and to engage with competence concerns on their own terms, has stymied the potential of the Presiding Officer's statement to engender a culture of legislative review within Parliament. There is a resulting risk, then, that legislative review will fold back in on a form of pre-legislative *bureaucratic* review where it is (de facto if not de jure) the assessments made by officials that make the most significant impacts on legislative proposals, and where the cost of that impact is transparency and accountability. Underpinning this risk, however, are questions of behaviour and not law. A culture shift on the part of the Presiding Officer to provide more by way of reasons where there are real risks to legislation and a culture shift on the part of legislators to look behind positive statements of competence and to interrogate those risks on their own terms, would have the effect of further enhancing the scrutiny of legislation by an executive motivated to legislate via the path of least resistance, of better informing the Parliament about risks to *its* legislation that might further be explored during the passage of a bill and of providing to Parliament a source of legal advice that is robust in its review of legislative proposals and independent of the executive's own assessment. To revive meaningful legislative review, in other words, is to enable pre-enactment scrutiny by the legislature and in so doing to empower legislators, by the provision by parliamentary lawyers of information and advice, to contest – with equality of arms – the view of the executive.

NOTES

1 On the nature of acts of the Scottish Parliament, see Aileen McHarg, "What Is Delegated Legislation?" *Public Law* (2006): 539–61.

2 *Scotland Act 1998*, s. 29 and Schs. 4 and 5.

3 For their varying perspectives on the operation of rights vetting in these jurisdictions see, for example, Stephen Gardbaum, *The New Commonwealth Model of Constitutionalism: Theory and Practice* (Cambridge: Cambridge University Press, 2013); Janet L. Hiebert and James B. Kelly, *Parliamentary Bills of Rights: The Experiences of New Zealand and the United Kingdom* (Cambridge: Cambridge University Press, 2015); Ruth Dixon, "An Australian (Partial) Bill of Rights" *International Journal of Constitutional Law* 14, no. 1 (2016): 80–98; Alison Young, *Democratic Dialogue and the Constitution* (Oxford: Oxford University Press, 2017).

4 Indeed, the statement of competence by the responsible minister must be cleared by the Scottish government's law officers (the Lord Advocate and the Solicitor General for Scotland) before introduction; see the *Scottish Ministerial Code (2018 edition)*, para. 3.4. There is no such requirement on the responsible person introducing a non-governmental bill.

5 House of Lords Debate, 28 July 1998, column 1353, per Baroness Ramsay of Cartvale. The Scotland Bill debate on 28 July 1998, https://hansard.parliament.uk/lords/1998-07-28/debates/40be2d00-8ae3-4a1f-ba48-95856398ac57/ScotlandBill.

6 House of Lords Debate, 28 July 1998, column 1350, per Lord Mackay of Drumadoon.

7 Ibid.
8 *Anderson v. Scottish Ministers* [2001] UKPC D 5, 7, per Lord Hope.
9 *Imperial Tobacco v. Lord Advocate* [2012] UKSC 61, 7, per Lord Hope.
10 House of Lords Debate 9 November 1998, column 532, https://hansard.parliament.uk/Lords%E2%80%8F/1998-11-09/debates/46ed7046-469c-4f24-bff2-3ced9f329934/ScotlandBill.
11 Reference by the Attorney General and the Advocate General for Scotland – United Nations Convention on the Rights of the Child (Incorporation) (Scotland) Bill [2021] UKSC 42, 77.
12 Ibid., 77.
13 Ibid., 74.
14 A parallel bill in Wales – that became the (now repealed) *Law Derived from the European Union (Wales) Act 2018* – was introduced with a positive statement by the Presiding Officer. Reflecting the contestable nature of the legislation, the positive statement was accompanied with a statement of reasons, available at https://senedd.wales/laid%20documents/pri-ld11431/pri-ld11431-e.pdf.
15 Alan Page, *Constitutional Law of Scotland* (Edinburgh: W. Green, 2015), 204.
16 Ibid.
17 The Scottish Parliament, UK Withdrawal from the European Union (Legal Continuity) (Scotland) Bill, Statements on Legislative Competence, 27 February 2018, https://www.parliament.scot/-/media/files/legislation/bills/s5-bills/uk-withdrawal-from-the-european-union-legal-continuity-scotland-bill/introduced/statements-on-legislative-competence-withdrawal-from-the-european-union-legal-continuity-scotland-bi.pdf.
18 The UK Withdrawal from the European Union (Legal Continuity) (Scotland) Bill – A Reference by the Attorney General and the Advocate General for Scotland [2018] UKSC 64, at 85. See Chris McCorkindale and Aileen McHarg, "The Supreme Court and Devolution: The Scottish Continuity Bill Reference," *Juridical Review* 2 (2019): 190–7.
19 Bruce Adamson, "The Protection of Human Rights in the Legislative Process in Scotland," in Murray Hunt, Hayley Hooper, and Paul Yowell, eds., *Parliaments and Human Rights: Redressing the Democratic Deficit* (Oxford: Hart Publishing, 2015), chap. 13.
20 For a counterpoint that considers committees to be more engaged in rights scrutiny than our interviews suggest, see Douglas Jack, "Defending the Scotland Act 1998 as a 'Third Way' Bill of Rights" (PhD diss., Strathclyde University, 2022).
21 A more rounded discussion of the vetting process in Scotland, that includes discussion of the SGLD and Scottish and UK Law Officers' roles, can be found in Chris McCorkindale and Janet Hiebert, "Vetting Bills in the Scottish Parliament for Legislative Competence," *Edinburgh Law Review* 21, no. 3 (2017): 319–51.

Contributor Biographies

G. Elizabeth Bergman, (JD, PhD, MA, BMus)

Erin Crandall, Associate Professor, Department of Politics, Acadia University

Brendan Dell, PhD Candidate, Department of Political Studies, Queen's University

Minh Do, Assistant Professor, Department of Political Science, University of Guelph

Winsome Hall, Barrister, Alinea Chambers, JD (University of New South Wales), LLM (Cantab)

Mark S. Harding, Assistant Professor, Department of Political Science, University of Guelph

Janet Hiebert, Professor Emeritus, Department of Political Studies, Queen's University

Nancy Hills, PhD Candidate, Department of Political Science, University of Waterloo

Andrea Lawlor, Associate Professor, Department of Political Science, McMaster University

Emmett Macfarlane, Professor, Department of Political Science, University of Waterloo

Chris McCorkindale, Reader, University of Strathclyde Law School

Andrew McDougall, Associate Professor, Department of Political Science, University of Toronto

Kate Puddister, Associate Professor, Department of Political Science, University of Guelph

Troy Riddell, Associate Professor, Department of Political Science, University of Guelph

Tamara A. Small, Professor, Department of Political Science, University of Guelph

Grégoire Webber, Canada Research Chair in Public Law and Philosophy of Law, Faculty of Law and Department of Philosophy, Queen's University

George Williams, Distinguished Professor and Vice-Chancellor and President, Western Sydney University

Selected Bibliography

Adamson, Bruce. "The Protection of Human Rights in the Legislative Process in Scotland." In *Parliaments and Human Rights: Redressing the Democratic Deficit*, edited by Murray Hunt, Hayley J. Hooper, and Paul Yowell. Oxford: Hart Publishing, 2015.

Baker, Dennis. "Criminal Justice and Criminal Law." in *Canadian Federalism: Performance, Effectiveness, and Legitimacy*, edited by Herman Bakvis and Grace Skogstad. Toronto: University of Toronto Press, 2020.

——— *Not Quite Supreme: The Courts and Coordinate Constitutional Interpretation*. Montreal: McGill-Queen's University Press, 2010.

Bakvis, Herman, and Jennifer Smith, "Third-Party Advertising and Electoral Democracy: The Political Theory of the Alberta Court of Appeal in *Somerville v. Canada (Attorney General)* [1996]." *Canadian Public Policy* 23, no. 2 (1997): 164–7. https://doi.org/10.2307/3551483.

Barsh, Russell Lawrence, and James Youngblood Henderson. "The Supreme Court's *Van der Peet* Trilogy: Native Imperialism and Ropes of Sand." *McGill Law Journal* 42, no. 4 (1997): 993–1009.

Barsh, Russell Lawrence, Michelle Fraser, Faye Morning Bull, Toby Provost, and Kirby Smith, "The Prairie Indian Vote in Canadian Politics 1965–1993: A Critical Case Study from Alberta." *Great Plains Research* 7, no. 1 (1997): 3–26.

Bateman, Thomas M.J. "The Supreme Court of Canada as Moral Tutor: Religious Freedom, Civil Society, and Charter Values." in *Liberal Education, Civic Education, and the Canadian Regime*, edited by David W. Livingstone. Montreal: McGill-Queen's University Press, 2015.

Bilson, Beth. "The Voice from the Trenches: Administrative Tribunals and the Interpretation of the Charter." *Saskatchewan Law Review* 69, no. 1 (2006): 3–38.

Bird, Brian. "Federal Power and Federal Duty: Reconciling Sections 91(24) and 35(1) of the Canadian Constitution." *Appeal: Review of Current Law and Law Reform* 16, no. 1 (2011): 3–14.

Borrows, John. *Recovering Canada: The Resurgence of Indigenous Law*. Toronto: University of Toronto Press, 2002.

——— "Sovereignty's Alchemy: An Analysis of *Delgamuukw v. British Columbia*." *Osgoode Hall Law Journal* 37, no. 3 (1997): 537–96. https://doi.org/10.60082/2817-5069.1522.

Braden, Alexander. "Decision Instruments of the Federal Cabinet: Legally Exercising the 'War Prerogative.'" *Journal of Commonwealth Law* 3, no. 1 (2021): 157–217.

Bredt, Christopher D., and Ewa Krajewska. "Doré: All that Glitters Is Not Gold." *Supreme Court Law Review* 67, 2nd ser. (2014): 339–359. https://doi.org/10.60082/2563-8505.1292

Bryant, Alan, Marc Gold, H. Michael Stevenson, and David Northrup. "Public Attitudes Toward the Exclusion of Evidence: Section 24(2) of the Canadian Charter of Rights and Freedoms." *Canadian Bar Review* 69 (1990): 1–45.

Cairns, Alan C. *Charter versus Federalism: The Dilemmas of Constitutional Reform*. Montreal: McGill-Queen's University Press, 1992.

Cameron, Jamie. "Collateral Thoughts on Dialogue's Legacy as Metaphor and Theory: A Favorite from Canada." *University of Queensland Law Journal* 35, no. 1 (2016): 157–69.

Campbell, Kathryn M. *Miscarriages of Justice in Canada: Causes, Responses, Remedies*. Toronto: University of Toronto Press, 2018.

Carter, Mark. "Diefenbaker's Bill of Rights and the Counter-Majoritarian Difficulty: The Notwithstanding Clause and Fundamental Justice as Touchstones for the Charter Debate." *Saskatchewan Law Review* 82, no. 2 (2019): 121–46.

Choudhry, Sujit, and Claire E. Hunter. "Measuring Judicial Activism on the Supreme Court of Canada: A Comment on *Newfoundland (Treasury Board) v. NAPE*." *McGill Law Journal* 48 (2003): 525–62.

Chowdhury, Tanzil. "Taming the UK's War Prerogative: The Rationale for Reform." *Legal Studies* 38 (2018): 500–13.

Christie, Gordon. "A Colonial Reading of Recent Jurisprudence: *Sparrow*, *Delgamuukw* and *Haida Nation*." *Windsor Yearbook Access to Justice* 23, no. 1 (2005): 17–53.

Cottrill, Edward. "Administrative "Determinations of Law" and the Limits of Legal Pluralism after *Vavilov*." *Alberta Law Review* 58, no. 1 (2020): 153–86. https://doi.org/10.29173/alr2614.

——— "Novel Uses of the *Charter* Following *Doré* and *Loyola*." *Alberta Law Review* 56, no. 1 (2018): 73–118. https://doi.org/10.29173/alr2498.

Coulthard, Glen. *Red Skins, White Masks: Rejecting the Colonial Politics of Recognition*. Minnesota: University of Minnesota Press, 2014.

Crandall, Erin, and Andrea Lawlor. "Third Party Policy and Electoral Participation after Harper v. Canada: A Triumph of Egalitarianism." In

Policy Change, Courts, and the Canadian Constitution, edited by Emmett Macfarlane. Toronto: University of Toronto Press, 2018.

Crandall, Erin, Andrea Lawlor, and Kate Puddister. "Charter Talk: How Canadian Media Cover Rights and Politics." In *Constitutional Crossroads: Reflections on Charter Rights, Reconciliation, and Change*, edited by Kate Puddister and Emmett Macfarlane. Vancouver: UBC Press, 2022.

Dabin, Simon, Jean François Daoust, and Martin Papillon. "Indigenous Peoples and Affinity Voting in Canada." *Canadian Journal of Political Science* 52, no. 1 (2019): 39–53. https://doi.org/10.1017/S0008423918000574.

Daly, Paul. "Prescribing Greater Protection for Rights: Administrative Law and Section 1 of the Canadian Charter of Rights and Freedoms." *Supreme Court Law Review* 65, 2nd ser. (2014): 247–90.

——— *A Theory of Deference in Administrative Law: Basis, Application and Scope.* Cambridge: Cambridge University Press, 2012.

——— "The *Vavilov* Framework and the future of Canadian Administrative Law." *Canadian Journal of Administrative Law & Practice* 33 (2020): 111–44.

Dawood, Yasmin. "Democracy, Power, and the Supreme Court: Campaign Finance Reform in Comparative Context." *International Journal of Constitutional Law* 4, no. 2 (2006): 269–93. https://doi.org/10.1093/icon/mol005.

Dell, Brendan. "Rights Review and the Institutional Roles in Sentencing: A Study of Harper-Era Mandatory Minimum Sentences." Master's thesis, University of Guelph, 2022.

Dixon, Rosalind. "The Supreme Court of Canada, Charter Dialogue, and Deference." *Osgoode Hall Law Journal* 47, no. 2 (2009): 235–86. https://doi.org/10.60082/2817-5069.1150.

Do, Minh. "Throughout Legitimacy and the Duty to Consult: The Limits of the Law to Produce Quality Interactions in British Columbia's EA Process." *Canadian Journal of Political Science* 53, no. 3 (2020): 577–95. https://doi.org/10.1017/S000842392000027X.

Docherty, David. *Legislatures*. Vancouver: UBC Press, 2005.

Dodek, Adam. "The Canadian Override: Constitutional Model or Bête Noire of Constitutional Politics?" *Israel Law Review* 49, no. 1 (2016): 45–65. https://doi.org/10.1017/S0021223715000187.

Dyzenhaus, David. "The Politics of Deference: Judicial Review and Democracy." In *The Province of Administrative Law,* edited by Michael Taggart. Oxford: Oxford University Press, 1997.

Esselment, Anna Lennox, Alex Marland, and Thierry Giasson. "Permanent Campaigning: Changing the Nature of Canadian Democracy." In *Permanent Campaigning in Canada*, edited by Alex Marland, Thierry Giasson, and Anna Lennox Esselment. Vancouver: UBC Press, 2017.

Feasby, Colin. "*Libman V. Quebec (Ag)* and the Administration of the Process of Democracy under the Charter: The Emerging Egalitarian Model." *McGill Law Journal* 44 (1999): 5–38.

Feldman, Charlie. "Beyond Charter statements: Constitutional Communications in the Parliamentary Context." *Journal of Parliamentary and Political Law*, 2018: 37–66.

——— "Preliminary Observations on Parliamentary and Judicial Use of *Charter* Statements." *Journal of Parliamentary and Political Law* 13 (2020): 587–601.

Franks, C.E.S. *The Parliament of Canada*. Toronto: University of Toronto Press, 1987.

Gagnon, Alain-G. *Le Choc Des Légitimités*. Montreal: Presses de L'Université Laval, 2021.

Gardbaum, Stephen. *The New Commonwealth Model of Constitutionalism: Theory and Practice*. Cambridge: Cambridge University Press, 2013.

Gee, Graham, and Grégoire C.N. Webber. "What Is a Political Constitution?" *Oxford Journal of Legal Studies* 30, no. 2 (2010): 273–99. https://doi.org/10.1093/ojls/gqq013.

Glendon, Mary Ann. *Rights Talk: The Impoverishment of Political Discourse*. New York: The Free Press, 1991.

——— *A World Made New: Eleanor Roosevelt and the Universal Declaration of Human Rights*. New York: Random House, 2001.

Glover, Kate. "The Supreme Court in Canada's Constitutional Order." *Review of Constitutional Studies* 21, no. 1 (2016): 143–64.

Greene, Ian, Carl Baar, Peter McCormick, George Szablowski, and Martin Thomas. *Final Appeal: Decision-Making in Canadian Courts of Appeal*. Toronto: Lorimer, 1998.

Harding, Mark S. "The Political Purposes of the Charter: Four Decades Later." In *Constitutional Crossroads: Reflections on Charter Rights, Reconciliation, and Change*, edited by Kate Puddister and Emmett Macfarlane. Vancouver: UBC Press, 2022.

Hausegger, Lori, Danielle McNabb, and Troy Riddell. "Provincial Courts of Appeal and s. 24(2) of the Charter." In *Constitutional Crossroads: Reflections on Charter Rights, Reconciliation and Constitutional Change*, edited by Kate Puddister and Emmett Macfarlane. Vancouver: UBC Press, 2022.

Heckman, Gerald. "Developments in Administrative Law: The 2014–2015 Term." *Supreme Court Law Review* 72, 2nd ser. (2016): 1–74.

Hennigar, Matthew A. "Conceptualizing Attorney General Conduct in Charter Litigation: From Independence to Central Agency." *Canadian Public Administration* 51, no. 2 (2008): 193–215. https://doi.org/10.1111/j.1754-7121.2008.00015.x.

——— "Expanding the 'Dialogue' Debate: Canadian Federal Government Responses to Lower Court Charter Decisions." *Canadian Journal of Political Science* 37, no. 1 (2004): 3–21. https://doi.org/10.1017/S0008423904040041.

——— "Exploring Complex Judicial-Executive Interaction: Federal Government Concessions in Charter of Rights Cases." *Canadian Journal of*

Political Science 43, no. 4 (2010): 821–42. https://doi.org/10.1017/S0008423910000739.

——— "*Reference re Same-Sex Marriage*: Making Sense of the Government's Litigation Strategy." In *Contested Constitutionalism*, edited by James Kelly and Christopher Manfredi. Vancouver: UBC Press, 2009.

——— "Unreasonable Disagreement? Judicial-Executive Exchanges about Charter Reasonableness in the Harper Era." *Osgoode Hall Law Journal* 54, no. 4 (2017): 1245–73. https://doi.org/10.60082/2817-5069.3189.

——— "Why Does the Federal Government Appeal to the Supreme Court of Canada in Charter of Rights cases? A Strategic Explanation." *Law & Society Review* 41, no. 1 (2007): 225–50. https://doi.org/10.1111/j.1540-5893.2007.00296.x.

Hiebert, Janet L. *Charter Conflicts: What is Parliament's Role?* Montreal: McGill-Queen's University Press, 2002.

——— "The Charter, Policy, and Political Judgment." *Policy Change, Courts, and the Canadian Constitution*, edited by Emmett Macfarlane. Toronto: University of Toronto Press, 2018.

——— "The Charter's Influence on Legislation: Political Strategizing about Risk." *Canadian Journal of Political Science* 51, no. 4 (2018): 727–47. https://doi.org/10.1017/S0008423918000884.

——— "Compromise and the Notwithstanding Clause: Why the Dominant Narrative Distorts Our Understanding." *Contested Constitutionalism: Reflections on the Charter of Rights and Freedoms*, edited by James B. Kelly and Christopher P. Manfredi. Vancouver: UBC Press, 2009.

——— "Elections, Democracy and Free Speech: More at Stake than an Unfettered Right to Advertise." In *Party Funding and Campaign Financing in International Perspective*, edited by Keith Ewing and Samuel Issacharoff. Portland, OR: Bloomsbury Publishing, 2006.

——— "Governing Like Judges?" In *The Legal Protection of Human Rights: Sceptical Essays*, edited by Tom Campbell, K.D. Ewing, and Adam Tomkins. Oxford: Oxford University Press, 2011.

——— "The Human Rights Act: Ambiguity about Parliamentary Sovereignty." *German Law Journal* 14, no. 12 (2019): 2253–75. https://doi.org/10.1017/S2071832200002765.

——— "A Hybrid-Approach to Protect Rights? An Argument in Favour of Supplementing Canadian Judicial Review with Australia's Model of Parliamentary Scrutiny." *Federal Law Review* 26, no. 1 (1998): 115–38. https://doi.org/10.22145/flr.26.1.5.

——— "Interest Groups and Canadian Federal Elections." In *Interest Groups and Elections in Canada*, edited by F. Leslie Seidle. Toronto: Dundurn Press, 1991.

——— "Interpreting a Bill of Rights: The Importance of Legislative Rights Review." *British Journal of Political Science* 35, no. 2 (2005): 235–55. https://doi.org/10.1017/S000712340500013X.

——— "Is it Too Late to Rehabilitate Canada's Notwithstanding Clause?" *Supreme Court Law Review* 23, 2nd ser. (2004): 169–89.

——— *Limiting Rights: The Dilemmas of Judicial Review*. Montreal: McGill-Queen's University Press, 1996.

——— "Money and Elections: Can Citizens Participate on Fair Terms Amidst Unrestricted Spending?" *Canadian Journal of Political Science* 31, no. 1 (1998): 91–111. https://doi.org/10.1017/S0008423900008696.

——— "New Constitutional Ideas: Can New Parliamentary Models Resist Judicial Dominance When Interpreting Rights." *Texas Law Review* 82, no. 7 (2004): 1963–88.

——— "Notwithstanding the Charter: Does Section 33 Accommodate Federalism." In *Canada at 150. Federalism and Democratic Renewal*, edited by Elizabeth Goodyear-Grant and Kyle Hanniman. Montreal: McGill-Queen's University Press, 2019.

——— "Parliament and the Human Rights Act: Can the JCHR Help Facilitate a Culture of Rights?" *International Journal of Constitutional Law* 4, no. 1 (2006): 1–38. https://doi.org/10.1093/icon/moi051.

——— "Parliamentary Bills of Rights: An Alternative Model?" *Modern Law Review* 69, no. 1 (2006): 7–28. https://doi.org/10.1111/j.1468-2230.2006.00574.x.

——— "Parliamentary Bills of Rights. Do They Alter the Norms of Legislative Decision-Making?" In *Comparative Constitutional Theory*, edited by Gary Jacobson and Miguel Schor. London: Edward Elgar Publishing, 2018.

——— "Parliamentary Engagement with the Charter: Rethinking the Idea of Legislative Rights Review." *The Supreme Court Law Review* 58, no. 1 (2012): 87–107. https://doi.org/10.60082/2563-8505.1249.

——— "Rights and Public Debate: The Limitations of a 'Rights Must be Paramount' Perspective." *International Journal of Canadian Studies* nos. 7–8 (1993): 117–35.

Hiebert, Janet L., and James B. Kelly. *Parliamentary Bills of Rights: The Experiences of New Zealand and the United Kingdom*. Cambridge: Cambridge University Press, 2015.

Hillmer, Norman, and Phillippe Lagassé. "Parliament Will Decide: An Interplay of Politics and Principle." *International Journal* 71, no. 2 (2017): 328–37. https://doi.org/10.1177/0020702016638679.

Hogg, Peter W., and Allison Bushell. "The Charter Dialogue between Courts and Legislatures (or Perhaps the *Charter of Rights* Isn't Such a Bad Thing After All)." *Osgoode Hall Law Journal* 35, no. 1 (1997): 75–124. https://doi.org/10.60082/2817-5069.1612.

——— "Reply to "Six Degrees of Dialogue." *Osgoode Hall Law Journal* 37, no. 3 (1999): 529–36. https://doi.org/10.60082/2817-5069.1521.

Hogg, Peter W., Allison A. Bushell Thornton, and Wade K. Wright. "Charter Dialogue Revisited – or 'Much Ado About Metaphors.'" *Osgoode*

Hall Law Journal 45, no. 1 (2007): 1–65. https://doi.org/10.60082/2817-5069.1254.

Horner, Matthew. "Charter Values: The Uncanny Valley of Canadian Constitutionalism." *Supreme Court Law Review* 67, 2d ser. (2014): 361–90. https://doi.org/10.60082/2563-8505.1293.

Howe, Paul, and Peter H. Russell, eds. *Judicial Power and Canadian Democracy*. Montreal: McGill-Queen's University Press, 2001.

Huscroft, Grant. "Constitutionalism from the Top Down." *Osgoode Hall Law Journal* 45, no. 1 (2007): 91–104. https://doi.org/10.60082/2817-5069.1256.

Hutchinson, Allan C. *Waiting for Coraf: A Critique of Law and Rights*. Toronto: University of Toronto Press, 1995.

James, Patrick, Donald E. Abelson, and Michael Lusztig, eds. *The Myth of the Sacred: The Charter, the Courts, and the Politics of the Constitution in Canada*. Montreal: McGill-Queen's University Press, 2002.

Jansen, Harold J., Royce Koop, Tamara Small, Frédérick Bastien, and Thierry Giasson. "Democratic Citizenship: How Do Canadians Engage with Politics Online?" *Digital Politics in Canada: Promises and Realities*. Toronto: University of Toronto Press, 2020.

Jochelson, Richard, David Ireland, Ryan Ziegler, Erika Brenner, and Kirsten Kramar. "Generation and Deployment of Common Law Police Powers by Canadian Courts and the Double-Edged Charter." *Critical Criminology* 28 (2020): 107–26.

Kahana, Tsvi. "The Notwithstanding Mechanism and Public Discussion: Lessons from the Ignored Practice of Section 33 of the Charter." *Canadian Public Administration* 44, no. 3 (2001): 255–91. https://doi.org/10.1111/j.1754-7121.2001.tb00891.x.

——— "Understanding the Notwithstanding Mechanism." *The University of Toronto Law Journal* 52, no. 2 (2002): 221–74. https://doi.org/10.2307/825966.

Kam, Christopher J. *Party Discipline and Parliamentary Politics*. Cambridge: Cambridge University Press, 2009.

Kelly, James B. "Bureaucratic Activism and the Charter of Rights and Freedoms: The Department of Justice and its Entry into the Centre of Government." *Canadian Public Administration* 42, no. 4 (1999): 476–511. https://doi.org/10.1111/j.1754-7121.1999.tb02037.x.

——— *Governing with the Charter: Legislative and Judicial Activism and Framers' Intent*. Vancouver: UBC Press, 2005.

——— "Legislative Capacity and Human Rights in the Age of Populism – Two Challenges for Legislated Rights: Discussion of Legislated Rights – Securing Human Rights Through Legislation." *Jerusalem Review of Legal Studies* 21, no. 1 (2020): 94–111. https://doi.org/10.1093/jrls/jlz024.

Kelly, James B., and Kate Puddister. "Criminal Justice Policy during the Harper Era: Private Member's Bills, Penal Populism, and the *Criminal Code of Canada." Canadian Journal of Law and Society* 32, no. 3 (2017): 391–416. https://doi.org/10.1017/cls.2017.25.

King, Jeff. *Judging Social Rights*. Cambridge: Cambridge University Press, 2012.

Knopff, Rainer. "Populism and the Politics of Rights: The Dual Attack on Representative Democracy." *Canadian Journal of Political Science* 31, no. 4 (1998): 683–705. https://doi.org/10.1017/S0008423900009604.

Kristjanson, Freya, and Morgana Kellythorne. "Charter Cases before Administrative Tribunals and on Judicial Review." *National Journal of Constitutional Law* 25 (2008): 217–32.

Ladner, Kiera. "Up the Creek: Fishing for a New Constitutional Order." *Canadian Journal of Political Science* 38, no. 4 (2005): 923–53.

Lagassé, Philippe. "Parliament and the War Prerogative in the United Kingdom and Canada: Explaining Variations in Institutional Change and Legislative Control." *Parliamentary Affairs* 70 (2017): 280–300. https://doi.org/10.1093/pa/gsw029.

Lawlor, Andrea, and Erin Crandall. "Policy versus Practice: Third Party Behaviour in Canadian Elections." *Canadian Public Administration* 61, no. 2 (2018): 246–65. https://doi.org/10.1111/capa.12266.

——— "Understanding Third-Party Advertising: An Analysis of the 2004, 2006 and 2008 Canadian Elections." *Canadian Public Administration* 54, no. 4 (2011): 509–29. https://doi.org/10.1111/j.1754-7121.2011.00190.x.

LeBel, Louis. "Some Properly Deferential Thoughts on Deference." *Canadian Journal of Administrative Law & Practice* 21, no. 1 (2008): 1–20.

Liston, Mary. "Administering the *Charter*, Proportioning Justice: Thirty-Five Years of Development in a Nutshell." *Canadian Journal of Administrative Law & Practice* 30, no. 2 (2017): 211–46.

Macfarlane, Emmett. "Conceptual Precision and Parliamentary Systems of Rights: Disambiguating 'Dialogue.'" *Review of Constitutional Studies* 17, no. 2 (2012): 73–100.

——— "Conservative with the Constitution? Moderation, Strategy, and Institutional Distrust." In *The Blueprint: Conservative Parties and Their Impact on Canadian Politics*, edited by J.P. Lewis and Joanna Everitt. Toronto: University of Toronto Press, 2017.

——— "Dialogue or Compliance? Measuring Legislatures' Policy Responses to Court Rulings on Rights." *International Political Science Review* 34, no. 1 (2012): 39–56. https://doi.org/10.1177/0192512111432565.

——— *Governing from the Bench: The Supreme Court of Canada and the Judicial Role*. Vancouver: UBC Press, 2013.

——— "Public Policy and Constitutional Rights in Times of Crisis." *Canadian Journal of Political Science* 53, no. 2 (2020): 299–303. https://doi.org/10.1017/S0008423920000256.

——— "'You Can't Always Get What You Want': Regime Politics, the Supreme Court of Canada, and the Harper Government." *Canadian Journal of Political Science* 51, no. 1 (2018): 1–21. https://doi.org/10.1017/S0008423917000981.

——— "Revisiting Judicial Activism." In *Constitutional Crossroads: Charter Rights, Reconciliation, and Change*, edited by Kate Puddister and Emmett Macfarlane. Vancouver: UBC Press, 2022.

——— "Terms of Entitlement: Is there a Distinctly Canadian 'Rights Talk'?" *Canadian Journal of Political Science* 41, no. 2 (2008): 303–28. https://doi.org/10.1017/S0008423908080451.

Macfarlane, Emmett, Janet Hiebert, and Anna Drake. *Legislating under the Charter: Parliament, Executive Power, and Rights*. Toronto: University of Toronto Press, 2023.

Macklem, Patrick. *Indigenous Difference and the Constitution of Canada*. Toronto: University of Toronto, 2001.

Macklin, Audrey. "Charter Right or Charter-Lite? Administrative Discretion and the *Charter*." *Supreme Court Law Review* 67, 2nd ser. (2014): 561–88. https://doi.org/10.60082/2563-8505.1300.

Maddison, Sarah. "White Parliament, Black Politics: The Dilemmas of Indigenous Parliamentary Representation." *Australian Journal of Political Science* 45, no. 4 (2010): 663–80. https://doi.org/10.1080/10361146.2010.517180.

Malloy, Jonathan. "High Discipline, Low Cohesion? The Uncertain Patterns of Canadian Parliamentary Parties." *Journal of Legislative Studies* 9, no. 4 (2003): 116–29. https://doi.org/10.1080/1357233042000306290.

Mancini, Mark. "The Conceptual Gap between Dore and Vavilov." *Dalhousie Law Journal* 43, no. 2 (2020): 793–834.

Mandel, Michael. *The Charter of Rights and the Legalization of Politics in Canada*. Toronto: Thompson Education Publishing, 1994.

Manfredi, Christopher P. "Conservatives, the Supreme Court of Canada, and the Constitution: Judicial Government Relations, 2006–2015." *Osgoode Hall Law Journal* 52, no. 3 (2015): 951–84. https://doi.org/10.60082/2817-5069.2960.

——— *Judicial Power and the Charter: Canada and the Paradox of Liberal Constitutionalism*. 2nd ed. Oxford: Oxford University Press, 2000.

Manfredi, Christopher P., and James B. Kelly. "Dialogue, Deference, and Restraint: Judicial Independence and Trial Procedures." *Saskatchewan Law Review* 64 (2001): 323–46.

——— "Misrepresenting the Supreme Court's Record? A Comment on Sujit Choudhry and Claire E. Hunter, 'Measuring Judicial Activism on the Supreme Court of Canada.'" *McGill Law Journal* 49 (2004): 741–64.

——— "Six Degrees of Dialogue: A Response to Hogg and Bushell." *Osgoode Hall Law Journal* 37, no. 3 (1999): 513–27. https://doi.org/10.60082/2817-5069.1520.

Manfredi, Christopher P., and Mark Rush. "Electoral Jurisprudence in the Canadian and Us Supreme Courts: Evolution and Convergence." *McGill Law Journal* 52, no. 3 (2007): 457–94.

Marland, Alex. *Brand Command: Canadian Politics and Democracy in the Age of Message Control*. Vancouver: UBC Press, 2016.

——— *Whipped: Party Discipline in Canada*. Vancouver: UBC Press, 2020.

Mathen, Carissima. *Courts without Cases: The Law and Politics of Advisory Opinions*. Oxford: Hart Publishing, 2019.

McCorkindale, Christopher, and Aileen McHarg. "The Supreme Court and devolution: the Scottish Continuity Bill Reference." *Juridical Review* 2 (2019): 190–7.

McCorkindale, Christopher, and Janet Hiebert. "Vetting Bills in the Scottish Parliament for Legislative Competence." *Edinburgh Law Review* 21, no. 3 (2017): 319–51.

McCormick, Peter. *Supreme at Last: The Evolution of the Supreme Court of Canada*. Toronto: Lorimer, 2000.

McCrossan, Michael. "Shifting Judicial Conceptions of 'Reconciliation': Geographic Commitments Underpinning Aboriginal Rights Decisions." *Windsor Yearbook Access to Justice* 31, no. 2 (2013): 155–79. https://doi.org/10.22329/wyaj.v31i2.4418.

McGregor, Michael, Cameron Anderson, and Scott Pruysers. "Partisanship, motivated reasoning and the Notwithstanding Clause: The Case of Provincially Imposed Redistricting in the City of Toronto." *Commonwealth & Comparative Politics* 59, no. 1 (2021): 94–117. https://doi.org/10.1080/14662043.2020.1800294.

McHarg, Aileen. "What Is Delegated Legislation?" *Public Law* (2006): 539–61.

Meiklejohn, Alexander. "The First Amendment is an Absolute." *Supreme Court Review* (1961): 245–66. https://doi.org/10.1086/scr.1961.3108719.

Moon, Richard. "Limits of Constitutional Rights: The Marginal Role of Proportionality Analysis." *Israel Law Review* 50, no. 1 (2017): 49–68. https://doi.org/10.1017/S0021223716000327.

Moore, Kathryn. "Police Implementation of Supreme Court of Canada Charter Decisions: An Empirical Study." *Osgood Hall Law Journal* 30, no. 3 (1992): 547–77. https://doi.org/10.60082/2817-5069.1713.

Morton, F.L., and Rainer Knopff. *The Charter Revolution and the Court Party*. Toronto: University of Toronto Press, 2000.

Mullan, David. "Reasonableness Review Post-*Vavilov:* An 'Encomium for Correctness' or Deference as Usual?" *Canadian Labour & Employment Law Journal* 23 (2021): 189–219.

Murphy, Michael. "Culture and the Courts: A New Direction in Canadian Jurisprudence on Aboriginal Rights?" *Canadian Journal of Political Science* 34, no. 1 (2001): 109–29. https://doi.org/10.1017/S0008423901777839.

Newman, Dwight. "Canada's Notwithstanding Clause, Dialogue, and Constitutional Identities." In *Constitutional Dialogue: Rights, Democracy, Institutions*, edited by Geoffrey Sigalet, Grégoire Webber, and Rosalind Dixon. Cambridge: Cambridge University Press, 2019.

——— "The Limitation of Rights: A Comparative Evolution and Ideology of the *Oakes* and *Sparrow* Tests." *Saskatchewan Law Review* 62, no. 2 (1999): 543–66.

Nichols, Joshua, and Robert Hamilton. "In Search of Honourable Crowns and Legitimate Constitutions: *Mikisew Cree First Nation v Canada* and the Colonial Constitution." *University of Toronto Law Journal* 70, no. 3 (2020): 341–75. https://doi.org/10.3138/utlj.2019-0115.

Nicolaides, Eleni, and Dave Snow. "A Paper Tiger No More? The Media Portrayal of the Notwithstanding Clause in Saskatchewan and Ontario." *Canadian Journal of Political Science* 54, no. 1 (2021): 60–74. https://doi.org/10.1017/S0008423920000876.

Pal, Michael. "Is the Permanent Campaign the End of the Egalitarian Model of Elections." In *The Canadian Constitution in Transition*, edited by Richard Albert, Paul Daly, and Venessa MacDonnell. Toronto: University of Toronto Press, 2019.

——— "Three Narratives About Canadian Election Law." *Election Law Journal: Rules, Politics, and Policy* 16, no. 2 (2017): 255–62. https://doi.org/10.1089/elj.2016.0410.

Parfett, Julianne. "A Triumph of Liberalism: The Supreme Court of Canada and the Exclusion of Evidence." *Alberta Law Review* 40 (2002): 299–332.

Parkes, Debra. "From Smith to Smickle: The Charter's Minimal Impact on Mandatory Minimum Sentences." *Supreme Court Law Review* 57 (2012): 149–72. https://doi.org/10.60082/2563-8505.1235.

Peacock, Anthony A. "Strange Brew: Tocqueville, Rights, and the Technology of Equality." *Rethinking the Constitution: Perspectives on Canadian Constitutional Reform, Interpretation, and Theory*, edited by Anthony A. Peacock. Oxford: Oxford University Press, 1996.

Penney, Steven, and James Stribopoulos. "'Detention' under the Charter after *R. v. Grant* and *R. v. Suberu*." *Supreme Court Law Review* 51, 2nd ser. (2010): 439–77. https://doi.org/10.60082/2563-8505.1201.

Penney, Steven, and Moin Yahya. "Section 24(2) in the Trial Courts: An Empirical Analysis of the Legal and Non-legal Determinants of Excluding Unconstitutionally Obtained Evidence in Canada." *Osgoode Hall Law Journal* 58 (2021): 509–66. https://doi.org/10.60082/2817-5069.3711.

Potes, Veronica. "The Duty to Accommodate Aboriginal Peoples Rights: Substantive Consultation?" *Journal of Environmental Law and Practice* 17, no. 1 (2006): 27–45.

Puddister, Kate. "How the Canadian Sentencing System Impacts Policy Reform: An Examination of the Harper Era." *Law & Policy* 43, no. 2 (2021): 149–69. https://doi.org/10.1111/lapo.12163.

——— "Protecting against Cruel and Unusual Punishment: Section 12 of the Charter and Mandatory Minimum Sentences." In *Policy Change, Courts, and the Canadian Constitution*, edited by Emmett Macfarlane. Toronto: University of Toronto Press, 2018.

——— *Seeking the Court's Advice: The Politics of the Canadian Reference Power*. Vancouver: UBC Press, 2019.

Radmilovic, Vuk. "Governmental Interventions and Judicial Decision Making: The Supreme Court of Canada in the Age of the *Charter*." *Canadian Journal of Political Science* 46, no. 2 (2013): 323–44. https://doi.org/10.1017/S0008423913000504.

Régimbald, Guy. "Correctness, Reasonableness and Proportionality: A New Standard of Judicial Review." *Manitoba Law Journal* 31, no. 2 (2005): 239–79.

Riddell, Troy. "Measuring Activism and Restraint: An Alternative Perspective on the Supreme Court of Canada's Exclusion of Evidence Decisions under Section 24(2) of the Charter." *Canadian Journal of Criminology and Criminal Justice* 58 (2016) 87–111.

Riddell, Troy, and Dennis Baker. "The Charter Beat: The Impact of Rights Decisions on Canadian Policing." In *Policy Change, Courts and the Canadian Constitution*, edited by Emmett Macfarlane. Toronto: University of Toronto Press, 2018.

Roach, Kent. *Canadian Policing: Why and How it Must Change*. Toronto: Irwin Law, 2022.

——— "Not Just the Government's Lawyer: The Attorney General as Defender of the Rule of Law." *Queen's Law Journal* 31, no. 2 (2006): 598–643.

——— *The Supreme Court on Trial: Judicial Activism or Democratic Dialogue*. Rev. ed. Toronto: Irwin Law, 2016.

Rose, Jonathan. "Government Advertising and the Creation of National Myths: The Canadian Case." *International Journal of Nonprofit and Voluntary Sector Marketing* 8, no. 2 (2003): 153–65. https://doi.org/10.1002/nvsm.209.

Rothstein, Marshall. "Section 1: Justifying Breaches of Charter Rights and Freedoms." *Manitoba Law Journal* 27 (2000): 171–83.

Rousseau, Guillaume, and François Côté. "A Distinctive Quebec Theory and Practice of the Notwithstanding Clause: When Collective Interests Outweigh Individual Rights." *Revue Générale de Droit* 47, no. 2 (2017): 343–431.

Russell, Peter H. "Canadian Constraints on Judicialization from Without." *International Political Science Review* 15, no. 2 (1994): 165–75. https://doi.org/10.1177/019251219401500208.

——— "The Political Purposes of the Canadian Charter of Rights and Freedoms." *Canadian Bar Review* 61 (1983): 30–54.

——— *Recognizing Aboriginal Title: The Mabo Case and Indigenous Resistance to English-Settler Colonialism*. Toronto: University of Toronto Press, 2005.

——— "Standing Up for Notwithstanding." *Alberta Law Review* 29, no. 2 (1991): 293–309. https://doi.org/10.29173/alr1563.

Savoie, Donald. *Governing from the Centre: The Concentration of Power in Canadian Politics*. Toronto: University of Toronto Press, 1999.

Sigalet, Geoffrey, Grégoire Webber, and Rosalind Dixon, eds. *Constitutional Dialogue: Rights, Democracy, Institutions*. Cambridge: Cambridge University Press, 2019.

Simpson, Jeffrey. "Rights Talk: The Effect of the Charter on Canadian Political Discourse." *Protecting Rights and Freedoms: Essays on the Charter's Place in Canada's Political, Legal, and Intellectual Life*, edited by Philip Bryden, Steven Davis, and Peter Russell. Toronto: University of Toronto Press, 1994.

Sirota, Lèonid. "Canadian Administrative Law and Good Governance." *Canadian Journal of Administrative Law & Practice* 31 (2018): 285–305.

——— "'Third Parties' and Democracy 2.0." *McGill Law Journal* 60, no. 2 (2015): 253–93.

Slattery, Brian. "A Theory of the Charter." *Osgoode Hall Law Journal* 25, no. 4 (1987): 701–47. https://doi.org/10.60082/2817-5069.1833.

Small, Tamara. "Promises, Promises: Assessing the Liberal's Electoral Reform Agenda." *Études Canadiennes/Canadian Studies* 89 (2020): 41–64. https://doi.org/10.4000/eccs.3874.

Snow, Dave, and Eleni Nicolaides. "Notwithstanding the Media: Section 33 of the Charter after *Toronto v. Ontario*." In *Constitutional Crossroads: Reflections on Charter Rights, Reconciliation, and Change*, edited by Kate Puddister and Emmett Macfarlane. Vancouver: UBC Press, 2022.

Sossin, Lorne, and Mark Friedman. "Charter Values and Administrative Justice." *Supreme Court Law Review* 67, 2nd ser. (2014): 391–430. https://doi.org/10.60082/2563-8505.1294.

Sriskandarajah, Anuppiriya. "Race, Space, and Media: The Production of Urban Neighbourhood Space in East-End Toronto." *Canadian Ethnic Studies* 52, no. 1 (2020): 1–22. https://doi.org/10.1353/ces.2020.0004.

Stacey, Richard. "A Unified Model of Public Law: Charter Values and Reasonableness Review in Canada." *University of Toronto Law Journal* 71 (2021): 339–75. https://doi.org/10.3138/utlj.2020-0056.

Stribopoulos, James. "In Search of Dialogue: The Supreme Court, Police Powers and the Charter." *Queen's Law Journal* 31, no. 1 (2005): 1–74.

Sunstein, Cass R. *Legal Reasoning and Political Conflict*. New York: Oxford University Press, 1996.

Trakman, Leon E., William Cole-Hamilton, and Sean Gatien. "*R. v. Oakes* 1986–1997: Back to the Drawing Board." *Osgoode Hall Law Journal* 36, no. 1 (1998): 83–149. https://doi.org/10.60082/2817-5069.1569.

Trimble, Linda, and Shannon Sampert. "Who's in the Game? The Framing of the Canadian Election 2000 by the Globe and Mail and the National Post."

Canadian Journal of Political Science 37, no. 1 (2004): 51–71. https://doi.org/10.1017/S0008423904040028.

Turner, Dale. *This Is Not a Peace Pipe: Towards a Critical Indigenous Philosophy*. Toronto: University of Toronto Press, 2006.

Tushnet, Mark. *Taking the Constitution Away from the Courts*. Princeton, NJ: Princeton University Press, 1999.

——— *Weak Courts, Strong Rights: Judicial Review and Social Welfare Rights in Comparative Constitutional Law*. Princeton, NJ: Princeton University Press, 2008.

Twomey, Anne. "The Prerogative and the Courts in Australia." *Journal of Commonwealth Law* 3, no. 1 (2021): 55–101.

Vermette, D'Arcy. "Dizzying Dialogue: Canadian Courts and the Continuing Justification of the Dispossession of Aboriginal Peoples." *Windsor Yearbook Access to Justice* 29, no. 1 (2011): 55–72. https://doi.org/10.22329/wyaj.v29i0.4480.

Waldron, Jeremy. "Some Models of Dialogue between Judges and Legislators." *The Supreme Court Law Review* 23, no. 2 (2004): 9–21.

Walters, Mark D. "Respecting Deference as Respect: Rights, Reasonableness and Proportionality in Canadian Administrative Law." In *The Scope and Intensity of Substantive Review: Traversing Taggart's Rainbow*, edited by Mark Elliott and Hanna Wilberg. Oxford: Hart Publishing, 2015.

Watt, Daniel W. "General Warrants Take the Wrong Path: Challenging the Constitutionality of Section 487.01 of the Code." *Canadian Criminal Law Review* 12, no. 3 (2008): 297–326.

Webber, Grégoire. "Human Goods and Human Rights Law." *The Cambridge Handbook of Natural Law and Human Rights*, edited by Tom Angier, Iain Benson, and Mark Retter. Cambridge: Cambridge University Press, 2022.

——— *The Negotiable Constitution: On the Limitation of Rights*. Cambridge: Cambridge University Press, 1999.

——— "Proportionality, Balancing, and the Cult of Constitutional Rights Scholarship." *Canadian Journal of Law and Jurisprudence* 23, no. 1 (2010): 179–202. https://doi.org/10.1017/S0841820900004860.

Webber, Grégoire, and Paul Yowell. "Introduction: Securing Human Rights through Legislation." In *Legislated Rights: Securing Human Rights through Legislation*. Edited by Grégoire Webber et al. Cambridge: Cambridge University Press, 2018.

Weiler, Paul C. "Of Judges and Rights, or Should Canada Have a Constitutional Bill of Rights?" *Dalhousie Review* 60, no. 2 (1980): 205–37.

Weinrib, Lorraine. "Learning to Live with the Override." *McGill Law Journal* 35, no. 3 (1990): 541–71.

Whyte, John D. "On Not Standing for Notwithstanding." *Alberta Law Review* 28, no. 2 (1990): 347–57. https://doi.org/10.29173/alr1606.

Williams, George. "The Power to Go to War: Australia in Iraq." *Public Law Review* 15, no. 1 (2004): 5–9.

Williams, Meaghan, and Robert Schertzer. "Is Indigeneity like Ethnicity? Theorizing and Assessing Models of Indigenous Political Representation." *Canadian Journal of Political Science* 52, no. 4 (2019): 677–96. https://doi.org/10.1017/S0008423919000192.

Witten, Lauren. "Proportionality as a Moral Process: Reconceiving Judicial Discretion and Mandatory Minimum Penalties." *Ottawa Law Review* 48, no. 1 (2016): 81–134.

Wolfson, Matthew. "Public Opinion and Excluding Evidence under Section 24(2) of the Charter: A Recent Poll." *Windsor Review of Legal and Social Issues* 2 (2016): 40–79.

Wright, Wade. "Against Privileging the Charter: The Case of Federal Pre-enactment Constitutional Review." *Review of Constitutional Studies* 25, no. 1 (2020–2021): 49–78.

Young, Alison. "Dialogue and Its Myths: 'What Peoples Say I Am, That's What I'm Not.'" In *Constitutional Dialogue: Rights, Democracy, Institutions*, edited byGeoffrey Sigalet, Grégoire Webber, and Rosalind Dixon. Cambridge: Cambridge University Press, 2017.

Young, Lisa. "Money, Politics and the Canadian Party System." In *Canadian Parties in Transition: Recent Trends and New Paths for Research, Fourth Edition*, 4th ed., edited by A. Brian Tanguay and Alain-G. Gagnon. Toronto: University of Toronto Press, 2016.

Young, Lisa, and Harold J. Jansen. "Cartels, Syndicates, and Coalitions: Canada's Political Parties after the 2004 Reforms." In *Money, Politics, and Democracy: Canada's Party Finance Reforms*, edited by Lisa Young and Harold J. Jansen. Vancouver: UBC Press, 2011.

Index

Cases

Canada

United Kingdom

www.ingramcontent.com/pod-product-compliance
Ingram Content Group UK Ltd.
Pitfield, Milton Keynes, MK11 3LW, UK
UKHW041905020326
468479UK00003B/27

9 781487 559533